FROM COAL MINE TO
FINISH LINE

JAMES MCLATCHIE

ISBN-978-1-945587-50-4
Library of Congress: 2020903683
James McLatchie
From Coal Mine to Finish Line
1. Running; 2. History; 3. Scotland; 4. Coaching

Book Design: Dancing Moon Press
Cover Design: Dancing Moon Press
Cover Art: Austris Augusts on Unsplash

Dancing Moon Press
Bend, Oregon USA
dancingmoonpress.com

DANCING
MOON
PRESS

ACKNOWLEDGEMENTS

I must thank the following people for prompting me to sit down and put my past history to print.

My two daughters, Heather and Amy, for getting me on the right track to start writing.

Taylor Vandenborn for reminding me to think and start composing.

Heather for editing what I wrote as I typed along.

Carol, my wife, for keeping me at the task and making me get up from the chair and do some exercise.

Contents

Prologue

After having endured prostate cancer, heart attack and a stroke, my daughters Heather, Amy and some friends told me to sit down and start writing about my past history. This book is about my life story. The details are correct, but some of the dates might be off a bit. My memory may be like an internal picture book, but these pages have been stained with tea and lager/ale/IPA over the years.

The first part is about me growing up and depicts my life from an infant living in a one-room house with my parents and seven siblings. The story concludes with winning the National High School Cross Country Championships in 2018, where, I along with my wife, Carol, were named Coaches of the Year.

The second part of the book contains several different training schedules for the runners I coached. During the past 50 years, I have produced over 150 USA National Champions who won titles ranging from high school level to Masters.

I coached the following athletes in the Olympic Games:

Year	Name	Event	Country
1984	Midde Hamrin	Marathon	Sweden
1996	Justin Chaston	Steeplechase	GB
1996	Sean Wade	Marathon	NZ
2000	Justin Chaston	Steeplechase	GB
2004	Justin Chaston	Steeplechase	GB

World Championship Competitors:

Year	Name	Event	Country
1985	Carol McLatchie	15K	Gateshead
1987	Carol McLatchie	Marathon	Seoul
1989	Charlotte Thomas	Marathon	Milan
1991	Carol McLatchie	Marathon	London - World Cup

1991	Joy Smith	Marathon	London — World Cup
1991	Joy Smith	Marathon	Tokyo
1991	Joy Smith	1/2 Marathon	Gateshead
1995	Justin Chaston	Steeplechase	Gothenburg
1997	Patty Valadka	Marathon	Greece
1997	Jon Warren	Marathon	Greece
2003	Sylvia Mosqueda	Marathon	Paris
2006	Max King	Cross-Country	Fukuoka
2008	Max King	Cross-Country	Edinburgh European Championships
1982	Midde Hamrin	Marathon	Athens
1994	Justin Chaston	Steeplechase	Helsinki

I was national coach for the following events:

1986	USA Men's IAAF World Relay Championships	Yokohama, Japan
1989	USA Women's International Road Relay Championships	Hiroshima, Japan
1991	USA Women's IAAF World Cup Marathon	London
1994	USA Women's International Road Relay	Yokohama, Japan
1996	USA Women's International Road Relay	Seoul, Korea
1998	USA Women's International Road Relay	Beijing, China
2002	USA Women's International Road Relay	Beijing, China
2004	USA Men's IAAF World Half Marathon Championships	New Delhi, India

I was involved with Committees and Action Groups:

1984 — 1994: Worked with Nike as coach of regional athletes to raise them to a level where they could compete nationally. The women's team won the cross-country title in 1988. I was a member of several committees with associated coaches to develop a master plan to try to improve distance running in the USA.

1985 — 2002: Member of the Women's Long Distance Running Committee where I was one of the selectors for international competition. I also held a post lecturing and coaching marathon development at the Olympic Training Centre.

1990 — 1993: Member of the USA Track & Field Development Committee to develop a plan for distance running. I received an award from the USA Women's Track & Field for outstanding service to the sport.

1994 — 1999: Member of the USA Women's Cross-Country Committee to promote the development of sport for women.

1999 — Present: Member of the Great Britain elite coaching squad for the steeplechase.

2003 — 2009: Volunteer Coach at Pilot Butte Middle School, Bend, Oregon.

2010 — Present: Distance Track Coach at Summit High School, Bend, Oregon.

Chapter 1
Growing Up in Glenbuck, Ayrshire, Scotland

I was born on July 11, 1941, and grew up in Ayrshire, Scotland in a coal mining village called Glenbuck, which was famous for producing soccer players. I was the third eldest child in a family of five boys and three girls. My mother was from Huddersfield, England.

When my mother fell pregnant with my dad prior to World War II, they were married in Coventry, England and moved to Glenbuck. Glenbuck was an eye-opener for my mother, moving from all amenities to none.

7 Grasshill Row was a "single end" made up of one room. The houses were all attached, 33 in one row. The whole row was white. Most houses were two rooms, a couple of houses were three and we had the only one room house in the row.

I never knew I had an older brother called David for several years. He lived with my grandparents in Torhill, which was about three miles from Glenbuck. My parents would never mention David. I believe that my grandparents took my brother away from my mother to keep her from returning to England which was very weird.

When my mother baked, it was on a small oven attached to the fireplace called the "open grate." One could never regulate oven temperature.

Laundry facilities consisted of one wash house per four dwellings and the coal fired boiler had to be lit early in the morning so there would be warm water to wash clothes. Each family was assigned a "laundry day," which meant lighting the boiler, scrubbing clothes, and then inserting them in the boiler, and when we were finished, we had to run the clothes through a hand-wringer before hanging them outside to dry. If it was raining, the clothes had to be dried around the fire in the house.

We shared one room with no running water, bathroom or electricity. When David visited, the siblings slept four to a bed—two at the top and two at the bottom. My parents had their own bed. After my eldest brother moved away to live with my grandparents, there was more room in the bed.

I used to run all over the place, which made it easier to get around. I played soccer nearly every day. On Saturdays, my elder sister and I were given six pence—about five cents—to attend a movie matinee in Muirkirk, another village three mile away. Three pence for the bus, which ran every hour, and three pence was for the movie. To have money to buy sweets, I would run the three miles to Muirkirk, and we would watch the movie and return home by bus.

Since there was hardly money in the house, we went hungry many a time. We used to have a bowl of "SAPS"—which was white bread in a bowl with sugar and margarine covered with hot water (milk if you were lucky). Sometimes we received a sandwich of white bread and dripping (the lard from the chip pan). Chips were sliced potatoes like French fries cooked in a pan.

My grandparents lived just outside Muirkirk and I would bypass their house when I ran to the movies on Saturdays. I was worried that I would get into trouble if they saw me running past their door, so I would make a detour and run out of sight. Needless to say, that I, as a nine- and ten-year-old, was very fit.

Sometimes I would run to Torhill to visit my brother. He had one set of boxing gloves and I always landed with the left glove. Now I know how I became a southpaw. We were not permitted to hit with the ungloved hand.

All children over the age of ten were bused to Muirkirk to attend school until their 15th birthday. That was a big change from Glenbuck, which had a one-room classroom where multiple grades were taught.

My brother David attended the same school and a couple of times he stepped in to defend me when an older boy would be harassing me. It was great having someone keeping their eye on you.

I made the soccer team as a ten-year-old. At the age of 11, I was 5 feet, 10 inches tall. I played at "left-half." Today that position would be called a mid-field player. While at school, I played trials to make the national boy's team and represented the area a couple of times, but as I got older, I enjoyed running more.

Once per year, they had a sports day which consisted of several events: 100, 200, 400, high-jump, long-jump, shot-putt, and throwing a cricket ball. My elder brother won the event prior to me. I followed up by only losing one event—the 100 yards.

Later on, one of my younger brothers and two sisters won the same championship. In all, five McLatchies were crowned "Sports Champion of the Year."

Glenbuck had no industries. It was a coal mining village, and after the mines were closed, Glenbuck had nothing. Nearly all the adults worked in the mines in Muirkirk. There was a plan to move all the families in Glenbuck to Muirkirk, which took a few years as they had to build houses to accommodate large families.

We were on the wait list for a four-bedroom house, which took longer to build. Slowly, Glenbuck began to die. In the latter years, our family was one of the few who still lived in the village and all my friends were gone. I spent a lot of time kicking a ball against a wall, which improved my soccer skills.

In 1952, we received word that our house was ready and we had to move to Muirkirk into a house with four bedrooms, two bathrooms, and three fireplaces. I thought we had won the Pools (lottery).

Chapter 2
Coal Mine Muirkirk Ayrshire

It was 1952 and we were living in a new house with four bedrooms, running water, and electricity. Must be a dream. My mother used to get upset when all the kids would pile into the sitting room rather than being in their own bedroom. We were not used to so much space. We played "hide and seek" with so many rooms.

While at school, I delivered newspapers for two years, which was good for my fitness as I ran the route. Newspapers in Scotland were different as people subscribed to different papers: *Mirror, Herald, Bulletin, Express*, and the *Mail*. I had to sort them in street address sequence before I took off. It was good for one's memory as you had to know who received the paper that they had ordered; if not you received an "ass-chewing."

In 1954 when my brother David had his fifteenth birthday he came to live with the rest of the family. The reason being that he found a job as a "Carpenter's Assistant." By having a paid job, he could work and contribute to the family's household.

I was told to move to Torhill to live with my grandparents. I asked why did I have to move and was told that they needed someone to run errands. I was pretty upset about the whole arrangement. David my brother was living with the family and I had to move. How was I ever going to get to know him?

After nine months of living with my grandparents I told them I was returning home to live with the rest of the family and I would get their eggs from the farm on Fridays and groceries on Saturdays. I moved back in with my family and finally had a chance to get to know my brother. Talk about a lonely existence in Torhill with no boys to play with. My brother must have had a tough life growing up in those surroundings. I know I couldn't handle the existence.

I attended school to the end of the school year, which was June 1956. I was 15 in July, and believe it or not, I had to report to the coal mine for a physical and start work the following week. I was assigned to the wood yard with Wull (William) Russell. We were given a task list to take wood to the mine entrance. The wood came in different sizes—10, 8, 6 and 4 feet. Our orders might say the following: 20x10, 30x8, 60x6 and 100x4. We loaded the wood on a "bogey," which ran on the rail line. We loaded the bogey, pushed it about 200 yards to the mine shaft, unloaded, returned to the wood yard and worked until the order was complete. We worked in snow, rain and sun. Awful job.

No one could work down the mine or do shift work until they were 16 years old. The next step was to train you to work underground. At 16, I was sent to a coal mining school called Dungavel, about ten miles from Muirkirk, where we were trained to work underground. The students came from all over the west of Scotland. We were divided into four groups. I was named captain of my group, which was called Garron. We played a lot of sports and games between learning how to work down a mine. I played soccer, boxed, and ran on the school team. Sometimes down the pit, you heard someone shout, "Roof falling." You didn't know which way to run.

Going for a run outside the "pit" showers after working all day.

After coal mining training I was placed on second shift from two until ten p.m. on the "tables" (conveyor belt). As the coal came up the mine (pit) in tubs, which held about 500 pounds of coal, they were put on a conveyor belt where a team of boys picked out the stones. The conveyor belt emptied into a wagon, which, when full, was hauled away by a train. A monotonous job. I decided, "I am out of here as I cannot work in this shit!" I left after one year and found a job working for the railroad.

The Kames coal mine (pit) was deemed a safe mine and people were allowed to smoke! Canaries and the Davy lamp, which is a safety lamp for use in flammable atmospheres, were the safety protocols. The lamp was created for coal mines, to reduce the danger of explosions due to the presence of methane and other flammable gasses, which were called firedamp or mine damp. If a canary died, then you knew to get out of that area quick or you were dead.

Now smoking in a mine just blew my mind. In November 1957, 17 miners were killed by an explosion. The conclusion was that two men went into the heading to check out the previous work with a naked light. It was natural for them light a match as smoking was permitted while on the job. It was concluded this was the cause of the explosion. Poor buggers. After the disaster, smoking was prohibited in the mine.

After school, I decided to give up playing soccer and started training for running. Our village had no running track. We had a couple of soccer fields where I could get about 220 yards around the field. I had no idea of pace. I did my 400s alongside the railway track; 400 into the wind and 400 with the wind in my back. Times were all over the place. I raced mostly the 800, and as a 15-year-old managed a 2:05 and later improved to 2:03.

Cross-country was a different kettle of fish as I went unbeaten for several years. We had hills surrounding the village, which was a great background for running. I ran in boots, which I wore in the pit and weighed about four pounds each, full of studs with heel and toe plates. Did all my running with boots on except for faster stuff or races. I lifted weights three times per week.

My Dad was a poacher, living off the land. He made snares to catch hares (jack rabbits) and fed corn with needles to the ducks. The duck would get the needle stuck in its throat and all you had to do was go early the next day and pick up the dead ducks. I used to go for runs on the hills and carry snares that my Dad made. I used to carry six snares hoping that I would never catch six hares. Once I did and nearly shit myself. Luckily, I wore a long coat like "Jack the Ripper." I had some string where I tied the back legs together and hung the hares around my neck. Another way of doing weight training and feeding the family.

One winter, I was going for a run and told my brother, Colin, I was going to catch a hare (jack rabbit). He told me I was crazy, I said, "No way, as there is over one foot of snow, hares cannot run too fast in the snow, plus they will be easy to track." So, he decided he would come with me, and sure enough I raised a hare (jack rabbit). The chase was on. All I had to do was keep it in sight. After about 20 minutes, the hare was exhausted and could run no more. As it lay there looking at me, Colin said, "What are you going to do now?" I replied, "Eat the bloody thing."

Working for the railroad I did a variety of jobs. I shoveled coal from a coal wagon into engine tenders which held the coal, cleaned the engines, and was a "fireman" who stoked the fire to produce steam. I was making more money than I had earned working in the coal mine. Some weeks I was giving my mother more money that my dad was contributing to the household. He didn't like me telling him that he needed to contribute more.

I started a running club for some of the locals. We met twice per week at the Community Center, where we lifted weights, ran outside when the weather was cooperating, and played games when it wasn't. In the winter, it was tough with the weather, but great having an indoor facility. In the fall, we would meet for cross-country runs, which usually ended up being a handicap race. I would start a stopwatch when the first runner would take off and count down the handicap allowance for the next runner and so on. Since I was always the last runner, I placed the watch in a safe place and every runner knew the location. The first runner to return to the start line would pick up the watch, check his time, and be responsible for timing the other runners as they returned. Great fun. It didn't matter if anyone was cheating. Who cares?

My running was improving as I was winning most of my races. I competed as a youth through my 17th birthday. As a junior (age 17-19), I started running the mile, which was a new adventure. I had very little idea of pace as I did not have a track.

I bought a motorcycle which was a 350cc Velocette, which I used to transport me to track meets, especially in the Glasgow area. Otherwise it was usually by bus which travelled every four hours. Having transportation, I would be able to leave later and be able to travel back home without having to hang around a bus stop waiting for a bus.

In championship races, I would go to the front and hang on the best I could. In open events, which were handicapped, you started on the track which depended on your time. In reality, you never raced a mile. As a junior, I used to run from a handicap mark that was off ten yards, which meant I raced ten yards short of one mile. In my junior year, I won the National Scottish Junior Cross-Country Championship over a six-mile course. I was invited to compete in Brussels against some of the best runners in Europe. I was not allowed to attend as the Scottish Federation said I was too young. Oh boy, politics at its best.

Winning Scottish National Junior cross-country championships.

In 1958, I received some devastating news. My eldest brother, David, was diagnosed with Hodgkin's cancer, which at that time had no cure. The doctors gave him iodine and mustard to try and kill the cancer. Nothing worked. I watched him waste away to skin and bone.

I would visit David in hospital as often as I could, knowing full well that he was not going to survive. It was tough on me. He was my big brother; someone I hardly knew. He lived with my grandparents from the time he was one year old until he was 15. I could never understand why he didn't live with us in Glenbuck, and no one would give me an explanation. It was like an Agatha Christie mystery.

One day while I was at home alone, a policeman arrived at our house. He informed me that my brother was dying and he did not have much time left to live. I jumped on my motorcycle and took off for the hospital. When I arrived, I was informed that David had just died. I was not so sure how I would have handled the situation if he had still been alive when I arrived and died while I was there. Phew!

I learned another lesson. My mother and other females along with my younger siblings were not allowed to attend the funeral. I can imagine what anguish my mother went through when she was told she could not attend the funeral of her son. I attended the funeral and after the service I went for a long walk with my uncle Jackie while the others went to a pub. My dad and relatives stayed out of my way as they knew not to mess with me.

David died on December 23, 1958 at the age of 19. A bloody waste.

David at 17 years age — he played a good trumpet.

In 1959 I had to give up riding the bike after one day I fell off and landed on my butt. I had just started the bike and went about 20 yards when I hit some black ice and went into a skid. Down I went. The kick stand came down and the bike turned around and ran over me while I was lying on the road. I was so mesmerized that I could not move. I checked my leg where the bike had run over me and I could see the white of the shin bone. No broken leg and no more motorcycle.

Lesson learned. "Do not ride a motorcycle on ice."

Most of my running in the winter was done on the roads accompanied by my brother, Ian, who rode a bicycle. On downhills where he could free wheel, he would give me a rough time as I couldn't keep up with him. I was grateful for the assistance, which helped my training tremendously.

As my running was improving, I was also told to apply for an office job, which I did. I was told to report to Pollockshields, which was just outside Glasgow. Now I had to figure out where I was going to live. I had an aunt and uncle with three girls who lived in Milngavie outside Glasgow. Arrangements were made and I was on my way to a new life.

Chapter 3
Glasgow, Scotland

Once I was in Glasgow, I had a new start with a new job. My own room and finally I could train on a 440-yard track.

I travelled by bus from Milngavie to Glasgow and then ran like hell to catch the train to work. In the new job, I had to read meters which showed consumption for water and electricity. I also had to calculate coal consumption for each steam engine located at Pollockshields. I prepared reports on usage for water, coal, and electricity. I had to walk alongside the railway line to read water meters each week, which were situated about a half-mile from work. I noted the reading, which was used to prepare reports and graphs showing monthly consumption by engine. These reports were used to determine the efficiency of the engines.

Not too far from work was Haggs Castle golf course, where I ran each lunch time. I used the course to run Fartlek. Hard from tee to green, jogged from green to next tee on Tuesday and Thursday with easy runs on Monday and Wednesday. Then I'd return back to work after having a shower and I finished around 4:30 p.m.

Monday and Wednesday, I trained either at Glasgow University or with Western Track Club, which had 440 cinder tracks. Finally, I could work on pace, which was a big change from running alongside a railroad track. Other days I would run on the streets in my aunt's neighborhood. Sundays, I would take off and run up hills and around the local reservoir. Saturdays, if not racing, it would be easy run. Sometimes in the winter, when the weather was bad, I would train indoors doing mostly weights, core, and circuit training.

By 1959, I was the leading miler in Scotland. Raced in all the big meets, ran for Scotland in several meets in Poland, Germany, Ireland, England, and Iceland. I was selected to compete in Krakow, Poland, in an international track meet. What a journey. I took a train to Harwich, a ferry to the Hook of Holland, and then a train to Krakow. Like the rest of the team, when I arrived, I was worn out. After a good night's sleep and some easy running, I was ready to roll.

I did not race very well. I guess too much travelling.

The organizers arranged several trips for us, one being a visit to a salt mine. They must have known I had worked in the mines. Once we were underground, I was amazed at the size of an area they had taken us into. They explained that the Germans were using this area of the mine to build airplanes. Seemingly they built components in the mine and reassembled the parts above the ground into the end product, an airplane.

One thing I noticed was that there were hardly any men visible. Women were doing most of the work. On inquiring, I was informed that most of the men had been killed in World War II and the women were the main workforce.

I improved from 4:19 to 4:08 for the mile in a short time. I won the Junior and Senior cross-country championships on the same day at the 1961 South West Scottish Championships. I believe no one else in Scotland achieved that double. I also went on to win the Scottish Junior cross-country championships that same year.

A lot of our races were held on grass tracks, which were normally five laps to the mile. I ran barefooted. During some of the big soccer matches, with crowds nearing 90,000 rabid fans, I was invited to run a mile. I always knew never to wear a singlet the same color as one of the teams that was playing as they would throw stuff at you and curse you as you raced past them. A great experience.

Running barefoot in mile race — Scotland — Holland finished second.

I visited Berlin in 1961 on my way to compete in in a European cross-country race in Leipzig, East Germany. On that trip, we travelled by train, stopping at Berlin to board another train to the eastern sector of Germany.

UK team leaving for Leipzig. Walter Wilkinson is 3rd on left.
Dom Keily last on right, and I am the tall guy behind two women.

What a journey! I was taking a picture of the insignia on the Berlin to Moscow Express when I was hit on the head. Looking around, my attacker was a soldier who kept shouting, "Nein, Nein." Great introduction.

Picture below is me giving him a "salute."

When we approached the East German border, the train was stopped and the engines were changed. Seemingly, it was to accommodate a different rail gauge. On the way back to Berlin, the train was stopped again, but this time, soldiers and German Alsatian dogs walked through the train and anyone whose papers were not in order were taken off the train. It was very depressing, with people crying and probably having no idea what was going to happen to them.

Berlin was a drab city, as everything was painted grey and dull with the wall dividing the East from the West. It was strange to see a wall, and between the wall, a barbed-wire fence and an area which was considered no-man's land, where mines were placed. Chances were no one was going to make it safely to the West. A person trying to escape had to negotiate a mine field and then be able to climb over a ten-foot wall without being shot.

In 1961, while racing at a meet in Edinburgh, I was approached by Colin Ridgeway, who was a high jumper from Australia. He was attending Lamar University in the USA. He told me I needed to come to the States and get an education and compete for Lamar. I told him I wasn't interested as I was happy doing what I was doing.

In 1962, we had the Scottish Championships, which selected a team for the Commonwealth Games that were going to be held in Jamaica. I finished second in the mile behind Mike Berisford, an Englishman who was selected for Scotland due to birthrights as his grandmother was born in Scotland. Berisford ran 4:06.8 I ran 4:08.3.

Berisford leading me with 200 yards from the finish.

After the Scottish nationals, I bumped into Ridgeway, who was competing again in the same meet as me. Once again, he hit me up with going to the States. This time, I decided, "I am going to apply."

I was running well and getting a bit fed up with the weather, which was nearly always raining, making it hard to train.

I filled in the necessary papers and took an exam which was necessary to go to college. A few months later, I was accepted and could go to university in January 1963.

I continued training and racing, making plans to fly to Texas. When the word got out that I was leaving the country to take up a new life in the States, all hell broke loose. I was invited to appear on BBC TV for an interview to state why I was leaving Scotland. I explained it was to get educated and a better life.

It was amazing how many companies offered me a job to stay. During the past few years, NO ONE had offered me a job as they assumed, I was happy!

Heading to America.

Chapter 4
1963, Beaumont, Texas USA

One must remember that in the 1960s, communication was mainly by mail. Between the USA and Scotland, it took several weeks if mailed regular, which meant your letter went by sea.

I booked a one-way ticket from Prestwick to Houston on January 26, 1963. What a journey. It was snowing when I left. I took off for Houston via Gander, New York, and Atlanta. I was met in Houston by Colin Ridgeway on Monday, January 28th. It was 78 degrees. I couldn't believe it as the temperature never got this high in Scotland. I thought, "Oh, jeez, what have I done?"

Colin met me at the Houston airport and drove me to Beaumont from Houston, a journey just over 90 miles. I was amazed at the terrain. Flat as a pancake, no hills, and hot. Colin took me straight to the track, where the team was working out along with the coach.

He introduced me to the coach, Ty Terrell, who had a stopwatch around his neck, a clip board in his hand, and a cigar in his mouth. My first impression was bad. I said to myself, "Holy shit, this guy cannot coach me." After introductions, I was taken to the dorms for room assignment. I was assigned a room with two others and in the adjoining room, three other students. Six people sharing a bathroom, just like living in Muirkirk.

I was assigned a bed which was the middle of three. Looking at the bed, there was no pillow, sheets or blanket. So, I asked where the bedding was. I was informed you had to supply your own. I had none. One of the suite-mates gave me two sheets and a pillow case. I went to the track and took a piece of foam rubber from the pole vault pit for a pillow. When it got cold, I put a towel and jacket over me to keep warm. Later that week, my other roommate showed up: Peter Nimmo from London, England. He threw the discus and played basketball.

The next day, I signed up for class, taking the basic freshman classes along with accounting, which, according to my test scores, was a suitable degree. Classrooms were hot and depended on fans to move the air around. It was challenging trying to pay attention to lectures in a room that was not air-conditioned. The library was air-conditioned, which made a great escape to get away from the heat and humidity.

When I went to the track for a workout, I decided to approach the coach, and ask, since he was the only coach and was really busy with the sprinters and field event athletes, if I could take some of the load from him and coach the distances. He said, "Sure" and "That was great."

Attending classes was difficult after leaving school in Scotland six years earlier. One day, while attending a class, I was told that I had to report to the Dean of Students. Hoffman was his name. He told me I couldn't attend any classes until I paid a student fee. I responded that I was on scholarship and the athletic department paid the fees. He was quite adamant that I should pay and could not go to classes until the fee was paid. My response was, "If I cannot go to class, I need a one-way ticket back to Scotland." Finally, he called the coach, who stated that there had been a misunderstanding and he would take care of the fee.

A couple of weeks later, I ran in an indoor meet in Fort Worth, Texas. It was right after the rodeo. They took a bulldozer and fashioned out a track in the rodeo arena, 11 laps to the mile. It was a challenge as the place stunk of shit. I finished second to a runner from the University of Texas, in 2:17.3 minutes over 1000 yards.

My next race was a week later in Houston. It was over a half-mile and I won in 1:52.2. It was raining, which reminded me of home. I won in a new school record. Two weeks later, I travelled to Laredo, Texas, where I won the mile in 4:10.8 (school record) and the 880 in 1:54.8.

While racing in Laredo, seemingly it is a ritual to cross the border into Mexico and visit Nuevo Laredo. Unwittingly, I had no means of identification as I did not bring my passport. Not realizing the severity of such a mishap, I mentioned it to one of my teammates, Tony Guillory, a black athlete on the team, who told me, "Don't worry." Tony gave me his driving license, and I thought, "No way in hell is this going to work." He told me he would be standing behind me at customs and said, "Don't speak." Approaching customs, the inspector looked at the license, looked at me, and while he was debating, Tony said, "He doesn't speak good English," and pushed me through the gate. I was now back in the USA via a black driving license.

Running the 880.

Tony went on to play football for the Los Angeles Rams, what a guy.

All our travelling was by road with no air-conditioning, which made the journey uncomfortable in 90-plus heat with humidity around 100 percent. The room that I had in Campbell Hall was not air-conditioned, which made studying tough. I usually ended up in the library to cool off.

There was a strange rule when I was competing as a freshman. NCAA would not let freshmen compete in championship races. I was fortunate enough to get invites to compete against the best milers. In some cases, the coach made me run a relay before competing in the mile.

I was invited to run the mile invite at the Drake Relays against Dyrol Burleson. This was good news, until I was told I would be travelling with the team by car to Des Moines, Iowa. I thought, "Jeez, the coach must be joking. Traveling in a car 920 miles before a race."

Boy I was surprised when he told me I had to run the anchor legs in the DMR and Sprint Medley before the mile. The DMR was on Friday evening, where I ran 4:09.8 for the mile. On Saturday, it was raining. The track was muddy and heavy. I ran the 880 leg in 1:50.2 and came back for the invitational mile in 4:12.6, finishing fourth. Burleson won the race. We finished fourth in both relays.

I am in fourth place.

I had to run two races before the invitational mile: Sprint Medley and DMR. I gave it all I had, but I was buggered. I am in fourth place in the photo.

Shortly after the race, we piled into a vehicle heading back to Beaumont, only stopping for gas and something to eat. This was a tough weekend. I was asking myself, "What have I done?"

Near the end of the season, I raced Jim Ryun over a mile in Houston at the Meet of Champs on a cinder track. I took off from the gun and managed to win in 4:07.9. Ryun was second. About 100 yards from the finish, I could hear someone beginning to puke, and I thought, "They are going to throw up on me," which motivated me to keep in front. Crossing the finish line, I looked over, and it was Ryun puking his guts out.

The following weekend, I ran a mile in the Texas National Championships, where I won in 4:10.7. In this race, I decided to run behind until 700 yards and then let it go. I ran 65, 67, 60, 58.7 to win. The following week, I ran 4:12 for a mile in Houston. This was my last race for the season. Boy, was I tired! Before some of the home meets, I would stand under a cold shower to bring my temperature down before a race. There were a lot of meets where I doubled by running the mile, and twenty minutes later, I ran the half. In the 1960s, there were no women's events. Doubling was wicked.

During the school year, in the evening, I used to attend some of the local black night clubs and listen to some of the great singers from the Gulf area: Jimmy Reed, Bobby "Blue" Bland, Fats Domino, Percy Sledge, and Joe Tex. At one of Fats Domino's shows, I was standing about six feet from him and was amazed after he finished singing a song, he would turn to his guitar player and ask, "What's next?" I was never sure if Fats had an idea what was going on until he was informed by the lead guitar player what the next song was. I believe he was in another world! The guitar player kept him on the straight and narrow.

Hardly any white people attended shows performed by black artists. I guess I was different. No one bothered me and left me alone to enjoy the music.

I was soon educated to racism and the Ku Klux Klan. We had one black kid in the distance group, and on travels, he and I would share a room. Shortly after arriving in Texas, we were going to a meet in West Texas. Since we had a black man on the team, we were not allowed to eat in cafes or in a restaurant. We had to eat at the roadside or in a park. The main food was fried chicken, which we were given each meet. After one season of eating chicken, I disliked chicken so much it took me several years to start eating chicken again.

Once we stopped at a gas station and I noticed two drinking faucet signs: "White" and "Colored." So, I took a drink out of the one marked Colored and then White. I thought they tasted the same, then one of the team said, "Don't be drinking out of the 'nigger' water." I asked what he meant, and he stated one was for whites and the other for colored. He then asked, "Don't you have colored people in Scotland?" I responded, "Coalminers come up from the mine black, go to the showers, and wash off the coal soot, even though they were once black, but now they are white. It didn't change them one bit. They are still human, and 'niggers,' as you call them, are also human."

At one of the local track meets, my black friend was running the 4x400 relay on the third leg when he fell down exchanging the baton to the anchor. I ran on to the track and helped him, when I heard, "Leave him alone, you nigger-loving bastard." I didn't think much of it. On Monday, I was called into the coach's office and was informed that the KKK was going to kill me if I didn't stop running around with the blacks. I said, "They're joking." He said, "No, they are serious, so pay attention."

Helping a black person in the south in the 1960s was a "no-no." I did not grow up experiencing prejudice and had no idea about segregation, but did I get an education during my first six months in the South.

I took six weeks off from running, and since I had very little money, I needed to work. My first job was as a lifeguard at the local swimming pool, where I was paid $1 per hour. I had to sit in a chair with no shade waiting for someone to drown so I could dive in and relieve them. Sitting in the sun getting roasted was not my cup of tea. I called my coach and said I need to do something different.

Where I grew up in Scotland, all the kids were able to swim. The process was simple. An adult would throw you into the water and see if you could manage to get out safely. If not, they helped you out. A couple of the adults taught you how swim or tread water. I guess it must have worked as nobody ever drowned. We had a couple of rivers in the neighborhood which were used in the summer for swimming.

I got a job in Port Arthur on second shift at a shipyard as an assistant to a mechanic, where the pay was $1.50 per hour. We worked on barges and boats fixing engines. If there was nothing to fix, I worked in the machine shop assisting engineers. I enjoyed the job as the workers were down to earth, mostly "coon-asses" (Cajuns). Great sense of humor and fun to be around.

One night, I was asked to make coffee. The coffee in the urn was usually made of chicory. Bloody awful for a tea drinker. Anyway, since this was my assignment, now was my turn to make something that I could drink. I made the coffee and stood back from the urn knowing full well that all hell would break loose. Sure enough, when one of the older workers sipped his first taste, he spat it out and yelled, "You, Scottish bastard, I'll kill you! You are poisoning me." He grabbed a spanner and chased me around the workshop. The rest of the work crew were doubled up laughing. Finally, he gave up, and told me that I would never make coffee again. I stuck to water as I couldn't stomach what they made.

Work was slowing down and I was released from the job. I called the coach and explained my situation. He said he would find me another job. I received a call later and was told to report to where a new football stadium was being built for Lamar.

I reported to work, which consisted of spreading concrete for the new building. One day, the superintendent told me to run and do something. I looked at him and said, "I don't want to run on the job as I might get hurt, but if somebody needed help in an emergency, there is nobody here that can run faster than me." He looked at me and said, "I am only kidding."

I started training in August as cross country would be starting in September. I was only running about 30 miles per week with one speed work. The season in the south was short as there were not too many cross-country races, whereas in Scotland it would last about five months.

During the first week in October, I ran a two-mile cross-country race held on the roads, where I finished 12th. What a joke. I was informed by Coach Morris of the University of Houston that he would be taking a team to the US Federation cross country championships in November and I could run the trials.

I was running three times per day and slowly getting in shape. Each morning, I would get up around 6:30 a.m. and jog to South Park football stadium and run barefooted on the grass to loosen up, return to the dorms, have a shower, attend classes, go for an easy run of four to five miles, eat lunch, have a nap, and then meet the distance group for a workout.

I had another race at the end of October over four miles, where I finished fourth. The following week, I went to Austin to run in a three-mile race. I was surprised that the course had mile markers. They had a clock at the half-mile, where I went past in minutes 2:12, the mile in minutes 4:24, and finished second in 9:14 minutes. In Scotland, I was used to running six miles on grass. Racing two through four miles instead in America was a new experience for me.

My next race was over four miles in Houston, where I finished fourth in 19:46. The following week, I raced in Houston again, this time over a 10,000-meter course, which was a selection race to pick a team to run in Chicago the following month in the US Federation cross country championships. I finished second in 30:42 behind John Macy.

I was on the Houston Track Club team to compete in Chicago in the American Track & Field Federation Championships. I was informed that the team would pick me up in Beaumont and continue to East Lansing, Michigan, where the University of Houston was competing in the NCAA cross country championships.

We left on Thursday and drove to Bloomington, Illinois, where we stayed the night. I managed to get a slow three-mile run on an indoor track. While driving into Bloomington, we heard on the radio that John Kennedy had been shot in Dallas, Texas. We were wondering what was going to happen to us as we were driving with Texas plates. Luckily nothing happened and we continued to East Lansing the next morning, where we arrived later that Saturday.

I went out for a ten-mile easy run to loosen up from sitting in a station wagon. The race was over four miles on November 26, 1963. Victor Swolak won from John Camian and San Jose State won the team title. I was not allowed to compete in this race due to being a freshman. I felt I would have raced well, but was never given the chance.

Due to Kennedy's death, the race was delayed a day and was held on Thursday, November 28, 1963 in Washington Park over 10,000 meters. I was ready to get racing after being cooped up in hotels and a station wagon for a week. I took the lead at the four-mile mark and started to push the pace. With 200 to go, I was still leading with Tom O'Hara breathing down my neck. I kept wishing for the finish line as I was running out of gas. O'Hara went by me with 150 to go and won in 30:12 minutes, I was second in 30:17, and Jeff Fishback was third in 30:22. Houston beat San Jose with a score of 25 to 34. San Jose had just won the NCAA by 15 points, beating Oregon.

We headed back to Texas on Friday morning and arrived Saturday morning in Beaumont, where I went out and jogged a mile with a few strides.

I was still keeping in shape because I was informed that I could run in the Sugar Bowl over a mile in New Orleans at the end of December.

The coach at Lamar put on a meet in the middle of December, where I ran in a 1500-meter race which I won in 3:50.1. Then four days before the race in New Orleans, I ran a 1320-yard time trial in 3:02 (62, 61, 59), then five minutes later ran a 440 in 57.4. I knew I was in shape to compete well.

The 1500-meter race in New Orleans was loaded with Tom O'Hara, Morgan Groth and Norm Hoffman. I moved into the lead with 800 to the finish where I was still leading with five yards from the tape when Tom O'Hara went by me winning in 3:51.3 to my 3:51.4. Lap splits were 66, 63, 60, and 42.4.

Track & Field News

World Wide Coverage of Track and Field

December 1963, Vol. 16, No. 11   P.O. Box 296, Los Altos, Calif. $3.00 per year

VIC ZWOLAK holds the trophy he was presented for winning the NCAA cross country championship.

JOHN MACY (who eventually placed fourth) leads the field in the USTFF cross country championship followed by GEOFF WALKER (who placed fifth), TOM O'HARA (first), ROBERT BROUILLET (eleventh), unidentified runner hidden, JAMES McCLATCHIE (second), and JULIO MARIN (sixth). (Photo by Don Sparks)

AAU CROSS COUNTRY
Kidd Returns, Wins
by Mike Lester

New York City, Nov. 30 -- Bruce Kidd amply demonstrated his return to top condition by scoring a thrilling victory over veteran Pete McArdle in the National AAU cross country championships at Van Cortlandt Park on a cold and windy afternoon. The 20-year-old Canadian ace was timed in 30:47.2 for the hilly 10,000 meter course as he defeated McArdle, the defending titlist, by the slender margin of three yards in a driving finish.

The Los Angeles Track Club, although without the services of the injured Ned Sargent, easily captured the team championship for the second straight year. Mihaly Igloi's powerful squad, paced by Ron Larrieu who finished fourth, collected 47 points to outdistance the host New York Athletic Club, which had 74. The Toronto Olympic Club was third at 81, as the first three teams finished in the same order as they had in 1962.

McArdle, a 34-year-old Irish-born New Yorker, figured that his best chance of winning would be in a fast race, and accordingly he rushed into the lead soon after the start. He covered the first mile in 4:33 and only John McDonnell, the latest Irish import of the New York AC, cared to follow him. Kidd was well-placed among the first ten runners, as were Larrieu and Chris Williamson, a 19-year-old Canadian from the University of New Brunswick.

As the runners headed up into the rugged hills after the one-mile mark, McArdle began to increase his tempo. At two-and-a-half miles the Pan American 10,000 meter champion had lengthened his lead to seventy yards over Kidd, who had moved into second place. Billy Mills of the Marines had worked his way now running fifth, and Larrieu had fallen a few yards back.

McArdle continued to force the pace and still held his wide lead at the four-mile mark, having passed the 5000 meter checkpoint in 15:12. On the long upward slopes of Cemetery Hill, however, Kidd began to close the gap steadily and set the stage for the epic duel that followed. In that half-mile stretch Kidd regained all but ten yards of McArdle's advantage and shortly thereafter he moved up to the leader's shoulder.

In the last mile of hills, hidden from the view of the spectators, Kidd challenged for the lead several times, but McArdle would not be passed and fought him off. The pair continued to run together until only 400 yards from the finish, when Kidd managed to break away with a desperate sprint that opened up a lead of three or four yards. McArdle battled back and chased Kidd down the finishing straightaway to the tape, but he could not gain in the
(Continued on page 4)

USTFF CROSS COUNTRY
McLatchie Pushes O'Hara
by Paul O'Shea

Chicago, Nov. 28 -- The carrot-topped Irishman did it again. Making use his fourth start of the cross country season, Loyola University's Tom O'Hara kicked home to win the second annual United States Track and Field Federation cross country championship, in Washington Park.

Under bright skies and in moderate temperature, O'Hara clocked 30:12.1 for 10,000 meters on a rather slow course.

Johnny Morriss' Houston Track Club successfully defended its title against the just-crowned NCAA champions, San Jose State.

Left in O'Hara's wake were Scotsman Jim McClatchie, Polish-born John Macy, Costa Rican Julio Marin and Australian Geoff Walker and Laurie Elliott.

Macy was on top at three miles in 14:45 but McClatchie took the lead at four in 20:01. Jeff Fishback had moved up with the leaders by the fourth mile and six runners were within a four-second spread of 20:01-20:05.

Macy began to fade a bit in the fifth mile as did Marin, leaving Brown, McClatchie, O'Hara and Fishback in the front-running group. Macy, however, wasn't finished. Reminiscent of his national AAU six-mile against Peter McArdle this
(Continued on page 3)

NCAA CROSS COUNTRY
Zwolak Nips Camien
by Larry Middleman, The Detroit News

East Lansing, Mich., Nov. 25 -- Vic Zwolak is an old Marine who gave up "total war" for the values of limited action.

The 25-year-old Villanova senior said he played it safe in winning the NCAA cross country title today. He covered the four miles in 19:35.

"I went out and tried to bomb everyone the last two years and got beat," said Zwolak, who last two years ago and fourth last fall. "This time I ran just to win."

Zwolak still set the pace most of the way, but not until past the two-mile mark did he and John Camien of Emporia State try to pull away from the pack of 167 starters. "If Camien wanted to pass me I'd have let him," Zwolak said. "But I didn't want everyone there at the finish."
(Continued on page 4)

Track and Field News

Chapter 5
1964 Beaumont, Texas USA

I took two weeks off from training and enjoyed the down time. I started training again by doing some slow running. In one session, I was barefoot running on the grass and cut my toe pretty badly and had to take three days off from running.

JAMES MCLATCHIE

I was named captain of the 1964 Lamar track team.

The team decided to run for one hour on the track to see what distance they could cover in an hour. I ran 11 miles, 587 yards, which was tough on me and left me sore. Rather than take some time off to recover, I kept training, which was a BIG mistake. After a few days, I could hardly walk. The injury persisted and I had to take three weeks away from training. By the middle of February, I was back running. I had missed quite a lot of base training, and as the outdoor season was getting ready to start, I had to figure out what I was going to do.

My main intent in coming to the States was to train hard and get in shape for the Olympic Trials. Now, I wasn't too sure about this goal. I was reminded a few times, "You are on scholarship and you need to compete."

The first meet I competed in was the following week, where I won the two-mile in 8:50.2 and the mile in 4:12.2. A couple of weeks later, I won the mile at the Laredo relays in 4:12.2.

Once again in Laredo, some of the team members decided to visit Nuevo Laredo in Mexico. This time I brought my passport to get me back into the States, but never realized that I would end up in a Mexican jail.

Jail in Mexico is quite an adventure. The journey was something else.

We had rented a buggy/taxi to take us sight-seeing and had decided on a price with the driver. We kept the poor man longer than the time we had rented his services. He told us we had to pay extra to get us back to the border.

As it happened, a police car roared up. Out jumped a couple of cops with guns drawn, who told us we would have to pay or go to jail. Before we knew it, we were in a paddy wagon and taken to jail which was on the outskirts of Nuevo Laredo.

We were escorted into the jail, which was teeming with people. Jeez, a mass of humanity. We were lined up facing a wall with hands above our heads. The police started frisking our bodies. Peter Nimmo, who is 6' 4", was standing next to me and when he was being frisked, he turned around to see what was going on. The policeman, who was about 5' 6" stood on his tip-toes, hit Peter on the head with his gun. Peter slithered down the wall to the ground. I burst out laughing thinking about the "Keystone Cops."

Finally, we were taken to the booking officer's area, where he read the charges. If we paid an extra dollar each (there were five of us), we could leave, which we did.

I asked if we could get a ride back to the border. We were told "No," so we had to hoof the six miles back to the border. We arrived back at the hotel as the team was loading the vehicles back to Beaumont.

What an adventure for an extra dollar. Lesson learned.

The following week, I was entered in the USA Track & Field indoor championships in Milwaukee, Wisconsin. I had to travel to Houston and then fly to Chicago, but all the flights were cancelled to Milwaukee, so I had to catch a train, which got me to Milwaukee tired and worn out. I raced in the mile finishing in 4:12.5 with splits of 60, 61, 64, and 67.5. I was so tired with all the travelling and racing. It was a tough few days having raced on Saturday evening, then travelling to Milwaukee on Sunday and racing on Tuesday evening.

Over the following few weeks, I competed in Texas Relays, Kansas Relays, and Drake Relays with a couple of meets in between. I was running so slow, getting my "arse" kicked, and not enjoying racing. I dropped out of a couple of races later and was looking forward to going home to Scotland to visit my family, knowing full well my dream of the Olympics was at an end.

I had booked a flight from New York to Glasgow, Scotland on June 14, 1964. Now I had to figure out how I was going to travel from Beaumont to New York. I found a group of students who were going to New York to work during the World's Fair and they offered me a ride. Boy what a journey with four of us in a car going to New York via Florida. We slept at the side of the road, I jogged when I could, and was getting out of shape with no consistent training.

I finally managed to return home to Muirkirk, tired and out of shape. I was not strong enough to race a mile and ran several half-mile races, where I managed to finish second over a half-mile in the Scottish Championships in 1:56. I made the Scottish team and ran for them against Ireland over the half-mile, where I recorded 1:53.9. I raced a couple more times and then decided to quit for the season.

I could run a decent 880 as I didn't have the base to race over a mile. It's amazing if you don't do the work you cannot race very well.

In retrospect, I was not zeroed in to trying to make the Olympic Team due to having being injured with too much travelling and racing while in Texas, then having really no idea how I was going to catch a plane from New York to Scotland. Adding up all the missteps, there was no way I would have any chance of running fast enough to qualify for the Olympic Trials.

Me winning an 880-yard race while I went home for the summer.

The time with the family was enjoyable. I visited old friends. Living in the village, I was restless. I ran in the hills most days trying to get some sanity back. I was not sure about what I was going to, but I knew I couldn't stay in Muirkirk or Scotland. I had experienced a whole different world and a lot of different cultures. Segregation, the Ku Klux Klan, night clubs, hellish heat and humidity, sitting on my arse in class. I realized there was a big world out there and it was not in Scotland.

I wondered, "Now what do I do?" It was like being in a rudderless boat, drifting along with no idea where it was going. I had lost my enthusiasm for training hard and racing. Now I had to figure out what was next. I decided to return to the States and see if I could get my old enthusiasm back and enjoy running.

Chapter 6
Fall 1964 — Spring 1965

I started classes in September and was doing some easy running, which was difficult as the temperature was around 90 degrees. After a few weeks of easy running, I ran a three-mile cross country race in Houston in 15:14. Two weeks later, I raced in Lake Charles, Louisiana over three miles and finished second in 14:12. I was running around 45-50 miles per week.

I ran several more cross-country races, and started to sharpen up as I was scheduled to run two 1500-meter races in December. In the first race, I won in 3:55 (63, 64, 68, and 40). I then ran a leg of the 4x440 in 51:5. The next 1500 race was in New Orleans at the Sugar Bowl, where I finished third in 3:54, running the last 880 in 1:56.

Driving back to Beaumont with a friend, we were stopped by a State Trooper, which at that the time was hilarious. He kept changing his mind on the driving infractions (my friend was driving). First, it was speeding in a 25-mph zone, and he said we were driving 32 mph, which didn't fly. Next, he said we'd crossed a double yellow line. We asked where the lines were as we didn't see any. Anyway, we were taken to the police station and he told us he would put us in jail until the judge came on Monday as he was off fishing and didn't want to be disturbed. So, we asked what options we had. He replied, "Empty your pockets of money." He took everything we had except $1 to buy gas. Getting shook down cost us $9 and earned us an education about the Louisiana Police.

I took a break from training hard and was running some easy miles right up to my marriage to Mary Ruth Pleasant on January 27, 1965. We had been dating for about one year. Mary was in her final year of studies, so we decided to get married. Now, I was more committed to making a successful marriage than running.

I could feel that my running was improving. I was committed to running fast and making good grades in classes and being a good husband. I was more focused.

In February 1965, I raced indoors in Fort Worth, finishing second in the mile in 4:21. A week later, I anchored the distance medley, which

Lamar won. I ran the mile in 4:16. I raced again in the first week in March, winning the mile in 4:14 and the three-mile in 15:04 in very windy conditions. A week later, Lamar travelled to the Border Olympics, where I won the mile for the time and also managed to win the 880 in 1:54.8.

I raced a couple of relays and felt like I was just going through the motions. I raced again in April in a meet in Denton, Texas, where I won the mile in 4:13.5 (62, 66, 66, and 59.5) in 86 degrees. Hot, hot. A couple of weeks later, I had enough and quit the team.

While I was on the bus, the coach told me that I was not allowed to wear a short-sleeved football jersey. I told him since it was warm and the bus was not air-conditioned, I would wear the jersey. With a lot of shouting back and forth, I told him, "I quit the team," as I just lost interest in running for Lamar, where I was expected to run two races every meet. I was tired and I needed a break to get my head straight.

The disputed argument caused a commotion with the rest of the team. They were all leaning out of the bus windows trying to catch the verbal assault. I finally tossed my bag that contained my running gear at the feet of the coach and walked off.

I returned to my house and informed Mary that I had quit the team. She told me that I needed to keep running as that was part of my life. Since I quit the team, I was barred from the track. I visited the Athletic Director and had a discussion with him informing him that since I was a student, I was allowed to use the facility. A compromise was made that I could use the track after the team finished their workout. I trained in the evening when it was cooler and did not have to train with the team at 3 p.m., which was hot as hell.

I trained mainly for the half-mile which was easier in the heat and humidity. The Texas Championships were being held in Beaumont at the end of May. I entered the half-mile, where I finished second in 1:51.8 behind George Hunt, who went through the first 440 around 50 seconds. I ran 54.5 and thought he went out too fast, but he beat me at the finish by one second where I ran 1:51.1

After school finished, I had to find a job. Looking in the daily paper, I noticed a company was looking for workers to install a sewer line alongside a new road that was being built from Port Arthur to Groves. I was hired at $1.75 per hour. While visiting, I talked to a couple of men from Beaumont who said I could get a ride to work with them. The superintendent, the "drag line operator," and I were white. The rest of the crew were black. The car driver picked me up at the house and drove me to work for the cost of $3 per week to pay for gas.

I was assigned the task of driving a D47 bulldozer, which had an enormous roller on the back used to level out the new road. Each day, I would drive a water truck to the nearby bayou and pump water into the truck then return to the new road where I would spray water on the surface, then roll back and forth to level out the surface. I was getting tired with the job. Sitting in the sun all day with no shade.

One day, I went to the bayou to load the truck with water when I drove too near the edge of the bayou and the truck toppled into the water. I managed to get out and sat at the side of the bank knowing that someone would check me out. Sure enough, the superintendent showed up and when he saw what happened, he started cursing me out and told me I was fired. I said, "Best news I have heard all day." Boy he didn't have a sense of humor.

"Will" was one of my car mates from Beaumont who had fought in World War II alongside the British in the desert. He would tell stories about when under attack by the Germans and it was around tea-time, the English would stop for a cup of tea. He said it was crazy. I kept reminding him that Scots people didn't do that as they were always sent to the front of the troops playing bagpipes. For what! Stupid buggers were mowed down like grass.

Each Friday Will, John (driver), and I after work would stop at a store and buy a six pack of JAX beer and drink two each before we made the journey to Beaumont. It was awful tasting but wet.

Mary and I were trying to figure out what I was going to do since I lost my job and quit college. Mary had graduated from Lamar. I had a brother, Geoffrey, who was working in Luton, Bedfordshire, England and sent him a letter asking about job prospects in Luton. He replied there was plenty of work as there were several manufacturing companies located there. Mary and I had a discussion about locating to Luton, England.

We contacted Holland-America and were told we could travel on a freighter from Houston to La Havre, France. They said they took ten passengers and would take around 21 days as they stopped at several ports in the States on the way to Europe. We went ahead and booked our passage leaving Galveston in September.

Two weeks before we were due to sail, I had entered a two-mile country race in Houston, where I managed to win around 9:10. I ran away from the field over the last 200 yards. I was pleased with my fitness level but knew it would suffer being cooped up on a boat for three weeks.

The following week, we took sail for Europe, a 21-day and a new journey for both as we didn't have jobs and had no idea where we would be living. We made stops in New Orleans, Fort Lauderdale, and Savannah loading the ship with goods for Europe.

I managed to run around the small deck, which was about 150 yards, each day. I read a lot, stood on the deck clearing my head about my excursion and running in the USA, people I had met, and the experiences that I endured while there.

Crossing the North Atlantic going through The Azores was rough as we were being thrown around in the cabin. The best place was the bed. We managed to get off in Calais, France and board a ferry to Dover.

Chapter 7
England

Finally, in October after 21 days at sea, a ferry ride, and two different train rides, we arrived at the station in Luton, England, where my brother, Geoffrey, was waiting. We gathered our luggage and headed to 83 Reginal Street. My brother rented the bottom half of a terraced house where the landlord lived upstairs. We were so tired after a meal we went to bed.

The next morning, I went with Geoffrey to George Kent, where he worked, and applied for a job where I was hired as a forecaster, someone who determines what production lines would be working and how many items had to be produced.

George Kent manufactured measuring devices for movement through a meter—electricity, gas or water. Since I had taken courses in statistics, it was determined I should be able come up with production numbers for manufacturing. Armed with a slide rule and a calculator, I started my task of forecasting expected orders to be manufactured.

It took me several weeks to get situated. Work was interesting and within walking distance from the house. I joined a local running club, Luton United, and spent some time getting used to the surroundings. I did a lot of my running in People's Park, which was located at the end of Reginal Street. There was hill in the park which was ideal for strength training. As it was dark most evenings, for speed work I ran light poles, which were spaced about 60 yards apart. I would sprint one 60, jog the next. Some nights I ran 20x60. Cross Country races were starting up and I was looking forward to racing.

I kept working, learning as I was going on. I had to do quite a bit of research, gathering information on past sales. Studying the data, I came up with a formula using season sales which worked fairly well. There were no computers, just the calculator and a slide rule for calculations. My training was going well, and I was getting stronger every day.

We decided to drive up to Scotland for New Years and spend some time with my family. I ran some of my old routes out in the hills and through the heather, where I really enjoyed the freedom on the moors.

On the way back to Luton, we visited relatives in Huddersfield.

Two weeks later, I raced over seven and a half miles in Luton and broke the course record with a time of 37:40 running through snow and ice. I was getting fitter and starting to enjoy racing again. I finished ninth in the North of Thames race over a muddy and heavy-going seven and a half miles, where I had to run in flats as I forgot to pack my spikes.

I entered an indoor one-mile race on a 220 track in Cosford, which was located on an RAF base. I won the race in 4:15.6 with 440 splits in 62.3, 65.3, 65.4, 62.6.

I kept training and learning the ropes at work where my estimates on production were pretty accurate.

In April, I ran a road relay from Eton Manor to Southend-On-Sea. I ran the sixth leg and started 39 seconds down and managed to give Luton a lead of 34 seconds. I recorded 23:27 for the five-mile leg. I handed over to anchor runner Tony Simmons, who went on to win with Luton claiming the victory with a new course record by 24 seconds. At the end of April, I ran in the Regional Road Relay championships with a team of five running three and three-quarter miles. I recorded the sixth fastest time over the course in 17:32. Luton manage to finish fourth overall.

I had my first outdoor race the coming week in Leyton Buzzard, over 1,500 meters at 8 p.m. in the evening. It was cold and windy and I managed to win in 3:52 (61, 62, 63, 46). I felt strong throughout and was pleased with my run.

In March of 1966, I had to make a trip to Scotland as my Dad had a heart attack. I drove up, stayed for three days, and left when I was informed that he would be ok.

I entered a half-mile race at the end of May at the White City in London, where I raced in 1:52.3 (54.6, 57.7). I ran out of steam 150 yards from the tape. I guess the traveling back and forth to Scotland was catching up with me. The following weekend, I raced a mile in Bedford and ran 4:10 (60, 65, 64, 61).

A couple of weeks later, I ran a 1320-yard time trial in 3:01.4 (58.5, 62.0, 60.9) five days before the Scottish Mile Championships in Edinburgh. On the Friday, I ran 4:16 to qualify for the final next day. On Saturday, the conditions were not ideal, very windy, which was typical for Scotland. The first half-mile was run in a slow 2:07, when Ian McCafferty and I decided to pick up the pace and ran 62 then 59. Ian proved the stronger of us and went on to win in 4:7.5 and I finished second in 4:8.7.

Finishing 2nd in Edinburgh.

I was selected to race in Iceland on July 18 and 19, 1966. We flew to Reykjavik on the evening of the 15th, arriving at 2:30 a.m. on the 16th. I did some light jogging on the 16th and 17th to get the kinks out from traveling and sitting on my butt from Luton. I won the 1500-meter race in 3:54.6 and 25 minutes later, I had to run the 3000-meter steeplechase, where I finished second. The next day, I raced over 800 meters and managed to finish second in 1:53. Racing three times in two days was just like being back in the States. Scotland sent a small team and since I was a glutton for punishment, I ran three races.

A couple of weeks later, Mary and I drove up to Huddersfield to visit our old aunt and uncle who were in their nineties. Uncle Percy was a character. After lunch, he told me no talking for one hour as this was his quiet time. He suggested that everyone needed some quiet time with no distractions. I went for a walk and scouted the local area while he had his quiet time.

Later in the afternoon, he told me we were going to visit the local butcher, where he purchased a leg of lamb which we had for lunch. I asked why we were going to the butchers. Percy replied, "To take back the leg bone as you can't eat it." Seemingly this had been a ritual for the past ten years. Percy buys a leg of lamb, takes back the bone and he and the butcher have a spiritual debate, and Percy ends up with a pound of hamburger meat.

At my job, I was improving my statistical model for forecasting production and was able to get past sales trends in the years gone by. With past history and future sales, I was able to determine some good results.

I had to produce a monthly report for my immediate boss, who met with upper management to explain how we were hitting production targets utilizing the information that I had produced. He never mentioned how I had done it.

When I found out that he was bragging about how he produced the information, I said to myself, "I'll get him next month when I give him a report that contains data on the first page, and the rest of the report will be blank."

The next month rolled around, and after the meeting I asked him how it went. He replied, "They really like your report, which contains a lot of useful information." I said, "I'm not so sure of that since the report is blank after the first page." His face was priceless.

I had one more race, which was held in Paddington London on August 6th, one mile on a cinder track. The same track that Roger Bannister trained on where he broke the 4-minute mile. After the race I decided I needed a break. All my races prior to 1968 were held on cinder or grass. I ran 4:10 (59.8, 62.2, 62, 66). I was buggered as I could hardly move. Yup, I needed a break.

I jogged through the end of the month and played soccer for George Kent's work team until October 9th. Mary took a job with the local government as a Child Welfare Worker through a contact I made on the city council and we bought a semi-detached (duplex) house in Sundon Park. I was looking forward to a garden so I could grow vegetables and give me something to do. I bought a moped, which I used to travel to work, making it easier than waiting for and riding a bus.

I started weight training and ran a couple of cross-country races where I didn't run very well. I was sick a couple of times, and that, along with moving into a new house, buying furniture, and setting up a home changed my priorities from racing to being a home owner.

I raced a five-and-two-thirds-mile cross country race in Luton in the middle of January 1967 where I finished first in 30:31. I went to Bedford a few times and trained with a group of runners every two weeks. The Bedford runners would come to Luton the other week.

I raced a mile indoors in Cosford, where I finished third in 4:14.1 and a week later ran in the Easter Cross Country Championships in Peterborough—nine miles, where I finished fourth in 51:44, which was the longest race I had ever run. Then in the first week in March, I ran in the English Cross-Country Championships in Norwich—nine miles again and I lost my shoes in the mud and finished shoeless in 117th place out of 881 starters. I was in a bad state. My feet were all bruised and blistered and I could hardly walk. What an experience.

In April, I ran a leg on the National Road Relay in Leicester—five miles, 1600 yards in 29:25, where Luton managed to finish 18th. Later in the month, I raced another road relay in Ponders End, which was a five by three and three-quarter mile race. I ran 17:28 for my leg, which was the fastest Luton leg and third fastest overall. When I was not racing, I was playing soccer.

During the month of May, I ran a three-quarter mile time trial in 3:04.4 sec (61, 64.4, 59) on a windy night. Three days later, I ran a two-mile race in Welwyn Garden, where I managed 8:58 sec (4:27.8, 4:30.2). I felt good throughout and was beaten by Tony Simmons at the tape. I was also helping Tony, who at that time was one of the top Junior runners in England, with his training.

Tony was an apprentice painter by trade. I worked with a lady, Vera, who asked me to paint her outside windows and doors. Vera lived in a two-story house, which meant we needed a ladder, which Tony secured. I was painting some windows on the second floor when I dropped a can of yellow paint which landed in the middle of the Rhododendron bushes. Looking down, I started laughing as I had never seen yellow Rhododendrons before. I climbed down the ladder and told Tony what had happened. He started berating me, worried about what Vera would say. I replied, "I don't know but I hope she has a good sense of humor." We hooked up a hose and washed off as much of the yellow paint as possible. I thought, "Job well done." I explained to Vera what I had done and she wasn't too upset, but we never painted houses again. I guess Tony didn't trust me.

While I was coaching him, Tony ran a British Junior record for the mile in 4:04 and was one of the best Junior Cross-Country runners in the land. When I left to return to the States, Tony was coached by Harry Wilson, who also coached Steve Ovett. Tony finished fourth in the 10,000 meters at the 1976 Olympic Games. He also finished second in the European 10,000 meters championships, where he missed first place by four hundredths of a second.

I ran a few more races in July and August, I won first place in an 880 in 1:53.4, third in a mile in 4:14.1, and third in a handicap race where I raced off 20 yards (860 yards) in an 880 in Scotland in 1:52.8. Handicap races were popular back in the fifties and sixties. The national champion was usually the back marker and the field was handicapped with the idea of all finishing together. For spectators, it was a great event to watch. I won several big meets from the back mark, giving away 180 yards in a mile race. I won Ibrox Sports and Cowal Games mile races in two consecutive races.

Gambling was pretty popular in a lot of these track meets. No bookmaker, just some spectator saying, "I'll take McLatchie for ten pounds." My family made a few good bets backing me to win.

I played golf on a few occasions and attended Methyr Mawr in Wales for a training weekend with the British Milers Club. We slept in bunks and provided our own food. Most of the running was done on the sand dunes. Some of the dunes were pretty steep. We ran three times a day. The coaches were Frank Horwill and Harry Wilson—both UK national coaches. The training sessions were to develop camaraderie amongst the athletes and get an idea what hard training was all about.

At the end of November, I raced in a very foggy and cold 5.6-mile race in Luton, which I won in 29:20. It was two weeks later, I raced in Windsor—5.5 miles in snow which was about six inches deep. I managed to finish second in 30. I raced two more races in December. The first was a road relay, St. Neots to Bedford, where I ran the fastest leg for three miles, 1500 yards in 19:25. Luton managed to finish second overall. The following week, I raced in Shaftesbury, six miles cross country in slippery conditions, where I managed to win in 31:05.

Computers were starting to appear in lot of companies, which resulted in companies needing computer workers. I decided this was the future. The company where I worked, George Kent, was advertising for computer workers. I applied and took the required test, which I was informed I had failed. I thought, "This is bullshit," as I considered myself pretty good at logic questions. I told my brother, Geoffrey, that I had failed. He said he would apply and see what happened. He was informed like me he had failed. I went to human resources and asked if I could see the results of the test I had taken. I was informed that I had failed and I would not see the test results. I thought," These bastards don't like Scottish people."

Since I did not manage to secure a computer job with Kent's, I applied for a job with AC DELCO. I had to take a test, which was similar to the one I had failed at Kent's. After the test, a gentleman approached me and said I had aced the test and asked if I would be interested in working for AC DELCO.

I accepted the position on the spot and went back to Kent's and handed in my immediate resignation. Shortly after I had turned in my resignation, I was told to report to a senior manager, who wanted to know why I was leaving so abruptly. I explained, "I wanted to enter the Computer Data Processing field. Your company rejected me, telling me that I had failed the logic exam, which I took for the other company, which informed me that I had scored 100 percent." He said, "You left us in a bind, who is going to do your job?" I replied, "That is your problem as I am gone."

Chapter 8
1968 — Luton

I reported to AC Delco on January 2, 1968 to work the night shift from midnight until 8 a.m. I was being trained as a Computer Operator. I couldn't run for weeks as I was getting adjusted to working all night and trying to sleep through the day. During this time, I barely saw Mary as she was leaving for work as I was coming home. I tried to get around eight hours of sleep and get out for a run when I got up from bed.

Three weeks later, I raced a 5.6-mile cross country race in Luton, where I managed to run 30:56. I felt terrible, tired all over. Working night shift was taking its toll. After three months, I was placed on days, working 8 a.m. to 4 p.m. with one hour for lunch, which I used for training, running 30 minutes easy. I was enjoying this new life, learning about computers and having time at lunch to get in a run.

By April, I had done no racing. I was busy with the new job and taking a Computer Science course, which meant driving to London twice a week in the evening. At the end of the term, I received a diploma in Computer Science.

I raced in a few inter-club meets, but was not racing very fast because I was not training hard enough. I spent more time coaching Tony Simmons than training myself. I was barely running 1:55 for the half mile and 4:20 for the mile. It is easy to see what happens if you don't do the necessary work to race fast.

In August, Mary informed me that she'd had enough of England and the weather, and that I needed to find a job in America as she wanted to return to the States. I thought, "Jeez! This is a challenge." I was fortunate enough to find a job advertised in the London Times. An American company was interviewing for computer workers. I applied, received an interview, and was offered a job. The job was in Chicago and not in Texas. After the interview, I told Mary I had an offer from Blue Cross Blue Shield, which I'd accepted, but it was in Chicago. She said that was ok as it meant we would be leaving England.

That sounded simple enough and now the challenge. I checked on transportation and the best bet was by the Queen Mary ocean liner. I checked on sailing dates and found one that suited us and Blue Cross, so I made the booking. The journey was from Southampton to New York. Now I had to sell a house, furniture, and a car.

We had an offer on our house, but one week before we were due to sail, the deal fell through as the buyer did not qualify for a loan. I thought, "What the hell next?" I secured a lawyer and did the necessary paperwork assigning him the Power of Attorney.

In August, I entered a mile race in London at the White City and was surprised to find out that Ron Clarke from Australia was in the field. It was a handicap mile and I received a 20-yard start from Ron, who went past me like a train 200 yards from the finish to win.

I talked to him after the race. What an amazing man. He was going to attempt breaking his own two-mile record the following week at Crystal Palace and was asking fellow runners if they would help take him through the first mile in 4:08. It was all set up for the following week, where he ran 8:19.6 to break his world record by 0:0.1.

Later on, in 1983 while my second wife, Carol, and I were in Helsinki for the first IAAF World Championships, Ron was attending with the great Emil Zatopek, who had won multiple gold medals. After the games, Emil escorted Ron to the airport and gave him a package with Zatopek's final words, on the plane steps, "Open it when you are on the plane."

When Ron opened the package, there was a note with one of Emil's gold medals from the Olympics. It gleamed back at him. It was the medal he had won in the 10,000 meters at the 1952 Helsinki Olympics. It was even newly inscribed, "To Ron Clark, "Not out of friendship, but because you deserve it." Bravo, Ron Clarke. You bloody well did.

Sad to say that Ron passed away in June 2015 at the age of 78 from a brief illness. He will always be remembered as a man who gave his best. He told me that if you are fairly fit you should be able to race in a couple of weeks. He, like me, raced on grass and cinder tracks. Different story today.

A couple of highlights while living in England. I met Queen Elizabeth when she was attending some service at Luton-Hoo Estate, which is a traditional Estate that is included as one of England's finest stately homes.

I must admit the Queen was very patient and polite, and liked to chat with the local people. Like me, she loved horse racing and owns several race horses. No! She never gave me any tips.

The other person I met was Tina Turner, the famous singer. In 1966,

Mary and I attended a concert in Dunstable where Tina was performing, and after one of her songs I approached the stage and told her I really enjoyed her show in New Orleans at the 544 Club. She was surprised that anyone in England had seen her perform in the States.

She asked what song she could sing for me. I told her, "Proud Mary," which is my wife's name. Boy did she belt it out. This song was one of her biggest hits for years along with, "What's Love Got To Do With It" and "River Deep Mountain High."

Chapter 9
1968-1969 — Chicago

In September, we travelled to Southampton to catch the Queen Mary and sail to the States. I ran on the ship's deck each morning and just for fun would sit on the first-class deck with the "blue hairs" and listen to them talking about how the cabin class should stay where they belong. I would say, "I totally agree," with sweat dripping down my shirt. I don't think they liked regular people!

The trip was a new experience where I spent my free time exploring the liner, running and walking the decks, and reading a lot. The ship carried around 2,000 passengers and had 12 floors. It took five days to travel from Southampton to New York, where we arrived in the morning.

We had two steamer trunks which contained our clothes and souvenirs from England. Our luggage was picked up at the port in New York and transferred to Chicago. We headed to the airport and boarded a plane for Chicago and on arrival headed to the Sheraton Hotel, where we were given one week to find a place to live. After searching, we found a furnished apartment at 835 W. Buena, which was like a bed sitter, one big room with a bed and a separate kitchen. When our luggage arrived, we moved into the new digs.

Chicago had the famous Democratic convention, which had several riots. While in England, the Daily Mirror's reporter Margie Poops wrote an article about visiting her sister in the area and stated there were some hair-raising moments. I wrote her a letter telling her that we were about to move to Chicago and asked if it was really bad. She said no, there were some good neighborhoods with no problems. The article was sensationalized to sell papers.

I reported to work with Blue Cross Blue Shield as a computer operator working second shift. After a few days, I had a run-in with the shift supervisor as I was wearing a turtleneck sweater, which was fashionable at that time in England. Anyway, we ended up in the office of the person who hired me, and after a lengthy discussion, I was moved into the programming department. I really enjoyed the challenge. After a few weeks, like all of the hires from England, we found out that we were being underpaid. There was nothing we could do about the situation as we all had signed a contract which was binding for one year.

I searched out the local running club, which was Chicago Track Club situated on the south side. I trained at Washington Park and introduced myself to Ted Hayden, the coach, and some of the team members.

I had my first race on November 4th at Washington Park over four miles, where I finished fourth in 20:27. I raced the next two Saturdays, five miles, where I was sixth in 25:47 and four miles, where I was fourth in 21:03. I ran in an AAU Regional championship race over 10,000 meters where I finished second in 32:08. The month of December was a disaster as I came down with the flu, which kept me inactive for several weeks. I believe a new job and the change in temperature caught up with me.

I ran my first race in 1969 in January, indoors at the University of Chicago over 880 yards on a 220-yard unbanked track. I ran 1:59. I didn't race again until the middle of February, where I travelled to Champaign, Illinois to compete in an indoor mile where I ran 4:19 (62, 65, 69, 63), and later I ran a leg of the 4x440 relay at 52:6. A week later, I slipped on the ice and ended up with a bruised ankle, which incapacitated me for a week.

I raced again during the middle of March in two relay events. I ran a leg of a distance medley which was 880 in 1:57.5 and later ran a leg in the 4x880 in 1:58.2, where we placed first. A week later, we travelled to Kalamazoo, Michigan, where I led off in a 4x mile in 4:19.2, which we won. I came back later to run a 3000-meter steeplechase where the water jump was the long jump pit. I managed to finish second in 9:25.6. A week later, I won the Central AAU one-mile championships in 4:12 with splits of 62, 64, 65, 61, where I felt strong the whole race. The training I was doing was paying dividends. I travelled to the University of Chicago to train indoors.

The outdoor season started in April, where I raced a mile on Stagg Field at the University of Chicago in very windy and cold conditions. I won in 4:20.9 (63, 66, 66, and 64). I raced a few more times, nothing spectacular except in a medley relay, where I ran 1:55.3. During the month of June, I raced a couple more times—a four-mile race at Stagg Field, which I won in 19:45.3, and then a mile race in Sterling, Illinois, where I won in 4:19.3.

In July, I raced some cross-country races at Riis Park, where I won a three-mile race in 14:52, and a week later, a four-mile race in 21:05. At the end of the month, I raced over an hour for distance, where I recorded 11 miles, 382 yards, which left me sore for a week.

I played golf every week in the summer at Waveland Golf Course, and on occasion, would run there in the evening. Many a time, while having an easy run, I was chased in a golf cart by one of the workers. I used to enjoy being chased as it was good for my speed work. I always managed to climb the fence with no mishap and never was caught.

Mary and I drove to Guelph, Ontario, Canada to visit my brother Geoffrey, who was studying at the University. Like me, he decided he needed to move on and get an education and new life. We were gone for five days, a deserved break I needed with no running for four weeks.

Work was going well, but like most recruited workers from England, after a year, I decided to look a for a new job in the computer field where I could earn more money and have better benefits. I found a job at CPC International, which manufactured Mazola Oil, Argo corn starch, and Best Food mayonnaise. I was hired as the manager of the computer operations, which ran three shifts. The company was running two computers, and with the advent of the IBM 360, running three partitions. I decided to move all work from one computer to the other, getting rid of the other machine at a huge benefit to the company.

I also realized that to climb the ladder in a company in America, one needed a degree. I applied to North Park University to finish the degree I had started at Lamar University six years earlier. I decided on Economics with a minor in English. I must admit it was tough going. Attending night school, working, and trying to run was going to be a task.

We secured a new apartment on Jarvis Street, which was an easy walk to the 'EL' (elevated train service in Chicago), which took me downtown to work. We also bought a car which was a baby blue 1964 Mustang, which we only drove on weekends when we left the city to explore other neighborhoods.

In November, the cross-country season was starting and I was in good shape. The first race was in Washington Park, where I raced four miles in 19:42, finishing second. The following week I won over four miles in 19:47. A couple of weeks later, I came down with a sore throat which was caused by trying to run in the snow, and I missed a whole week of running. I managed to get in a race at the end of December, where I ran 1320 yards indoors, finishing second in 3:9.1 (62, 65, and 62.1). I was through racing for the year.

Chapter 10
USA 1970

In January, I raced an indoor mile in Chicago, where I won in 4:18.9 (62, 66, 68, and 62.9). A couple of weeks later, I anchored the distance medley, where our team finished second. I ran the mile leg in 4:15. A week later, I raced over a half-mile, where I finished third in 1:56.6. I managed to secure a key to the indoor track at Northwestern University, which was about five miles from our apartment. I travelled there twice a week, where I trained by myself. I was not as worn down as I had been travelling from the north side of Chicago to the University of Chicago.

During the first week of February, I travelled with the team to Kalamazoo, Michigan, where I anchored the distance medley, running the mile in 4:19, which we won. I came back later to anchor the sprint medley, where I ran a half-mile in 1:58.6 and the team finished second. I raced three more times that month: a half-mile in 1:57.9, a mile in 4:18, and two miles in 9:35.

Work at CPC International was interesting as I was travelling to other plants studying their computer installations and taking ideas and suggestions to management about how they might improve their facility. I was making inroads, introducing new techniques and eliminating old ones. Management was pleased with my work as I was saving them quite a lot of money.

I raced only once in March due to work commitments and university studies, where I was making 'A's' in most of my classes. I won the Central Illinois Indoor Championship mile in 4:16. I raced again in April in Columbus, Ohio in a one-mile indoor event, where I won in 4:16.1 (62, 66, 65, and 63.1). I raced a couple of times outdoors in May. I won a six-mile race in 30.05 with splits of 4:52, 5.00, 5.03, 5.10, 5.09, and 4.51. A week later, I won a three-mile race in 14:28.

I finished finals and work was progressing and I also learned I was going to be a father in December. I raced a couple of more times in June at Stagg Field. I won a half-mile in 1:55.9, and a week later won a mile in 8:18.6. I took a month of from racing. Workouts were easy, just jogging. I raced once in July at Riis Park, in a four-mile cross country race which I won in 20:15.

July through September, I hardly did much running as I was busy with work, and stuck to jogging easy with no speed work. In October, I raced a few times. I ran in a 30K race, which was the furthest I had ever attempted, where I won in 1:48:22. I then raced in a four-mile cross country race in Washington Park, finishing third in 20:08. I raced there again two weeks later to finish fourth in 20:20. A few days later, I ended up with a sore hip, which put me out of commission until July 1971.

I started University again, studying hard and edging towards a degree. I was very busy at work with new projects and ideas.

Heather was born on December 4, 1970 in and all of a sudden, my life changed. I had a newborn baby, and I was studying and working hard. The only thing missing from the American dream was owning a new house.

Chapter 11
USA — 1971

In April, I was told at work that I was being transferred to company headquarters in Englewood Cliffs, New Jersey, to be the manager of computer operations, which was a step up the ladder. Mary and I drove with Heather to look for a place to live, and we found one in Fort Lee on Valley Street. It was situated at the bottom of a hill, which meant it was hell to get out of the neighborhood in the winter. When it was snowing and slippery, the Mustang only had a rear wheel drive, so I had to back up the hill in. Another challenge.

It took me a wee while to get used to the new surroundings and the job. I was in charge of supervising three shifts of computer operators, schedulers, the tape library and 20 key punch operators. My new boss was a right bastard who knew very little about computers. I later found out that his mother owned a lot of shares in CPC International and part of the deal was to find him a managerial job. Lucky me, I was the one that had to report to him.

I joined the CPC indoor ten-pin bowling league and was part of the DP (data processing) team that met once a week, which was good for camaraderie and a chance to BS, plus drink a couple of beers. I was averaging 168, which wasn't too bad considering I was only playing once per week.

I had one course left to graduate and get a degree in Economics, and had to receive permission from North Park College to finish my degree at another school. I applied to Fairleigh Dickinson in Teaneck, NJ, where I was accepted. The course I had left was advanced English. I signed up, attended classes twice a week, and made an A at the end of the term, which entailed a lot of reading and writing essays. I was glad all the university studying was over. I now had a degree, which was a necessity in the States to advance in the job market, but later found out that knowing someone carried more weight than having a degree. My immediate boss was a good example.

We bought a 1972 MGB-GT, which was more or less a two-seater with a small seat in the back. When I had a break from work, we drove to Miami, Florida where we spent a few days lying in the sun and swimming. One day, we decided to go to the Gulfstream Horse race track and I was really surprised that security would not let us enter because Heather was under 21. I had a tough time with that decision as Heather wasn't even a year old. Ah well, rules. Returning back to Fort Lee, we took our time and did some sightseeing.

Returning to work, I had new challenges. One that incident stood out was when the supplier of our computer paper and supplies showed up and asked me to sign a blank sheet of paper for supplies. I chased him off and told him to come back with a quote for our requirements and make sure he sharpened his pencil. I was required to put supplies out for bid and then make a decision when I received the bids. Another company showed up and presented me with a quote, which I deliberated for a bit, when the rep said, "Give me the contract and you can have a new color TV." I told him, "You cannot buy me," and I realized that this is how business was conducted before. I told him that I had a few more quotes to look at before I made a decision. I chose his company because his prices were cheaper than others, and cheaper than the year before, but I did not take the TV.

I didn't do much running the rest of the year as I was still recovering from a hip injury, plus with no running, I had put on about ten pounds in weight. My new boss and I were at logger heads most of the times. I finally realized he didn't like other men who went toe-to-toe with him. I guess he thought that since he was the boss, his subordinates should cow down to him. I guess he never supervised a Scotsman.

Chapter 12
USA — 1972

Everything came to a head on January 1, 1972, when my second shift members were celebrating bringing in the New Year and had left some celebration bottles on top of the computer. When the night security guard noticed the bottles, he reported the incident to upper management. A day later, my drunken boss called me at night and told me to fire everyone that was involved. I told him I wouldn't do that, but I would reprimand them, and told him I would see him in the morning.

The next day, I guess things didn't work out, as I found out later that he wanted one of his buddies to take over from me. Later on, I had to report to the director of data processing, who informed me that I was being sent back to Chicago to design and implement a new payroll system and when complete, I had to leave and find another job. He then told me to go and report to my immediate boss, which I did. I approached his office and told his secretary that I had to report to him. I entered his office and he would not look at me. Finally, I said he was a conniving bastard and leaned across the desk and grabbed him by the tie and told him, "If I hit you it's your word against mine." When I left, his secretary said to me, "I wish you had hit him, because someone needs to kick his ass." She might have said he started abusing me if I had slapped him a couple of times. Ah well, another adventure. Now to arrange a place to live in Chicago.

In May, after we secured an address, I told work where to ship our furniture. Mary and I decided to drive back to Chicago as it would be senseless to arrive at Bosworth Street before our furniture.

We took our time and visited out-of-the-way places and enjoyed the lazy drive.

I had some vacation time and decided to take Heather with me to Scotland to visit my family. Boy was that a journey as Heather had to sit on my knee for the whole flight. When we arrived in Prestwick, I rented a car and we drove to Muirkirk, where we spent two weeks, which gave Heather a chance to get used to her new surroundings. It also gave me time to go for a run in the hills, which I enjoyed.

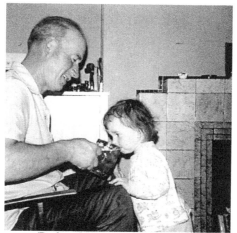

Dad and Heather having a sip.

Mum and Heather.

Chapter 13
1972 — Chicago

After two weeks, we headed back to Chicago, where I had to report to work and design and implement a computerized payroll system. I worked with Harold Carlson, who was told the same as me that when the system was implemented, we were terminated. I thought, "This is BS," and started looking for a job. In October, I found a job with Playskool Toys and started work as a Computer Analyst.

When I came back to Chicago, I was still not doing any running, nursing my hip, which still bothered me after six months. One of my former teammates suggested I go see the White Sox baseball team's physiotherapist. It was an interesting visit. After an extensive examination and putting me through a series of exercises, he told me I was okay to run. I told him that I still had some soreness when I tried to run. He looked at me and said, "What is hurting is your head, now get to hell out of here and start running." So, I started jogging again and after a few weeks, the pain disappeared. I guess it was in my head.

My first job with Playskool Toys was to design a labor incentive system for the production lines that manufactured toys. I had to work with the local union, which was a new challenge. I would time each line to find out how long it took from start to finish to produce the finished article. Mondays and Fridays were bad days to measure production as the workers just went through the motions. After several weeks, I came up with a formula which was accepted by both management and the union.

I calculated that to make a livable wage, they had to run at 100 percent each day, but to make a bit extra, just crank up the production belt. Monday and Friday were considered around 100 percent, running at normal speed, whereas the other days, the line would be running at 115 percent, which the workers cranked up to make extra money in their paycheck.

One of the benefits was that I received prototype toys for Heather to play with, and after a couple of weeks, I had to fill in a form answering questions that were used to make adjustments before the products were released to the market. It was a good way of doing quality control. Going to the offsite production plant also meant I could go for a run at lunch time in Horner Park.

One lunch time after a run I was having a shower when I dropped a contact lens. I was on my hands and knees looking for it when in walked the Harlem Globetrotters after their workout in the gym. Meadowlark Lemmon asked me why I was on my knees, I told him I had dropped one of my contacts, next thing I knew that he and some other Globetrotters were helping me retrieve my contact. It must have looked strange with one white guy and three black guys on their knees in the showers. A great bunch of guys. I saw them every lunch time when I went running. We had a great rapport. To them, I was the crazy white guy running in circles.

Working for Playskool was a nice, relaxed atmosphere. I had a good boss and good co-workers. After ten months, I implemented the labor incentive program. Working with the union and trying to convince the workers that with a little bit of effort they could make a decent living was an eye-opener. I was learning new procedures and developing new production systems.

I started racing again in October and my first race was over three miles cross country, which I won in 15:34. The following week, I raced again over four miles and finished fourth in 21:00. The following week, I raced again in Madison, Wisconsin over six miles and finished 12th in 32:01. I felt tired near end of the race. I guess three races in a row was taking its toll. Two weeks later, I raced over six miles in Parkside, Wisconsin where I finished 12th in 29:42. I should have finished better than 12th but I had a brain fart and didn't realize I still had 400 yards to the finish.

A week later, I raced in a five-mile race in South Bend, Indiana, on the Notre Dame campus, where I finished fifth in 25:25 in cold, damp conditions. Two weeks later, I raced in a Central AAU 10,000-meter championship in Washington Park, where I finished sixth out of 200 runners in 32:40. I stopped racing after that race and concentrated on work and ran easy most days.

Dogs off the leash are a runner's worst enemy, and I have been bitten a few times. While running with John Lesch, my training partner in the park near Foster Beach, there was a dog off the leash that started chasing us. John told the owner to get the dog under control, which he didn't, so John jogged back and punched the guy in the mouth. Now the owner took some action and started to run after us cussing obscenities and threatening what he was going to do when he caught us. We knew he would never catch us in 100 years. So, when he was out of breath and leaning over, John jogged back and hit him again. I had never done speed work before like this. Needless to say, the owner never caught us.

Another dog episode happened to a friend of mine. While running through a Chicago park, there was a man walking a dog on a length of rope and each time my friend ran past him, he would let the rope out and the dog would give chase, and just before the dog was going to bite, he reeled in the dog. My friend stopped and told him he runs in the park most days and if the dog chases him again, he will shoot the dog. The owner told him he was full of BS. Three days later while running, he passed the owner and the dog again and the owner let out the rope. My friend stopped, took out his revolver, and shot the dog dead. The owner hanging onto his dead dog said, "You just shot my dog." My friend said, "I told you I would." While he finished his run, the police arrived and took him to jail. As you are allowed one phone call, he called his good friend, the mayor of Chicago, Richard Dailey, who got him released him from jail and had the police write him a ticket for "discharging a firearm on city property," which was a slap on the wrist. I didn't race the rest of the year and concentrated instead on work and easy jogging.

Chapter 14
1973 — Chicago

I started out the New Year with a three-mile race indoors at the University of Chicago, where I finished second in 14:41.3. Three weeks later, I raced over 10 miles at Riis Park, where I won in very windy and cold conditions in 53:28. I alternated working indoors at the University Chicago and Northwestern University on Mondays and Wednesdays.

I raced in a five-mile cross country handicap at Riis Park, where I was giving starts up to five minutes and I finished ninth in 24:51, which was a new course record.

The weather was cold and there was a lot of snow, which made running outside pretty tough. Running along Lake Michigan was the toughest part with wind blowing off the lake. A couple of times, the wind chill dropped the temperature to -40° F. I wore glasses, which were a bugger in the winter. Once when running down Sheridan Road, I turned toward the Lake and came to lying on the sidewalk. Seemingly my glasses froze up and I ran into a telephone pole, which knocked me on my ass. Luckily, I was not hurt. I finished my run and the next day I was fitted for contact lenses.

In the middle of March, two teammates and I drove to Kalamazoo, Michigan for an indoor meet. I was driving the car of our coach, Ted Haydon. He was in New York with the 4x880 team and would meet us in Kalamazoo. Needless to say, we never made it. We hit a snowstorm around Albion and later a white out, where I couldn't see anything. I slowed down and when I could finally see, I saw cars and trucks strewn all over the freeway. I slowed down, and then all of a sudden, I was skidding. I had two choices: hit the people on the side of the road or the car in front of me. I chose the car in front. What a mess as the front end was demolished. Luckily, no one was hurt. Several other drivers headed to the median that had about two feet of snow. It was a disaster. We were transported to a school by the National Guard, where we were given something to eat and a cot. Later, I found out that 21 inches of snow had fallen and 1,600 people were stranded. What a mess.

We investigated the status of the car, which needed a new front end and had been towed to a local garage. I managed to contact Ted, who never made it to Kalamazoo, and explained the status. We had to rent a car to drive back to Chicago. The garages and rental companies did a great business. Amazing what snow, ice and winds does. Luckily no one was killed, and we only suffered a few scrapes and bruises.

Ted Haydon

20th Anniversary Dinner
June 6, 1970

Ted Haydon

Ted was the track coach at the University of Chicago and founder of the University of Chicago Track Club. He was an assistant coach for the 1968 and 1972 U.S. Olympic Teams and for the 1963 and 1979 Pan American Games. He was also inducted into the USA Track & Field Hall of Fame and the U.S. Track & Field and Cross Country Coaches Association Hall of Fame.

Ted taught me a lot about coaching and told me not to be too serious all the time, to have some fun. He kept a list of excuses that athletes would present to him if they missed a workout, like, "I couldn't find my spikes as the dog ate them!"

He was heard muttering one day about an elder runner who loved

69

to do long runs in Washington Park, saying," Every time he goes on one of his runs through the park, I worry that he's going to get arrested for loitering."

He coached numerous great athletes that included Rick Wohlhuter, who held the world record in the 880 yards at 1:44.10 (1:43.5 at 800 meters), and a world record in the 1000-meter event at 2:13.9, which remains the longest standing. He won the nation's top amateur athlete in 1974 for his achievements. He represented the USA in two Olympic Games and won a bronze medal in 800 meters in the 1976 Olympics.

Ted also coached Brian Oldfield, a shot putter who was 6'5" tall and weighed 275 pounds, a giant of a man. Brian made the 1972 Olympics, where he finished in sixth place. Like a few athletes that were lobbying to be paid, he competed as a professional throughout the 1970s with the International Track Association (ITA), and set several marks which would have been world records, had they been recognized by the IAAF. These included an indoor mark of 72-6½ and in 1975, he recorded a throw of 75 feet outdoors.

Brian and I would travel to compete in my 1964 Mustang. He was a hell of a guy, always up to something. I never knew what he was going to do next. He used to compete wearing speedo swim trunks or enter the ring smoking a cigarette.

I ran one more race indoors at the end of March at the University of Chicago, a 3,000-meter steeplechase, which I won in 9:11. The sand pit was the water jump. The following week, I raced outdoors in De Kalb, Illinois, in 30 mph wind. I remember leading in the first lap running into the wind, where I could hardly move, and still leading in the second lap, I just stopped and told the field that someone else had to take the lead. We all stood there for about five seconds before someone else decided to lead. I waited until the last 200, where I had the wind in my back and ran 28 seconds. The winning time was 4:24.

During the month of May, Mary, Heather, and I travelled to Houston to visit the in-laws. During my visit, I raced at Rice University in a 3,000-meter steeplechase, which I won in 9:34. It was a strange race as they forgot to put water in the pit. I later ran a mile in Chicago in the month of June, where I finished second in 4:18.9. At the end of the month, along with John Lesch, we raced in an eight-mile Paarlauf, which was a two-person team where each member raced alternate miles. I recorded 4:26, 4:22, 4:35 and 4:28 for an average of 4:27. John averaged 4:24. We won with a time of 35:28.

The next couple of months I ran easy and didn't do anything of note as I was busy with work and getting ready for our second child, Amy, who was born on August 14th. That put me out of commission for a few weeks taking care of Heather, household chores, and giving Mary a deserved break.

I kept doing some semblance of training and entered a five-mile cross country race in Washington Park, where I finished fifth in 26:14 in horrible conditions—pouring rain and mud. I raced again a week later at Washington Park over four miles where I finished first in 20:06. I had started running the seven miles home from work on Tuesdays and Thursdays. This really helped the household as I was through running for the day and helped with the kids, playing, getting them ready for bed, and reading stories. What a life—parenthood.

I raced a few more races but my head wasn't really into training hard with work and home life. I increased my run home from work to 12 miles and started to build some base.

I brought my mother over to Chicago from Scotland for a vacation and while she was here, we drove to Houston so she could meet the in-laws in Texas, where we spent a few days. Then we headed to New Orleans, visiting the Cajun sites and black nightclubs. On the way back to Chicago driving through Mississippi, someone had a pot shot at the car, hitting the windshield. Luckily it was BB not a bullet. It was not a stone from another car as we were the only vehicle on the road.

I was asked to be an usher at a friend's wedding and accepted. The wedding was to be held in a church. I was not so sure how I would react to being in a church, especially a wedding.

Growing up in Scotland as a youth in Glenbuck, I attended church and Sunday School three times a day on Sundays. Our area was the Church of Scotland, which is like the Presbyterian Church. In the winter, it was okay, as it got one out of the rain and snow and gave my old man and my mother time to themselves.

While I attended school in Muirkirk, we had religious instruction every day in class, except on Fridays, where all classes would meet and sing their hearts out.

Me as a wedding usher in 1973.

I hardly attended church in the following 16 years and was not so sure that I could follow protocol. I had to attend rehearsals on Friday, the day before the big day. I had never had to attend a rehearsal before. The minister showed up and told us where to stand, and all of a sudden, a light came on shining in my eyes. I said, "I cannot fuckin' see." All I heard was laughter from the groom and the best man, and then the minister asked, "Will he swear tomorrow during the ceremony?" Response, "No guarantee." Needless to say, I behaved myself and the wedding was a success.

Chapter 15
1974 — Chicago

At the end of January, I raced an 18-mile road relay at Riis Park, where I averaged 5 min 12 sec in weather that was very windy and 26 degrees, which was awful. I raced a couple more times in February—finishing second in a six-mile road race in 32:13, and winning an eight-mile road race in 42:18.

Racing in Chicago was miserable. Some days, it was blowing a gale and temperatures were under 35 degrees. That is why most racing is done on the indoor circuit. I liked running outdoors more so than indoors, although I trained indoors at least once per week trying to keep a semblance of pace.

I raced a couple of longer races in March on the roads in Riis Park, where the snow was always. I finished second in a 15K in 48:53 and fourth in a 25K, which was a long way for me, in 1:25:32.

With the longer runs, John and I decided to race in a marathon in Des Moines, Iowa. John was in good shape and could run all day, whereas I wasn't so sure about tackling a marathon, which seemed a long way. The course was one circuit around the city, and during the race, the temperature rose to 76 degrees. I made it to halfway and had to stop. Sitting on the curb at the side of the road popping blisters, I wondered what I had gotten myself into. Knowing that I had run/staggered 14 miles and the race was a circle around Des Moines, I decided I needed to plod on as the way I was going was toward the finish line. I finished in 2:50.10. John won the race in 2:26:03, six minutes ahead of the next finisher. I felt elated for him and confused for myself as to why I had entered.

One evening in May, driving home along Sheridan Road, I was waiting for a green light at the stop light at North Lake Shore Drive. I started moving forward, and in the middle of the intersection I was hit on the right front side by a car that had run the stop light.

I managed to get out with no injury and found I had a damaged right fender. Approaching the car that hit me, it looked like a penguin was driving. Then I realized it was a nun. The police were called and one arrived on the scene; his name was O'Brien. I thought, "Oh, shit, this is going to be interesting." I took him off to the side to look at the synchronization of the stop lights and after several minutes of discussion, it was deemed that the nun had run the stop sign.

So, I asked, "Are you going to give her a ticket for running a stop sign?" He said, 'You cannot give a sister a ticket." I thought, "Jeez, maybe I need to become a priest." The police called a tow truck to take my car to be fixed. After it was fixed, when I got it home, I checked the trunk and discovered the spare wheel was missing. I called the dealer, who told me that there was no spare when I left the car. Bloody liars. Now I was out a spare. I should have checked the MG before I left. Stupid.

One day at work, some top management from Milton Bradley, who owned Playskool, visited and had a meeting with our top management. My immediate boss was summoned upstairs and in about 20 minutes returned with a security guard. I asked what was going on and he told me he was fired and didn't know the reason. He was told to go back to his office put on his coat and leave. They told him they would send his personal belongings to his house.

I thought, "This is strange," so I went and asked to talk to someone from Milton Bradley to find out what was going on. I was informed there were some changes coming and not to worry as my job was safe and not to worry about my boss. I returned downstairs and had a meeting with my two programmers and informed them what was going on. I also said to them that if they could do that to our boss with little explanation, it could happen to us. I told them that I was going to look for a new job, and they both said they would do the same thing. We agreed that when we found one, we would all resign on the same day. We all found new jobs and two weeks later, the three of us turned in our resignation at the same time. Within an hour, I was summoned to the office of the acting data processing manager and told we couldn't do that as there was no one to take over our jobs. I told him "We just don't trust you and cannot work under the threat that we might be next to hit the door. Have a good day."

I obtained a new job with the City of Chicago's data processing management department as a project manager. The interview process was strange. I had an interview with four people and the first question was, "Are you a Democrat?" I said, "I am a Scotsman." They all looked at me and said, "Just a minute." In a couple of minutes, they responded, "You're hired." I thought, "This is strange, maybe since Dailey, the mayor, was Irish, they thought he and I were from the same tribe."

Not once did they ask me about what I could do or not do in the data processing arena.

The first job I was assigned to do was to deliver an envelope to the treasurer for the City of Oak Park. The envelope was not sealed, so I had a look inside. Mmm-hmm…a nice racket going on. Ah well, this is Chicago. I worked on several projects, and it was nice and easy to get to work. I walked up the road to Howard Street elevated station and rode the train to Monroe Street and walked to work, which was all underground. The facility was under the Picasso Statue on Dailey Plaza. The only time I saw daylight was to go upstairs and check the weather. It took a wee while to get used to working underground, but when you're busy, you don't notice daylight.

I raced a few times through August, nothing to brag about. In August, I acted as pace-maker for Rick Wohlhuter in an attempt to break four minutes for the mile. I took the field halfway in at 1:59 and then stepped off the track. Rick went on to record 4:1.2. He competed in the 1972 and 1976 Olympics, winning bronze in the 800 meters in the 1976 Olympics with a time of 1:44.12. He held the world record for 1000 meters for six years, after he ran 2:13.9. He was relieved of the record by Sebastian Coe, who ran 2:13.40. Rick also held the world record for 800 meters in 1:43.5 and 880 in 1:44.10.

Leading Wohlhuter through the 880 in 1:59.

The University of Chicago had a good core of half-milers. In 1973, they held the world record with a time of 7:10.4. in the 4x880 relay. The team was Tom Bach: 1:50.5, Ken Sparks: 1:47.1, Lowell Paul: 1:48.0, and Rick Wohlhuter: 1:44.8.

I raced a five-mile cross country race in Washington Park in October, where I finished second in 25:30. I raced a couple more times before the end of the year, but nothing exciting. I was getting used to my new job and being a father of two girls.

There is one thing about having young kids—you have to keep your eye on them all the time. I was in the park with Mary, Heather, and Amy. Heather was on a swing, and I sat down with Amy and noticed that Heather had lifted the safety bar and as she was going forward, she took off. I jumped up, dived, and caught her before she hit the ground, but the swing clattered me on the back. Luckily, I held on and Heather escaped unscathed. I had a bruised ego and back. I am sure parents need another set of eyes.

Lake Michigan — Heather and Amy.

Our three-story building was sold to a male hairdresser. I had a tough time with Heather, who imitated his speech, which was funny but could be embarrassing in front of the landlord. To save money on heating, he would turn the heat down, which made living uncomfortable. I had enough of his BS and called the health department. When they knew I worked for the city, action was swift, and the landlord was told to raise the heat or face a hefty fine.

I think he got back at me. When I returned from a run one night in the dark and was coming into the back of the apartment, I fell into the sewer as someone had removed the cover. Luckily, I didn't go all the way in, only one leg went into the hole. I managed to get myself out with just a bruise. I stood up, checked my leg, decided it was not broken, replaced the cover, and felt like kicking somebody's ass.

Chapter 16
1975 — Chicago

I didn't race much, as I was busy with my new job learning the ropes and finding out how a big city operated, which was an education. I was learning new procedures and how to be a father. It's amazing how one's life changes when you're married and have a couple of kids.

I used to take the kids to the local park and watch them on the swings and slide. Once when I was not paying attention, Heather came down head-first and had a slight gash on her head, which didn't need much medical attention. It was an education for me. "You cannot take your eye off young kids."

The last week in April, I received a call from home in Scotland and was told that my mother was dying from cancer. I approached my boss and stated that I needed to go to Scotland immediately and visit my mother. I was told to take as much time as possible. I booked a flight to Glasgow, Scotland then rented a car and drove to Muirkirk. My dad had my mother released from hospital while I was there, which made it easier than driving to Ballochmyle hospital every day. I found out that she had bone cancer which had spread to other organs in the body and she would not live too long.

After a week, she returned to hospital and on one of the visits, I had a talk with the oncologist about why there were so many deaths in the area from cancer. He told me most of it was from the fallout from the atomic testing in America in the forties and fifties that landed in Scotland and contaminated the water and grasses.

It really got worse when the Chernobyl disaster happened in 1986. Part of the fallout landed in Scotland and Muirkirk suffered a lot. Hares, rabbits, grouse, and all bird species disappeared from the hills. The local reservoir was closed and fresh water was piped in from the east of Scotland. Farmers were paid by the government to keep producing cattle and sheep which couldn't be eaten. It took over 20 years for the radioactive material to disappear and farmers were once again allowed to sell their animals for food. Now walking in the moors, one will say, "What was that, it sounds like a bird?"

My last visit with my mother was very emotional as we both knew that the end was near. We said our goodbyes and I returned to Chicago the next day. My mother died two weeks later on March 21, 1975, at 62 years old. This was the second member of my family to die from the scourge cancer. More to come.

I was just getting settled into the new job and upon returning to Chicago, Mary told me that she was fed up with living there and wanted to return to Texas. Oh boy! What next. Her mind was made up, and she drove the two kids to Houston and looked for a house which she found. She said that we needed to pack up and go. She left Heather and Amy with her parents and flew back to Chicago.

I thought, "This is going to be tough," as I liked Chicago and my job and now had to pack up and hit the road to Houston, where I didn't have a job.

Being a family man now, I turned in my resignation and told the landlord we were leaving—he was probably elated and happy to get rid of us. I booked a U-Haul and asked a couple of friends to help me load up the truck. Whatever belongings we couldn't fit in the truck we left at the side of the road.

I was so nervous about driving a truck in Chicago. Harold Carlson, who was my dear friend, offered to drive the truck to the freeway heading south and I would follow in his car, which we did. Then we exchanged vehicles, said our goodbyes, and Mary and I headed south, me as a cautious, sometimes white-knuckled driver at times.

Chapter 17
1975 — Houston, Texas

During the month of April, we drove south on US 55 and I was a nervous wreck crossing the Mississippi river in St. Louis. As the journey progressed, I became a bit more confident in my driving. We kept heading south until we hit US 10 and headed for our house in Houston, only stopping once.

We arrived at the house but couldn't move in until I signed some papers. We stayed with Mary's parents for the evening. I had missed the kids and it was sure great to see them again.

The next day, I signed the necessary papers, unloaded the truck, and tried to determine where we would put the furniture. After completing that task, I had to look for a job.

Not being the smartest guy on the planet, I decided to try the City of Houston, as I thought working for the City of Chicago would help. I was hired as a programmer and told my immediate boss, "I am not a programmer," but was informed that was the position I was hired into. One of the supervisors raised hell about me not wanting to program, so we finally ended with the manager and she was told I was the project leader for anything to do with planning.

After getting settled in with a home and a job, I noticed there wasn't much happening on the running scene and decided I needed to do something about the situation. I went to Memorial Park to do some running and meet the locals who were into running. The people I met thought it was a good idea to start up a club and try to organize the sport.

We met later and after a few beers, the Houston Harriers were born with the following people: Al Lawrence, who won the bronze medal in the 1956 Olympics 10,000 meters, Don Baxter, Len Hilton, who ran in the 1972 Olympics, Dan Green, a local runner, Simon McNamee, whom I went to college with at Lamar University, and Bob Cozens, an Australian I raced against while at Lamar. We formed the club and were given titles which didn't really mean much as I did most of the work. I was the treasurer, and who better to take care of the finances than a Scotsman.

We were always being chastised as being thrifty with a pound (British money).

We lived not too far from Houston Baptist University, which had a Mondo type track, which I used in the evening. I met Jim Massey, who was the Dean of Students, and asked him if it would be alright to hold some evening races for the local kids. He checked with the school, who thought this was a great idea. Now that I had been given permission to hold track meets, how was I going to get the word out? I decided to approach the sports editors of the two local papers—the *Houston Chronicle* and *Houston Post*. I told them what I wanted to do, but I said I needed help to advertise the event, which they both decided to do.

I went out and bought $100 worth of medals and decided to hold age-handicapped races with no distance greater than 200 yards. Everything went well for several weeks when I noticed one boy lining up to race, and thought, "He is older than the other runners." I asked his age, which he told me, and I informed him he was in the wrong race, so I didn't let him run.

When his dad noticed he wasn't in the race, he came out of the stand and made a bee line for me and started berating me about why his son wasn't in the race. I told him that his son was very honest and said his father had told him to enter that race. At the end of the discussion, I said there would be no more races as I don't have time for cheats. I gave him the medals that were left and told him to tell the other parents why there would be no more meets.

Work was interesting, learning about how things were being done. I knew that after working with the City of Chicago, I wouldn't learn too much more. One of my workmates suggested that I apply to Houston Community College to teach data processing. I did and started teaching two classes—RPG programming and Introduction to Data Processing. I taught in the evenings at Sharpstown High School which was about a mile from the house. Heather used to accompany me to classes on occasion and told me I was a meanie because I gave a few Fs to some students. Yes, I did, but they earned them.

I started scouting areas looking for a place to hold cross country races for the local kids. I found a grassy area on Brays Bayou off Allen Parkway at Montrose Blvd. I walked around and I thought, "This is an excellent location for racing and training."

I approached the newspapers again and sought some help to spread the word that the Harriers were holding cross country races and all were welcome. Most of the races I held were age-graded and on most occasions, there would be one for male and female.

I would send the results to the papers but nothing was printed, so I had to make another trip to the sports editors and told them it would mean so much for kids to see their name in the paper. One editor said I was the only one who visited him to ask for space. With some persuasion, he agreed to give me some space in the paper on Thursdays. Later on, they assigned a reporter to cover the sport.

I did a little bit of running, but spent more time coaching athletes that joined the club. I wrote schedules and kept training records of all athletes, which I could use later to decide what the next step would be in their progress.

Before one of the Rice University open meets, I told Len Hilton he would break four minutes for the mile. He looked at me as if I was crazy as no one had ever broken four minutes for a mile in Texas. I said, "Don't worry, it will happen." The day of the race, I had to go to the dentist to have a wisdom tooth extracted. I showed up for the race with a numb jaw and blood drooling out of my mouth. When Len saw me, he said, "Let's wait until next week when you will be healthier." I said, "No way. The race is on." I took him through the 880-yard mark in 1s:58. He went on to record 3:59.3 on a cinder track.

Len Hilton

Chapter 18
1976 — Houston, Texas

I had been training fairly hard, mostly easy runs and was getting in shape. In January, I was helping an athlete run part of the Houston Marathon, which was a three-loop course. I decided I would bail out at the 20-mile mark. I started out running easy. I went through 15 miles in 1:28, and at 18 miles the wheels fell off. I was toast. I covered the last two miles in 14:08. My 20-mile time was 2:01:28. What an experience. I wondered if race walkers hurt this much.

Two weeks later, Len Hilton and I raced in a two-person, ten-mile relay. Each runner runs alternate 440s and runs a total of 20 quarters. We won the race in 43:40; where I averaged 68 seconds per 440, Len averaged 62.5 seconds. Len started out running under 60 seconds per lap. I told him slow down as I wasn't getting enough rest. Once, I hid, and when Len was coming down the straight for the exchange, he couldn't see me on the track. All I heard was, "McLatchie, where the hell are you?" He was hell-bent on winning. He told me that the team from Rice University was not going to beat us. One has to remember that Len was an Olympian and he had that tenacity of giving it all.

In March, I ran a ten-mile handicap road race, which was a strange affair. The field took off from Memorial Park, heading out on Memorial Drive for five miles then turning and heading back to the park. Just before heading into the park, you crossed under a railroad track and then left into the park. As I made the turn, I noticed runners in front of me clambering up to the railroad track and then into the park, cutting around 200 yards off the course. Like an idiot, I stayed on the road and protested at the finish and was told, "On the way back, you can go any route as long as one gets back to the finish line." It was a strange rule and I was a wee bit wiser.

In April, I entered the Bayou Classic, which was a five-mile handicap race with a field of over 200 runners. I was the scratch runner and giving starts up to eight minutes. I kept passing runners and had no idea what place I was in. Approaching the entrance to Memorial Park I asked a spectator how many runners were in front of me, and he responded,

"Two." I caught one guy 100 yards later. One to go, and I could see him in the distance. I finally passed him with 200 yards to the finish, where I won in 26:08. Back then, there was no real certification of a race distance. Just jump in your car, reset the speedometer to zero and stop when you thought you had the correct distance. Hardly any races had miler markers, so you seldom knew how far to the finish line. It reminded me of racing in Scotland in cross country races held in a farmer's field where we just ran run like hell and hoped we didn't die.

I raced a two-mile cross-country race on Allen Parkway in 88 degrees, where I managed to finish first in 9:40 on a tough and challenging course. More later on this course...

I was still organizing races at Strake Jesuit High School. The only events I organized were a 440, and each week alternating between 880 and a mile, a mixed relay of one female, one male or female under fifteen, and two others, alternating with the high-jump and long-jump.

I was approached by a gentleman who accused me of being a racist. I replied, "I sure am, against sprinters, as sprinting takes up too much time with multiple false starts, whereas the others, I can line them up and fire the gun." Organizing a track meet gave runners an outlet to compete. There were no entry fees and I used a time-based system, i.e. the first heat of the 880 for runners under 2:15, and if that didn't work, we made it 2:20 until we got at least eight runners.

In my job, I decided I needed to make more money than the City of Houston was paying me. I found a job with Southwest Memorial Hospital as a systems analyst, where I was looking forward to the challenge of working in the medical field. My first assignment was to design a system for emphysema patients who sat in a body box (like a sealed container with a door and a seat) and wore a mouthpiece which was connected to a computer monitor that measured lung capacity. To get the parameters correct, I was the guinea pig, knowing full well that when blowing into the mouthpiece, I would be outside the high/low parameters. With trial and error, I came up with a formula to measure one's lung high and low capacity.

My immediate supervisor was a sneaky bugger. I was informed that he would check how a programmer wrote programs, which I thought was strange because the normal process worked. A program was written and tested by the computer for errors. If there were none, then it was run with input checking the output to determine if the results were what was required. If they matched, the program was put in production. Therefore, there was no need to check anyone's coding. It was a waste of time;

maybe he needed more work.

I was fortunate that the hospital was situated about 200 yards from the Houston Baptist University running track, where I did quite a bit of my track workouts. By getting my track running during the workday, it left me a bit more time to spend with Heather and Amy. The longer runs were along the Brays Bayou on the grass.

Along with the new job and teaching two classes most of the year, I had to spend quite a bit of time preparing lectures and tests, which left very little time for racing. I was getting more involved in the coaching aspects of running. I read a lot, examining what other coaches were doing and deciding what might work for the athletes I was coaching.

In December, I received a call from Ted Haydon, the coach from Chicago, that he had nominated me to be the race director for the 1977 National Cross-Country Championships. I asked, "Why me?" He said it was time for the race to be held in a warmer climate. I called a meeting with the Harrier board members and told them of our assignment. After a few discussions, we came up with a date—Saturday, November 26, 1977, and now had to put the plan in action.

Chapter 19
1977 — Houston, Texas

On a long run with Len Hilton, he said we should run the Houston marathon. We decided we, along with Tom Hoffman, would represent the Harriers. The marathon was held on January 22nd over a three-loop course designed by George Kleeman. I wasn't sure about this task as I had a couple of bad experiences racing long.

We lined up at the start, and didn't really know the course. When the gun went off, Kleeman took off like a rocket, leading the pack. Around the two-mile mark I noticed that Len was antsy and started pushing the pace. He covered the next mile in five minutes. I told him he was crazy and let him go. Approaching the 20-mile mark I noticed Len pull off to the side and hide behind a tree. As I approached the tree, he was doubled over as he was buggered. I told him in an abusive way to get his ass going as he made me run this bloody thing. We both staggered to the finish. I was knackered and hobbled the last mile in 10:20, recording 2:35 for the race. It was later announced that we had won the team race. I vowed, "Never again."

One teaching incident that stood out that year was during the final RPG programming test. The students had to write a program, then punch the written program onto cards that represented the program they had written. I supplied the data, which was attached to the cards they had keypunched representing their program. The assignment was to write a program that represented a seating chart on an airline and showed which seats had already been booked and what seats were available.

At the end of the class, I placed all the keypunched cards in a box, which would be run the next day on a computer. After running the programs through the computer and studying the results, I would know which programs were successful and grade accordingly. I walked to my car and drove home, and lo and behold I couldn't find the box with the keypunched programs. I drove back to Sharpstown and found the cards scattered all over the street. Seemingly, I had placed the box on top of my car, and drove off, causing the box to fall and creating a mess.

What a dilemma as this was the final test. The next time I went to class, I told them, "I have bad news and good news. The bad news—I cannot return your programs. The good news—everyone passed." Thank goodness there wasn't much discussion as most were pleased with their grades.

The summer dragged on and most of my energy was getting ready for the USA cross country championships. As I had run and walked over the selected course many times, I showed the group what I had come up with. Len, who was an engineer, wanted to be in charge of measuring the course.

A lot of work was put into designing the course. George Kleeman helped and Peter League provided stakes to keep the runners on the course. Don Baxter had two loads of dirt delivered at Waugh Bridge, which was scattered on the incline to make it tougher. Don also provided snacks and beer in the Holiday Inn for all runners after the race.

We had 280 runners sign up. The Friday before the race, we were relaxing in the hospitality room for the coaches when Joe Douglas and Billy Squires showed up, covered in mud. Both made a bee line for Don asking what the hell he was trying to do to the runners as this is a tough course.

Don smiled, pointed to me and said, "Raise hell with McLatchie." I listened to them going on about how Joe fell in one of the ditches and Bill had to pull him out. I looked at Joe and said, "You lucky bugger, you still have both legs. I guess the 'gators missed you." The next day, Bill was a no-show for the race.

The course was over two laps, which included some severe up and downs for about 60 meters, with two ditches about ten feet wide that had about 20 inches of water. Each side of the ditch had a decline and incline of about 30 feet, which were very slick.

The next day, Nick Rose approached me and said the course reminded him of a British course (a man's course). Nick went on to win, beating Craig Virgin, who had beat him a few times across the country, by eight seconds with a time of 30:14 to his 30:22. Salazar finished tenth in 31:07.

Toni Reevis kept reminding me that this was the toughest course he had ever seen. To the Harriers who trained on it weekly in the fall, it was a piece of cake.

Chapter 20
1978 — Houston, Texas

By 1978, I was still learning new procedures at work, taking care of the daughters, teaching, coaching a few athletes, and running a bit myself. I was still involved with track meets on Wednesday evenings.

In March I received a call from Bill Young, who worked for one of the local radio stations, KILT. He had been contacted by Playboy magazine to organize a local road race and the magazine said they would provide a Playmate and get local celebrities involved. I asked what date they were looking at to hold the race and said if the Harriers were involved, there would be a fee payable to the club.

A meeting was set up at the Doctors Club in Houston with the owner of the radio station, Dickie Rosenfeld, and Don Baxter, Len Hilton and myself representing the Harriers. We all arrived and I found out that Dickie was full of piss and vinegar. He asked if he could buy us a drink while we discussed what the club would do for the fee. I told him that we would take care of entries, police, results, and concessions. Dickie agreed and said, "Let's eat."

I said, "No. A handshake doesn't count because I really don't know you." Don and Len were squirming. Dickie said, "What do you want?" I produced a napkin and asked to him write a promissory note with his signature then we could eat. He looked at me and said, "You're a tough bastard." I retorted, "In this world, you have to be."

A date for the race was set. Dickie decided there would be no entry fee, we would give t-shirts to all runners, and the first male and female would get a trip to Germany to compete in Munich at Oktober Fest. He also had free beer, Pearl Light. Playboy flew in the Playmate of the year, plus invited a few celebs. I organized a 4x100 relay on the road for the celebs, which was a big hit. The Harriers received their fee and everyone was happy. I was stuck with cases of beer, which were good for killing caterpillars.

I convinced Al Lawrence to start training again as I thought he would shake up the over-forties in races. He started running again and was really running well. I approached him and told him I had bought him a ticket to compete in the masters cross country championships being held in Wisconsin. After some serious debate, Al decided to race, and he won in the over 45-49 age group. He went on to win the masters division in the Dallas Marathon. Al made reference in his book, Olympus and Beyond as to how I managed to get him back into racing.

Carol Urish, who had watched Len break four minutes for the mile back in 1975, decided to start training seriously. She was working on her Master's degree at Rice University. Carol had never competed in high school or college and with three years of running under her belt managed to win the Bayou Classic.

The Harriers Cross Country Championships were held in pouring rain and won by Jim Ewing. The beer, like the rain, flowed effortlessly.

As usual, in the fall, we trained on Buffalo Bayou, running up and down the inclines wearing a backpack that was supposed to contain ten percent of your bodyweight. A lot of guys cheated. I even threatened to bring out a set of scales to check their weight.

Don Baxter and I decided to travel to Edmonton, Canada for the Commonwealth Games. It was an exciting trip. At the airport, we met a couple of swim coaches who had attended the NCAA swimming championships in Texas and were heading to Edmonton to try and recruit some swimmers for college.

When we arrived in Edmonton and were going through Customs, Don was pulled to the side and had to open all his bags. He said, laughing at me, "I am wearing a suit and you look like a tramp. I get pulled over and you don't?" I replied back, "You look more like a bag man than me."

I hooked up with Tony Simmons, whom I coached while in England. Tony was running for Wales and we were introduced to some of his teammates, which included Steve Jones, who later became one of the best marathon runners in the world. Steve was 19 years old and was chosen to run the 1,500 meters.

Don had some friends in Houston that got us passes to the Athletes village. It was there that we met Brendan Foster, and when Brendan found out that Don was a foot specialist, he had him check his feet, which had a few blisters. Don patched him up and Brendan was able to finish first in the 10,000 meters in 28:13.65.

Alan Wells from Scotland won the 200 meters ahead of the Jamaicans. I was happy for our small nation to compete well and thought we also had a chance in 4x100 relay later in the meet.

Don and I would go for easy runs with Tony, Nick Rose, Tony

Staynigs and Steve Jones. Steve was designated to keep his eye on Don in case he got lost. Don nicknamed Steve, 'Boy Jones.'

After Don took care of Brendan Foster, all of a sudden, he was treating most of the British athletes. Wee later found out that the team doctor was always drunk, and the athletes avoided him like the plague.

Don and I went horse racing one day and since I was a student of the sport, he asked me who I fancied in one race. I said I was doing an exacta box with three runners, which means that I have to have the winner and second. Three runner box looks like this: 1-2,1-3, 2-1,2-3,3-1,3-2. So, if runner one wins and three is second, then I have the winner. Don took my three horse and bet a trifecta, where you must place all three horses in the correct position, and since the horse I picked finished 1, 2, 3 he won quite a lot of money that paid for our entertainment for days.

One night we were eating in a restaurant when a fight broke out during a Chinese wedding party. I thought I was in the wild west, with chairs being thrown all over the place and bodies scattering. When it quieted down a bit, we left by walking the stairs. On reaching the outside, we were surprised to see that police had arrived, but none entered the building. I guess they were waiting until the melee died down.

When we went to the track meet one day, there was an announcement made over the intercom, "Would Don Baxter please report to the training-room." I told Don, "I think Brendan wants you tape up his feet before the 5000-meter final." Don went to the dressing room and sure enough it was Brendan requesting Don to tape his feet. Brendan finished third in the 5000 behind Henry Romo and at the end of the race, came to where we were sitting and gave Don the singlet that he wore during the race. That singlet today is still displayed in Don's office.

The Queen visited the games, but the highlight for me was when Scotland won the 4x400 relay. When the Scottish national anthem was played at the medal ceremony, I stood up, and was promptly told to sit down. I turned around and said, "Fuck off. It's not every day that Scotland wins a medal at the games."

Chapter 21
1979 — Houston Texas

That January, Len Hilton and I were assigned the task of timing the Houston Marathon. It was a miserable day with temperatures dropping in the teens. The overhead clock at the finish line froze after three hours and the runners had to depend on Len and me to time them. What a laugh, but we survived. One of these 'fly by the seat of your pants' deals.

I was coaching quite a few more people and directing road races, which along with family and work, was keeping me more than busy. I had a garden and spent of lots time cultivating and growing vegetables. This activity gave me time to slow down and enjoy some peace and quiet, which was great.

The Harriers were growing in stature and beginning to show their muscle in races. I was coaching several married women with young children. It was like I was in charge of a nursery. Wiping noses, kicking ass, and keeping them off the track. I didn't think coaching entailed baby-sitting. A few of the Harriers were running well and letting people know we were a force to be reckoned with in the coming years.

Tom Birch won the Bayou Classic and 10,000 meters at Mt. Sac Relays in Los Angeles. Carol Urish was on a tear, winning the Bayou Classic, Bonne Belle, and 5,000 meters at Kansas Relays. Len Hilton recorded 13:51.7 at the Pre Classic in Eugene, Oregon. Ron Tabb won KILT's five-mile race in 23:56 and recorded 2:16:28 in the New York marathon. Al Lawrence broke the world age group record for the one-hour run on the track with a distance of ten miles, 817 yards. Toni Bernhard won the women's division of the Dallas marathon in 2:47.

In the fall, we would meet every Monday on Allen Parkway near Buffalo Bayou at Montrose for hill workouts. On an alternating basis, someone was designated to bring beer and snacks. What we didn't finish, we gave to the homeless people. Everyone who attended workouts thought this was a great idea. I told them it was a British and Australian custom after workouts to have beer, snacks, and a bullshit session.

During one of the workouts, I noticed the City of Houston parks department had planted trees all over the place where we did hills and ran our cross- country races. I thought some bugger was drunk as they had screwed up our course. The next evening, I took my spade and moved the trees in a straight line, which did not interfere with runners while racing or working out. I am not much of a horticulturist, but knew how to plant trees in a straight line. Those trees are still in a straight line today.

Chapter 22
1980 — Houston Texas

The year started off with a bang for the Harriers. Ron Tabb and Vanessa Vajdos both won the Houston marathon in 2:13:35 and 2:44:45. Donna Burge was beaten by one second by Vanessa.

Carol Urish won 11 consecutive road races, which included a 16:13:28 finish in the 5,000 meters at Texas Relays.

In the Boston Marathon, Ron Tabb finished third in 2:14:48.

Len Hilton recorded 3:42.1 sec for 1,500 meters at the Pre Classic.

One incident I remember was at a Miller Lite track meet held at the University of Houston. Don Baxter was the medical doctor for the meet, and back then, all shot putt thrower's hands had to be examined for tape or whatever the rules called for. Don had to make a ruling on tape that several shot putters had on their hands. When several 250+ pound athletes surrounded Don, he had no choice but to agree with them that the little cuts on their fingers were legit and required taping. I am glad he didn't piss himself.

I decided it was time to leave Memorial Southwest Hospital when I found out that the supervisor for data processing was checking out how an individual wrote code. I thought, "Why should he care, as long as the program worked and produced the end results?" It is a well-known fact that very few people solve a task the same way. I just have a problem with people that go behind one's back rather than confront them face to face.

I found a job at Geosource as a project manager. I was responsible for inventory and accounting systems. I had a couple of programmers working for me. We were a good team, worked well together, and enjoyed each other's company.

The Inventory was written in Assembly language, which I didn't understand and neither did my boss, Bill. The person who wrote the system would get called during the night when the system quit working. His solution was, "Start from step 1." Normally, it would quit again and he would work on solving the problem later when he showed up for work. Bill and I were fed up with this, as only one person knew

Assembly and when the system aborted, we had to depend on him.

Bill and I started to flow chart the program so we had a better understanding of how it worked. It took us several days to complete the task and when it was done, we assigned it to a COBOL programmer to be rewritten so that more than one person would know how it worked. When the program was complete and working, the original programmer was terminated. We were now able to have several programmers fix any problem as they all knew COBOL.

Heather and Amy were growing up and starting to have interests of their own. Mary decided she would like to have a beach house not too far from Galveston on the Gulf Coast. We found some vacant land and hired a builder to build the frame for a two-bedroom house. In the Gulf area, one had to build on stilts or the cabin would get washed away when the weather turned bad. I would have the electrical and sheetrock for the walls and ceiling done later.

My good friend, Curtis, said he would install the electric wiring, which he had done several times. I worked as his gofer, pulling wire and handing him tools when needed. He completed the job and now we had electricity but no walls.

My next task was to sheetrock the walls and ceiling. I had no idea how to install sheet rock, but boy did I learn quickly. My first attempt on the ceiling was like the Keystone Cops were turned loose. I was attempting this task on my own.

The ceiling was about ten feet high. I built a couple of TEE supports and would climb up the ladder with a piece of sheet rock which was six feet long, place it where it was supposed to go, and Mary would place one of the TEE supports to hold the sheet rock in place at one end. I would nail the end on my side to the jousts. I would climb down. Now I was ready to nail the sheet rock to the joist on the other side. Only one problem—there was nothing for me to nail. There are 16 inches between most joists and a piece of sheet rock is 72 inches, which means you would need 4.5 joists. So, I had to cut from 72 to 64 inches. Boy was I getting smart.

It took us several weekends to complete the walls and ceiling with sheet rock. The next task was to install a septic tank. Now I was smart. I thought, "No problem." Boy was I wrong.

I knew three Australians who were attending Houston Baptist University on an athletic scholarship. I asked them if they wanted to earn some money, and asked if they would they would help me install the septic tank They said yes.

We measured how big a hole we would have to dig to install the septic tank. We dug a hole and installed the tank with pipes from the house into the tank and a runoff pipe. We were drinking a beer, admiring our job, when all of a sudden, the tank started rising out of the ground like a prehistoric monster, taking the pipes with it. I thought, "What the hell!"

Looking at the hole, which now was beginning to fill up with water, I realized that the hole we dug was below sea-level and water was seeping into it. Had I done more research, I would have put enough water in the septic tank to keep it in place. We had to bail out enough water to let the septic tank reach the bottom of the hole, then put enough water in the septic tank to keep it in place. That was another couple of beer efforts.

My brother, Ian, sent me a note from Saudi Arabia, where he was working for Morris Knudson as an engineer, and said he was coming to Houston to clear his head as he had some marital problems at home in Scotland. I said, "No problem, come when you can."

Ian arrived in Houston in March, and later told me he was not going back to Scotland and would look for a job in Houston. My friend, John, offered him a job as a mechanic working on British cars.

His first task was to work on a Rolls Royce Silver Cloud, where he had to strip all paint from the top half of the car and have it ready for a movie shoot where it would be cut in two.

One Friday afternoon, John challenged him. He had a 1973 MGB that he could not get to run. He told Ian if he could get the car running, he would test-drive it Saturday morning, and if it was up to his standards, he would sign the car over to him. Ian took the wager, and around 5 p.m. John was ready to close the garage, and, laughing, shouted to Ian, "Sorry, Scottie! Have a good attempt at getting the car running, but you will lose."

Ian looked at him, smiling, and asked, "How many hours are there in a Texas day?" John responded, "24. Why?" Ian said the car would be running by 7 a.m. on Saturday. He got to work and had to rebuild the engine—pistons, rings, cylinder head, new valves and gaskets, the water pump, and reset the carburetors.

Ian rebuilt the engine but it still wouldn't start. After a few attempts, he thought, "No gas." He siphoned gas from another car and finally, the car started. Ian took another hour to synch the dual carbs and the car was running like a sewing machine. John came in on Saturday morning and made a beeline for Ian and asked if the car was running.

Ian said, "Let's go outside for a drive." John looked at him and said,

"No way is that car running." They took a spin around the block. John then signed papers, admitting that he never thought Ian would get the car running. John told him, "It's your car."

Chapter 23
1981 — Houston, Texas

As the year began, I was becoming busier with coaching. The Harriers now had 81 members. Toni Bernhard had a great run in the Houston marathon, where she recorded 2:42:28 seconds. The Harriers placed first, second, and third in the Women's Avon marathon, where Midde Hamrin won in 1:51:11.

Midde's story is quite unusual as she came to the States from Sweden on a basketball scholarship to Lamar University. Her boyfriend, now husband, whom I knew when I lived in Chicago, told her to contact me about coaching her. She was tough as nails and an easy person to coach.

Carol Urish won the Trevira Twosome, a ten-miler in New York, where they ran both male and females together in 55:59. Later that year, Carol was selected to represent the USA in Yokohama, Japan in an international relay.

Al Lawrence went on a record-breaking rampage with new world records for the over-50 age group—10:13.3 for two miles and 9:24.1 for 3,000 meters.

In the USA Master's Cross-Country Championships, the Harriers finished second with Bob Mohler, Phil Baker, Al Lawrence, and me as team members.

Karol Painter, a high school girl who attended Deer Park, won the Texas high school two-mile cross-country championship race in 11:11 seconds. Her coach at Deer Park contacted me about coaching her as she had no one to run with. I agreed and her dad drove her 30 miles each way on Mondays and Wednesdays for workouts.

Work at Geosource was going great as I was getting involved with a lot of new stuff. I was becoming quite an authority on computerized inventory, with over 1,000 items to monitor. I setup re-order points, which immensely helped our buyer with ordering.

Bill knew that I coached several athletes and told me about his son, Jon, who couldn't run much as he was diagnosed with a stress fracture. I gave him some workouts to do in a swimming pool. A couple of days later Bill came to work and started giving me hell about trying to kill his son. I told him I didn't understand until he told me that he climbed the fence to get into the neighbor's swimming pool and returned home a blue color. It was December, and I thought Jon would use an indoor pool. Now I knew you cannot expect high school kids to read your mind.

Jon went on to an illustrious career, winning the Texas state cross country championships the following year. He recorded a sub-four-minute mile, a 2:15 marathon, and represented the USA in the marathon in Greece in 1997.

In my garden, I had discovered that growing vegetables in Texas was quite different from the UK, where the growing season was not as long and one grew whatever would survive the season.

Ian was very well-educated in mechanical engineering and found it difficult to land a decent job in the USA. He said he needed to do something other than work on British cars.

One of the Harriers, Larry, owned a valve company and I spoke to him about Ian, explaining his qualifications and that he was having a tough time convincing American companies that he was educated and qualified to work as an engineer. Larry told me to tell him to report to his company for an interview. Ian was hired as the company's field technician and valve quality control engineer. The company made and renovated valves for oil companies that controlled the flow of oil. Ian travelled all over Texas and Louisiana testing and replacing valves in the oilfield. Like me, he had a tough time with the heat.

After talking to several companies about Ian, explaining his situation, I was told that if I sponsored him to get his Green Card he would probably get a decent job, but to do that I had to become a citizen of the States. I wasn't so sure if I really wanted to do that, but after talking to him, I decided to apply for citizenship.

One evening while attending Rice University for a track meet with Ian, he found out I needed someone to run on the 4x400 relay. I said to Ian, "You're on the team." He was looking at me, smoking a cigarette. "What are you talking about, me running a relay," he asked. I told him, "Get ready, you're on the team." The next thing I knew, he was on the running track in his skivvies. I said, "What are you doing?" He said, "I cannot run with my jeans on." Holy shit!! He ran like a brown streak.

Curtis and I would go fishing on the Galveston jetties. We didn't care whether we caught fish or not. We would buy a six-pack of beer, sit on the rocks, and try to solve the world's problems. We never solved anything, but the beer tasted good.

Tom Fatjo was a Rice University graduate and president of the neighborhood association in Willowbrook, the subdivision in the southwestern part of Houston, where he lived. One day, he listened to how difficult it was to get their garbage collected since the provider had quit. As a result, bags of trash were piling up in all the households. He then offered a suggestion of his own, "Since our garbage is not being picked up, why don't we buy a garbage truck and have our own service?"

He bought a garbage truck and later on bought and developed Brown & Ferris. He also built The Houstonian, which was a luxury type hotel. Tom was a great supporter of the Harriers and to show our appreciation, we had an award made for him. My task was to deliver the award to The Houstonian, where he was living in his house next to the hotel. It was dark and as I was walking to his residence, two men jumped out of the trees and started interrogating me. I told them I had an award for Tom Fatjo who was president of The Houstonian. They informed me that the vice president was living in the residence and I could not approach the house.

I told them, "I don't want to see the vice president," as I had no idea who he was. I thought they were talking about The Houstonian personnel. They informed me it was George Bush who was living there. I said, "I don't want to see him." They said they would deliver the award to Tom.

Chapter 24
1982 — Houston Texas

Carol Urish was being recognized as a force to be reckoned with in women's races. She finished fourth in the prestigious Sao Silvestre midnight run in Dao Paulo, Brazil, and then went on to win the Corrida International Leblon-Leme 8K race in Rio de Janeiro, Brazil and a 10K race in Aruba, Netherlands Antilles. She won the Bayou Classic for the fifth time and went on to win the Trevira ten-miler in New York in 55:14. She also recorded 16:00.1 on the track in Berkley, California for 5,000 meters. Carol and Midde Hamrin finished first and second in the Avon half-marathon, recording 1:13:42 and 1:14:53. The Harriers won the team race.

I had been training hard, getting myself ready for a new adventure racing in the 40-plus age group. The year before, I didn't do much but was ready to roll this year. On the track, I ran 4:09.8 sec for 1,500 meters and 2:03.95 for 800 meters. I later won the 3,000 meters in 9:34.10 at the USA Masters TFA in Wichita, Kansas. I went on later to record 16:00 for 5K on the roads.

The Harriers had an excellent meet in Wichita. Karol Painter won the under-17 800 meters in 2:11.13 and the mile in 4:53.20, which was one of the fastest times recorded by a high school girl. Mack Stewart won the over-40 400 meters in 58.80 and 800 meters in 2:14. Carol Urish won the over-30 age group in the 800 meters with 2:14.76 and 1,500 meters in 4:37.24.

Midde Hamrin finished second overall in the Woodland marathon, running 2:34:28. Later in the season, she finished seventh in the European Marathon Championships held in Athens Greece in 2:42:10 in very hot conditions, and recorded 32:21 for a 10K in Boston. Marty Froelick recorded 47:50 for ten miles. Al Lawrence ran an over-50 age group record for the marathon in 2:40:38. Carol Urish (later my wife) ran her first marathon in Dallas, winning in 2:47.

While working at Geosource, I coached the CEO, John Platt, who really loved running and was very competitive. I would meet him at Memorial High School at 6:30 a.m. one day a week for track workouts.

One day, I was installing a new computer system at one of our satellites in Seguin, Texas when in walks John and others. Seemingly they were inspecting the plant. He made a beeline for me when he saw me. "Jim, I need to talk to you about my schedule." He dragged me off to the side, where we had a discussion. A few minutes later, one of his aides said, "Mr. Platt, we need to leave as the helicopter is waiting." John turned around and said, "I am busy right now talking to my coach."

John used to pick me up and take me to a Houston Oiler football game where we would sit, not too aware of what was happening on the field. We would have a nice talk about running and life in general. I believe it was a great outlet for both of us to relax. For John, it was a time to forget the pressures of work, and for me, a chance to forget about developing training schedules and figuring out if I was on the right track.

Geosource decided to reorganize several areas within the company. All of a sudden, my group had a new manager who was a right bastard. He and I never hit it off as he was always telling me he was in charge and he knew more than me.

I thought, "If he knows more than me, let's find out how he will handle inventory when there will be no one around to solve any problems that will arise." I had talked to my two programmers and told them I was calling in sick on Friday. Immediately, they both said they would call in sick also.

So, on Friday, we didn't show up and suddenly there were questions about inventory. Lo and behold, there was no one to answer questions. Our new boss went ballistic. He called up Bill, my old boss, and told him he was going to fire me on Monday. Bill explained the sick policy, that no one could call in sick without having a doctor's certificate, and he should wait until Monday to see if I showed up.

Monday, I showed up bright-eyed and bushy tailed. Poor boss didn't know what to do as I hadn't broken any rules. I think he realized that he had a lot to learn.

We were doing year-end inventory, which had over 1,000 items. There would be a manual count of the items, which was compared against what the computer stated. For example: Item "A" started the year with 1,000 items, we used 300 and reordered 200, which made the computer total 900, but the physical count stated we had 890 on stock. If the price was $1 per item, and the computer showed $900 compared to $890, that was a difference of $10. In a sane world, $10 wasn't worth bothering about and it would be written off.

Our new know-it-all boss made us do re-counts and reruns on the computer trying to match dollar for dollar. As we were working on a weekend, I was getting flustered with his BS. I asked him how much we were out of balance. He gave me a number, which I took, and wrote a line of code in the computer program. I then reran the program, and lo and behold, we were in balance to the penny. Mr. 'know-it-all' came back and said we were in balance and could go home. I guess the dumb Scotsman knew a wee bit more than the boss.

I became an American citizen in early spring. Ian was married in April and he and Linette, who is Canadian, decided to move to Quebec. I was dumbfounded as I had become a citizen to keep him in the country and get a decent job and he was leaving, but he left me the MGB that he had rebuilt. Nice memory!

Chapter 25
1983

The Harriers started the season on a high note, which showed that I was coaching a good bunch of athletes who listened well. Other runners in the USA were beginning to notice that when a Harrier showed up to race, they were to be taken seriously.

Marty Froelick won the Las Vegas half-marathon. Carol Urish raced in Tucson, Arizona and came away with a win. Karol Painter set a new USA high school record for 1,600 meters with a time of 4:51. She is still ranked in the top Texas high school milers with a time of 4:53.39.

One day in March, John Platt called me up and said he had to fly to the east coast to Geosource's headquarters for an important meeting and was going to run the Cherry Blossom race in Washington. He asked if I would I like to attend, along with Marty and Carol. We all met at Intercontinental Airport and flew to Washington, DC, in John's company plane.

After we were checked into a hotel it was decided that Carol, John and Marty would go for an easy run along the Potomac River to loosen up for the race. While they were running, I went for a walk along the river and came across two old black men fishing. While I was watching them, one caught a fish and was struggling to get it ashore. I decided to help him, but as I did not have a net, I grabbed the line to take some pressure off the fisherman. The fish spat out the hook and took off. I thought, "Oh shit, what have I done." The poor old fisherman was nearly crying, "You let my big catfish escape." I apologized and started running, thinking, "I just lost that poor bugger's dinner."

Carol did not finish the race as she came down sick and was coughing her lungs out. Marty finished sixth in 47.59 and John had a great run.

We all went out for dinner and had a good chat about their race and my fish escapade. During the meal, John told me he had just gotten a mysterious phone call from Aetna, who purchased Geosource in April 1982. They wanted to meet with him in New York City. I told John I thought they were going to terminate him. I did not have a crystal ball but had that feeling, as the same thing happened to my boss in Chicago when Playskool was taken over by Milton Bradley.

John left for the meeting and said he would pick us up later in the week and fly us back to Houston. We had a quiet night, except for Carol, who coughed most of the night.

The next day, Bob, who worked with John, set up some sightseeing adventures in Washington while John was attending his meeting. When his meeting was over, John returned to Dulles airport, where we met him and headed back to Houston. I asked how the meeting went. John looked at me and said, "You were right. I resigned."

It was a terrible year for anyone who worked in oil-related jobs. Geosource, like other oil companies, was having a tough time financially and had to terminate personnel. On Thursday evening, John Platt called me on the telephone and told me what was going to happen the next day. He said he didn't think he could save my job as the decisions were coming from Aetna on the east coast, who now owned the company.

I witnessed a blood bath in respect to terminating workers. Bill had the tough job of deciding who stayed and who worked. It was not about John Smith or Peggy Sue. It was about money—dollars and cents. The company had to cut 'X' amount of dollars.

Management looked at salaries— as, 'If I cut these four, I have contributed 'Y' dollars." Then the top brass would come back and say, "You need to cut another 'X' dollars." In the end, I lost my staff and then finally I was told that I had to go. My boss said, "I can pay you as a consultant for several months as I have some money in the budget for a consultant and you can come to work on Monday."

My main assignment was payroll, since most of the manual workers were union and couldn't miss a payroll. I spent a lot of midnight oil fixing problems so that people could get paid. After three months, I was let go as there was no more money in the budget.

In the oil patch you could make big money, but job security was sparse. I, like others, found the hard end of the stick when I lost my job along with 45,000 in the Houston area.

That year, Len Hilton and I had surgery. Len had his Achilles scraped and I had plantar fascia release on my heel. The doctor did a great job with the surgery to correct the problem and I was back running in a week.

The Harriers had several good Master runners in the 40+ age group. Mack Stewart ran the 400 in 54, Bob Cozens in 58, and Don Baxter in 60. I ran the 1,500 meters in 4:19. We decided to travel to Dallas to compete in a Masters track meet. Mack won the 400 meters, Cozens the 800 meters, Baxter the javelin, and I won the 1,500 meters.

We also entered a 4x400 relay with Baxter, Cozens, Mack and me, the anchor. We won by a considerable amount. Cozens started reading out the splits and I ended up with the slowest leg. I said, "No way, how did you get the splits?" He said, "We all timed our legs and whatever is left is yours."

We won with a time of 3:46. The fictitious splits were: Mack, 54; Cozens, 54, Baxter, 58, and I got the remainder 60. I couldn't run that slow. Why argue?

We decided to go for a beer after the meet and found a bar near the track. On entering, we found out that we were in the dry part of Dallas, but if we joined their club, we could have a beer. We paid five dollars to join the club and then enjoyed a beer. We never got our membership's worth, but the beer was okay.

Mary Cullen called me up after the USATF convention and told me I was the race director for the USA Masters Track & Field Championships, which consisted of several age groups: 30-34, 35-39. 40-44, 45-49, and up to 75-79. I contacted Rice University seeking permission to hold the championships.

Prior to the meet, I received a call from the USATF headquarters in Indianapolis telling me I had to send them 50% of the revenue. I told them that was not going to happen and if they didn't like it, there would be no track meet. They backed off and the meet was on. I was not convinced I could do this as there was too much work involved. I called a meeting with the Harriers board and it was decided that since we were getting a fee for putting on the event, we should do it.

What an experience. I must have aged ten years in three days. I had to build a hammer cage, which took quite a bit of time. The hammer was held on the Friday, in an area where there were no lights. We had so many throwers that they were still competing in the dark. We had to use flashlights to measure throws. The judge near the cage would shout, "Hammer!" and the markers used their flashlights to record distance. I am sure there were a few age-group records. "The blind shall lead the world." Good thing no one was maimed.

Saturday was just another day with more problems and a chance to solve them the same way. The meet started off with the 10,000 meters. We had two heats, one for over 55 and the other for under 55. Sue 'Bonnet Sue' was in the first race, and we were on a timetable where the next heat had to start one hour from the start of the first race. Sue had several laps to 'wog' (walk/jog). I had to start the other race before she finished the first, and kept a watch going and a lap counter so she would be recorded.

The next problem was an elder lady in the high jump who said the pit was higher than she had jumped before. I told her the easy solution was to just jump into the pit as we cannot go lower. She came back and told me that she had just broken the world age group record. It's great what happens when there is not another alternative.

The next event was the 40-44 age group for the 400 meters. I was confronted by a gentleman from California who told me he was not running in lane two as he was the world champion and he should be running in lane five. I told him, "This is a heat section of the event and the computer will decide the running order in the first round," and if he didn't run in lane two, he wouldn't be running. Needless to say, he didn't run. Tough cookie.

Then in the pole vault, we were still running the event and it was getting dark. We had three vaulters left and they decided to keep going. I drove my car into the stadium and placed it at the start of the runway and had my lights hit the take-off area. I was so tired, having worked about 14 hours without any rest and limited intake of food and liquid. Jim Yarborough, who was helping me with the vault, had his wife help also. I sent her for a six-pack of beer, which I shared with the vaulters. The event concluded on a sober note.

We hurried over to the Cullen's house for a get-together, which was winding down when we arrived. We had some food and drink then left for the challenges the next day.

The meet started off with my first altercation, which was the 10,000-meter race-walk, when one of the officials who was a local race walker disqualified one of the competitors. If you received a yellow card three times for infringements, you were disqualified. One athlete received three cards, which meant he was disqualified, and when he was told he was disqualified, he refused to leave the track.

John, the official, pointed him out to me. I confronted him with John present and said he needed to leave the track, per the rules. He informed me that he was not leaving and would resist any attempt to remove him from the track. I replied that it was the best news I had heard in two days and if he didn't get off the track, I would kick his ass. He left. What would be my next challenge? Time would tell.

The Harriers had a wonderful National Championships winning several age-group titles: Carol Urish for 800 and 1,500 meters and

Melinda Carter for 5,000 meters in age 30-34, Mary Jo Gilaspy for 5,000 meters in age 40-44, Dave Rheinhart for 5,000 meters in age 35-39, and Al Lawrence for 5,000 and 10,000 meters in age 50-54.

Mary and I divorced and I felt devastated for Heather, who was 13, and Amy, who was nine. It's always the children who suffer the most, but normally bounce back quicker than the parents.

The whole year was devastating for me. I got a divorce, lost my job and my dad died. How much can a person take before putting their head in the oven? In Scotland all the ovens are gas-powered, and if life got too much for one, they would get a pillow, put it in the oven, turn on the gas, lay down and say, "Bye, bye." The biggest problem was for the poor bugger who later opened the front door smoking a cigarette.

Carol worked for Mobil Oil as a geologist, and Mobil sponsored the Grand Prix track meets. Since the Olympic Games were coming up in 1984, I had her contact them about working reduced shifts so she could train for the Olympics. Their response was a big fat, "No," as they didn't have a policy to allow this to occur. I told them I could write their policy, to no avail, and Carol handed in her resignation.

Being unemployed does a lot for one's morale, having to go stand in line at the unemployment office answering stupid questions. I made friends with a nuclear scientist who had a PhD in Physics. We were informed that to continue our benefits after three months, we would have to attend a class on how to write a resume, to which we both burst out laughing. The counselor informed us that we needed to attend so we could keep our benefits for six more weeks.

I was invited by the Cullen family to bring my daughters to their ranch to spend some time relaxing and enjoying the fresh air, when I received word that my dad had died on July 1st.

In 1982, I had booked with Track & Field News to travel to Helsinki in 1983 to watch the first World Track & Field Championships. I was taking Carol with me, and after the games, we were going to Scotland to visit my dad and spend some time with him as he had been on his own since my mum died in 1975. Then all hell broke loose when I lost my job, got divorced, and my dad died before we even left for Helsinki. I hadn't enough money to fly to Scotland for the funeral, which did not go over well with the family.

Helsinki was a great venue with plenty of exciting races. I was in a bookstore browsing through some books when I spotted Steve Cram, asked how he was doing, wished him luck, and asked where his coach was. He pointed out a gentleman who was reading a newspaper. I went up an introduced myself to Jimmy Hedley and we had a good old natter. Later that week, Steve went on to win the first world title for 1,500 meters.

There were several highlights of the meet. We watched Alberto Jauntoreno from Cuba jog through the finish line in the prelims of the 800 meters, turn right to look to see where the field was, step on the curb, and break his ankle, which took him out for the rest of the games. That race was won by Willi Wulbeck (GER) 1:43.65.

Jasmila Kratochivilova (TCH) broke the world record in the 400 meters in a time of 47.99 and then went on to win the 800 in 1:54.68. Carl Lewis (US) won both the 100 meters and long jump. Mary Slaney (US) won both 1,500 and 3,000 meters in times of 4:00.90 and 8:34.62. Greta Wetz (NOR) won the marathon in 2:28.09.

In the final of the men's 4x400 meter relay, we watched the USA drop the baton. The runner was too busy looking at the crowd when the baton hit his leg, flew up in the air, and bounced around before he retrieved it. The USA went on to finish sixth.

After the meet, Carol and I flew to Scotland, hired a car, and drove to Muirkirk. What a somber experience visiting where my dad lived and paying my last respects at the graveside.

I returned home with no aspects of obtaining a job, laid around the house with no ambition about much in life, and tried to figure out why, at 42, I was unemployed, divorced, had lost my dad, and came down with shingles. What the fuck.

I had to give myself a shake and try to get a job. I contacted a friend whom I'd worked with at the City of Houston and asked if there were any jobs. He informed me that the police department needed a programmer. I thought, programming…it's been so long." I applied for the job and interviewed with Don Hollingsworth, who hired me. He was more interested in what I was doing with the Harriers than my programming skills.

Carol decided to run in the Chicago marathon, which would be her third marathon. I was familiar with where the race would be run since I had lived there for seven years. I would get out on the course and be at various locations to cheer her on.

One incident from the event stands out. Anne Audain fell while running downhill, about one mile from the finish line. When she got back onto her feet, she started running the wrong way. The gentleman that I am took off running to get in front of her and wave my arms telling her she needed to turn around as she was going the wrong way.

I did not assist her manually, just verbally. She finally turned around and headed to the finish line to finish fourth in 2:32.15 behind the winner, Rosa Motta, who ran 2:31.12. Carol finished in tenth place in 2:37.57, which was her third race over the distance.

Chapter 26
1984 - Houston, Texas

I started with the police department and soon learned it was a great place to work and I had enough time to run during lunch. I started work at 7:30 a.m. and finished at 4:30 p.m., with one hour for lunch. The office was near Buffalo Bayou, which had plenty of grass for easy running. I went running nearly every day, had a shower, and then returned to my work. Working for the city one didn't make much money but the benefits were okay and normally you had a job for life.

One of my assignments was to install a new inventory system for the helicopter division of the city. I asked if it was possible to obtain a ride in one of their helicopters and have an aerial view of Houston. I had to sign a release form and was told to report next morning for a sightseeing tour of the city. The next morning, I was directed to a helicopter, where the pilot showed me how to strap myself in and communicate with him during the flight.

After getting situated, I noticed there were no doors. I thought, "Jeez, this will be interesting." On take-off, the pilot banked to right, which was my side of the helicopter. I thought I was going to fall out. I looked at the pilot, who had a big smile on his face knowing that he had got me. I did not pee myself and settled down to enjoy the tour of Houston from above. A great experience.

This was the year of the Olympic Trials, which was used to select the team for the Olympics that were going to be held in Los Angeles. The Harriers had seven women qualify for the marathon, which has never been surpassed by any club. The trials were held in Olympia, Washington. A few of the women had a tough time with Scotch broom, a shrub which caused breathing problems and irritated eyes. As the coach of the women, I was worn out before the finish. I had to cajole the runners that were having a bad day and convince them that they were doing okay, telling them they were part of history and emphasizing all the hard work and hours they had spent to get to the start line. Carol Urish finished 12th in 2:35:09.

She was very fit after training for the marathon and went to New

York and won the ten-mile Trevira Twosome in 55:14. She was on a roll.

Carol Urish finishing the Trevira Twosome.

Carol and I were married in March. The Harriers were getting bigger in numbers. If someone wanted me to coach them, they had to answer several key questions and if not to my satisfaction, they were not allowed in our training group.

Midde Hamrin competed for Sweden in the IAAF cross country championships, where she finished seventh and later went on to compete in the Olympic Games for Sweden. Getting there was some journey. We had decided to try the year before, when we asked the Swedish Federation what time would be required to make the team for the Olympics. They gave us a time of 2:35. I told Midde to ask if the Boston marathon would count as a qualifier. They informed her they would take the time from that race if she ran the qualifier.

Midde and I decided that all the training would be geared to April to get a qualifying time for the Olympic Games. Shortly thereafter, the fun started when officials from Nagoya, Japan asked Midde to run in the women's marathon in March. They offered airfare, accommodations, and pocket money. Midde called me and we talked. Since she wanted to compete in the first-ever women's marathon in the Olympic Games, she said no. A few days later, they called again and added an appearance fee of $10,000 dollars. Midde again said no.

The next day, they called again with the same deal plus they would fly her mother to the race. She called me again and I told her it was her decision—qualify for the Olympics or take the offer. She once again decided to head to Boston to try to qualify for the Olympics. She finished second to Loraine Moller in a time of 2:33:15 and was now on the team for the Olympic Games. She represented Sweden and finished 18th in 2:35:41 in hot conditions.

Midde Hamrin 1984 Olympics.

Prior to the Olympics, I received a call from Alberto Salazar, who had made the USA Olympic team. He was coming to Houston to train for the marathon. I told him that would be a bad move as Houston was hot and humid. Alberto said he was trying to emulate Los Angeles. I told him the big problem was that Los Angeles was not as humid. Needless to say, Alberto showed up.

I met with him to discuss what his protocol would be. He told me he was going to run a loop of Rice University, which was approximately three miles around. He was going to run four times (three miles at a five-minute pace, one mile on the track at 4:20 pace). I told him that was going to be tough. I told him that Marty Froelick would run the miles with him on the track. The first mile Alberto ran 4:22, the second mile, 4:30, the third mile, 4:40, and then he called it quits. A week later, he returned to the west coast and went on to run in 15th place in 2:14:19 under a hot sun.

The Olympic Trials in Los Angeles saw Renee Odom compete in the 1,500 meters, and Carol run in two exhibition events, where she finished seventh in the 5,000 meters in 15:45.28 which ranked her 22nd in the world, and seventh in the 10,000 meters in 33:03.06, ranking her 30th in the world.

Carol McLatchie in the Olympic Trials.

Carol and I flew up to Chicago to watch Steve Jones, a good friend of ours, run the marathon. He had dropped out of the race the previous year and had made up his mind to make amends, which he did by winning in a new world record of 2:08.05. The following year, he won again in 2:07.19, missing the world record held by Carlos Lopes.

Steve told me a story about forgetting the name he used as a guest in the hotel where he was staying prior to the marathon. Before a big race, he didn't want people bothering him, so he used an alias, and he didn't like running with a key. At the desk, he asked if he could leave the room key and retrieve it when he returned.

After his run, he went to the desk to retrieve his room key. The attendant at the desk asked for his room number. He replied, "I don't remember." He was asked for his name. He couldn't remember the name that he has used while booking into the hotel. And remember, this was before cell phones. While standing there at the front desk, someone walking past and said, "Hi, Jonesy." The person behind the desk asked if he knew Steve. He replied, "Sure do." After some time, they found his room number and gave him the key for his room.

Steve sent me this picture later. He called me the Baron as Don Baxter and I had nicknamed him at the 1978 Commonwealth Games "Sir Jones."

Steve Jones in the Chicago Marathon.

I have a dear good friend who is an orthopedic surgeon who asked me to come and take pictures of him doing a knee operation. I told him I wasn't too good with a camera. He told me it was easy, and all I had to do was point and shoot. The gig was arranged. I had to report to the hospital, then head toward the operating room, where I would be provided with green scrubs along with a mask and booties.

I received my directions, and off I went looking very officious but a nervous wreck. I found the operating theater and walked into the room. I heard this hammering, and was wondering what was going on, when out walks a man who looked like he worked in a butcher's shop. I asked where I could find my friend.

I found the room and saw a bunch of people around the operating table with someone lying there with an exposed knee that was wide open before orthoscopic surgery. Looking at tissue and bone, I said to myself,

"I cannot do this, but if I am going to pull it off, I need to suck it up and get on with the task at hand." My friend, the doctor, told me to take a chair and stand on it so I could shoot down on the procedure and get some good pictures.

As I was standing on the chair taking pictures, the anesthesiologist in the room asked what kind of film and what shutter speed I was using. I said, "Shit, I don't know any of this." My friend piped in, "He speaks Scottish and you will not understand him. He is on assignment for Sports Illustrated, just let him finish the job." I found out later that the anesthesiologist was a camera buff. Phew!!

Brian Scobie and I grew up in Milngavie and raced against one another while I was living in Scotland. Brian coached and guided blind runner Bob Matthews around the world, helping him break multiple world records.

While they were in Houston, I told them I would set up a race where Bob could attempt the world record for the mile. Marty Froelick agreed to be his guide and Bob went on to break the record with a time of 4:34.9.

One day, Bob was out sunbathing in the backyard, and I thought I would play a trick on him. I climbed upon the roof with a garden hose and sprayed him. He sat up, put out his hands to feel what he thought was rain, and then I turned off the hose. When he laid down again and got comfortable, I sprayed him again. Once more he sat up and felt for rain; watching his antics, I nearly fell off the roof laughing. Bob sat up and roared, "I'll get you, you big bastard."

Mike Peters, who lived near Bob, helped him in several races. Bob wanted to run a cross country race and Mike was his guide. In one race, they jogged the course early and Mike told Bob that there was a ditch at the bottom of an incline. As they were going downhill, he said, "Jump!" right before the ditch. During the race, they were approaching the ditch, Bob did not jump, and both he and Mike ended up in the water. Mike was furious and said, "Why didn't you jump?" All Bob said was "I didn't hear you."

Carol visited Bob in England and stayed with his family a few days while visiting friends. She said it was unique to be met by a blind person at the railroad station and then escorted to his home. Approaching the parking garage, she saw the rest of his family and said, "Thank goodness. I wondered how we were going to get to his house as I couldn't imagine a blind person driving a car."

Bob was a 'helluva' athlete who achieved several accolades: He won eight gold medals in seven Paralympic Games. In 1987, he became the first Paralympian to be appointed to the Member of the British Empire (MBE). He broke 22 world records, and won six world championship and 15 European championship gold medals. In 1986, he became the first blind runner to run the 800 meters in under two minutes. He was diagnosed with a brain tumor in 2017, and died in April 2018.

Chapter 27
1985 — Houston Texas

While working for the police department, I was approached by Garlon Rea from the customer service arm of the city's Public Works department, asking me to come work for them and straighten out the place. I said I would come for an interview and find out what I had to straighten out. He set up a meeting with his boss, Dick Brawner, which was a strange interview. He asked, "Are you still running and are you still an ass kicker?" I responded, "Yes, not much has changed."

I asked several questions on what they were trying to achieve. The real reason they wanted to hire me was that they wanted their own computer system to control the water billing system, meter reading, and repairs. This was going to be some challenge, and I love challenges, so I took the job.

I resigned from the police department and moved to customer service, which was located on Leeland Street. I was not officially on the Public Works payroll as my real boss was downtown with the City of Houston Data Processing Department. It was a terrible set up as I had two bosses, but nevertheless, I would make it work.

I didn't have an office or a desk. I sat on a chair, where my briefcase became my desk. I had three programmer/analysts, a computer operator, and a Honeywell 6000 series model 66 system that was so small it could barely run a program. The system badly needed an upgrade to be able to run the billing system that Public Works was buying from the City of Phoenix.

I laid out what we would require to the manager, and since the final decision was with the DP department downtown, we gave them our wish list. In return, if Public Works bought extra disks for the main computer, they would let us upgrade the present computer with equipment requested by me.

I received the requested additional equipment and started mapping out a conversion plan. I hired a couple more programmers and operators and started the conversion of the system purchased from Phoenix. The City of Phoenix provided an analyst to check the output as we converted programs to make sure the programs produced the correct results and we were on the right track.

I was told that I had a new boss downtown. He used to call meetings at 5 p.m. After a few weeks, I told him, "I have a lot of work to accomplish and I don't have time for meetings after 5 p.m. as my official day is over at 4 p.m." Lo and behold, he called me on the carpet and told me I was skating on thin ice. I smiled and said, "Sorry, I cannot skate. Now what?" He was a little bugger and used to crank up his seat so when you sat across from him, he could look down on you. I got his goat a few times when I would stand up and look down on him. Fortunately for both, he was fired and I was free to roam again, installing a new system and facing new challenges.

On the Harriers front, Marty Froelick started the season off well when he won the Houston marathon in 2:11:13. He represented the USA in the World Cross Country Championships, and finished first in the USA 30K Championships in 1:34.04.

Renee Odom was rounding into form and won the USA indoor mile title and later went on to run the 1,500 meters in 4:09.42 seconds.

The Harriers won the USA Women's 15K team championship with Carol in 52:04, Midde Hamrin in 52:12, and Debbie Warner in 56:36.

Carol went on to represent the USA in the IAAF world Championships in England.

Jim and Carol

Midde won Continental Homes 10K in 32:16 seconds and later went under the knife to have her Achilles repaired which was a success.

Chapter 28
1986 — Houston, Texas

Deon Dekkers showed up at one of our training sessions with his wife, Lorraine, son, Andre, and daughter, Michelle. Talking to him I learned that he represented South Africa prior to apartheid and gave up racing to concentrate on making a living. When the situation worsened in South Africa, he decided to sell everything and move to the States.

I must admit we were fortunate that he wanted to join the Harriers. It didn't take Deon too long to establish himself. He won the 5000 meters at the USA Masters in 15:28.1 and the 8k road race title in 25:37seconds.

The 'Javelin twins,' sisters Carol and Renee (Odom), represented the South in the Olympic Festival 10,000 meters on a hot and humid evening.

Carol McLatchie and Renee Odom.

Renee ran second behind Maricaca Puica in an indoor mile race in San Diego 4:34.

Carol and I were named as the women's and men's team managers for the IAAF World Relay Championships, which were held in Hiroshima, Japan.

This was one of the cities where the Americans detonated the atomic bomb during World War II, killing approximately 140,000 people. Large numbers of people continued to die from the effects of burns, radiation sickness, and other injuries.

One of our visits was to the steps, where the outline of a body was etched into the concrete, a terrible waste of a human life who had nothing to do with the war.

The steps in Hiroshima.

I was approached by Channel 2, the local NBC TV affiliate, to coach five rookies for the Houston marathon. Channel 2 picked the athletes, and I had no input in the selection process. Every Thursday evening, a crew showed up at the track to film the athletes and then showed it during the news later in the evening. This was a hell of a challenge as some of the people selected had never run before. One athlete was a retired sergeant major from the Marines. One was the son of a local judge and smoked a pack of cigarettes a day. The local six o'clock newscaster was another. Boy, this would drive you to drink.

After gathering data and running them a time trial over three miles, I came up with a plan. I was fortunate to ask for 12 weeks to try and get them fit enough to finish a marathon. Only one person did not make the finish line in the 1987 marathon—the newscaster, who twisted his ankle before the race.

I did several unpaid TV and radio interviews around the same time, answering a lot of stupid questions, just trying to promote the event.

Work was going along great. I managed to hire a really good computer person who could write machine code and solve machine problems. I also hired some more people. Programs were being converted and tested and we were progressing well. The next stage would be to hire a writer who would produce a user manual for all the users once that was complete, then we would start training and educating the users. We enlarged the computer room with enough space to build cubicles for the programmers and I finally got an office with no windows, but I had a door.

I hired Robert Stigers to help me implement a new system for Public Works that would eliminate keypunched cards, provide more information, and make the users more involved. Robert had worked for the meter-reading department since he left school and had a wealth of information that I could use.

The meter reader had a card for each meter and would write the read from the meter on each card, which was then keypunched, inserted into a card reader, and read into the computer, which then calculated a bill for the customer. I was looking at handheld readers manufactured by ITRON, which would download the customer's information onto the machine, where it would be read in sequence. All the meter reader had to do was start at the beginning of the route, punch in the information read from the water meter, and then go to the next customer.

At the end of the day, the information on the handheld devices would be uploaded to the computer, which would produce a water bill for each account read. By eliminating keypunching, it would also eliminate the use of keypunch operators and speed up the process with less errors.

What a year this was for the Harriers, winning major titles and me coaching people for Channel 2.

The over-40 master runners for Harriers were tearing up the roads. Deon Dekkers, Mack Stewart, and I won the USA Masters 8,000-meter team championships in Clearwater, Florida. The Harriers won the team race with a combined time of 82:09: Deon, 25:37, Mack, 30:12 and me, 26:19. Deon won the overall race and went on to later win the USA masters half-marathon title in 1:09:20.

Midde Hamrin won the women's 5,000-meter at the Texas Relays in 15:29.85, which is still a record today.

Heather, my older daughter, was 15 years old when her mother surprised her with a solo trip to England and Scotland, which really surprised me. Visiting Scotland from the USA was like going back in time, as in the States, we take a lot for granted. Scotland's pace of life is much slower. They don't rush, and their philosophy is, "We will to get to it later."

Heather in Scotland.

Transportation by bus or train was completely alien for most travelers. The local people did not have cars and traveled by bus, depending on where they were going. In Muirkirk, a bus traveled to Glasgow every four hours, and to Cumnock every hour, so you had to plan your journeys in advance. In England, transportation is more regular and one can get around much easier.

Heather navigated the system very well and got around to visit relatives. I realized when she decided to travel, she was like me; "Get out and see the world," which is an experience you will always remember.

One day, Mary Cullen called me on the phone and said they were having a function for Isabella Rossellini, the film actress, and I should bring Heather as she was interested in the movie industry and would probably enjoy meeting her. We went, and she got to meet her, which was special for her.

While attending the function, which was a fundraiser, I was asked by one of the attendees what I was doing there. I knew the asshole, who was an arrogant bugger when he competed for Rice University. I replied, "You had to make a sizeable donation to attend, I got in for free." He wanted to know how that came about. I replied, "It's who you know."

Another incident occurred while living in Houston. When one is growing up, boys want to emulate a doctor, wearing a little white coat and wearing a stethoscope around their neck. I had that opportunity as a grown adult. I made rounds at a hospital with a friend of mine, looking very officious with my white coat and stethoscope. I was introduced as a specialist from Scotland, touring the beds in a ward where all the patients were recovering well after an ailment. I would check the patient's chart at the bottom of the bed, take their pulse and said, "You are really looking well today and looks like you are progressing, keep up the good work." I thought I was in the MASH series for a while with Alan Alda.

Chapter 29
1987 — Houston, Texas

In the Public Works department, I used a system called Timeline to tie all the programs needed for the new system together and determine an estimated time when certain steps would be complete. It was a lot of work, but when it was finished, we would end up with one of the best systems in the country. I promoted Robert Stigers to the position of Computer Operations manager. His history as a meter reader would be beneficial for the new system.

The staff still worked in cramped quarters. The computer room was cold as we had to keep the temperature in the high 60s to keep the computer from overheating.

Still, within this environment, the staff worked diligently. Once I had an office, I could shut the door and concentrate on a plan to convert programs and implement a new billing system.

The Harriers continued to run well. Debbi Warner was chosen to represent the USA in the Pan Am Games marathon in New York. Marty Froelick won the Twin Cities marathon in 2:10:59. Prior to the race, I told him to run hard downhill after crossing the Mississippi River and keep it going uphill toward the finish line. When Marty took the lead, the TV commentators couldn't figure out who the guy was that was leading! He also recorded 44:25 for the 15K miler and won the San Diego half-marathon in 64:31.

Masters runner Deon Dekkers ran an amazing 10K in College Station, winning the overall race in 30:49. I put together a distance medley team that won the Texas Southern Relays over the younger university teams. Lou Vicenik, another master runner, recorded 2:01.1 for 800 meters.

Carol competed for the USA in the marathon in Seoul, Korea, where she recorded 2:39:39.

Carol and I went to Rome, Italy, to spectate the second World Track & Field Championships. I was not too impressed with Rome as it was hot and dusty. On the off days, we toured the normal attractions. When we decided to visit the Sistine Chapel, I was not permitted to enter since I wore shorts and my legs were bare. I was told that was the rule—no bare legs. So, I asked why women were allowed in with their legs uncovered and was told, "Because they are female." Since it was too late for a sex change operation, I decided I would sit outside on the steps in St. Peters Square.

While I was sitting on the steps reading and minding my own business, I was approached by this gentleman dressed in a strange garb, carrying a spear. He told me I could not sit there. I asked who he was and he said he was a member of the Swiss Guard and was responsible for the safety of the Vatican.

I also asked about his spear and was informed it was a Halberd, which is a two-handed pole and a weapon that had been used since the 14th century. I had to move on and find another refuge until Carol returned from the Sistine Chapel. I'm not sure if I received more knowledge than she did, but I know if you're tired, you DO NOT sit on the steps in St. Peters Square or you might have to deal with a Halberd.

While we were in Rome, the city put on a road race called the Vivicta World 12K. Roy Cullen entered the race and showed up at the start with his camera. I asked him why he had it, and he said since the race was going around Rome, he would be able to take pictures during the race which he probably would not be able to do otherwise. I kept waiting at the finish line for him. When he finally showed up, he told me he stopped for coffee and to chat with the natives and took some great pictures.

Sitting next to me on the marble seats at the stadium during the Games was Jock Semple, the legendary Scotsman who was involved with the Boston Marathon. Jock was famous for trying to tear the number off Katherine Switzer's back when women were officially barred from competing. Jock looked at me and said, "Sitting your arse on this concrete is hellish."

The other gentleman sitting next to us was Jeffrey Archer, the famed novelist who wrote several bestsellers. Jeffrey was also made a Lord (life peer) when he was involved in politics. He had a few financial scandals that left him broke, but was salvaged by selling over 300 million books worldwide.

Jeffrey ran for Oxford University and I used to rile him up about his sprinting prowess for Cambridge. After a few banters, he realized I was taking the piss. He did represent Britain in the 4x100 relay.

During the Games, Carl Lewis defended both his 100-meter and long jump titles. He set a world record in the 100 with a time of 9.94.

The men's 800 meters was great race between Konchellah (Kenya), who finished first with 1:43.06, Steve Elliott (Great Britain), who finished second in 1:43.41, and Jose Luis Barbosa (Brazil), who ran third in 1:43.76. Tatyana Samolenko (Russia) won both 1,500- and 3,000 meters in 3:58.56 and 8:35.73. Ingrid Kristianson (Norway) won the 10,000 in 31:05.85.

At work, after much hassling, I was finally transferred to the Public Works payroll so I would no longer report to the city's Data Processing department management. That was a step in the right direction where I no longer would have to deal with inter-department politics.

Amy, my younger daughter, asked me to drive her and one of her friends to a middle school sock hop, which was a dance for the kids who attended the school. I picked them up and drove them toward the school and she asked me to stop about 100 yards up the road from the entrance. Amy said they would get out here and walk up the road. I asked why I couldn't drive her to the school entrance and she said it wouldn't be correct for a parent to be seen dropping off kids at the school entrance, but I could pick them up after the dance at the entrance. As a parent you soon learn what is permissible in the age of children growing up.

Amy in 1987.

Chapter 30
1988 — Houston, Texas

Heather graduated from Sharpstown High School with Honors. She loved reading and had a very inquiring mind and was always debating subjects. She was very independent.

My staff converted the old card computer system that was running on the mainframe computer at the city's main installation to our new computer at Public Works, which was a challenge to make sure that all the customer records were transferred correctly. We worked many hours cross-checking to make sure that we didn't miss any records.

We ran a parallel system for a couple of weeks and when we were satisfied that we had the same results as the old system, we ran the system on our computer and eliminated the old system. We produced bills that were sent downtown to be sorted and placed into envelopes and mailed to customers.

My next plan was to have our own mail sorting system so that we would be responsible for mailing out bills. When someone else is doing that task, you don't have any control of the process.

The running season started off with a bang. Carol and Charlotte Thomas finished first and second in the Las Vegas Half-Marathon.

Six Harriers qualified for the Olympic Marathon Trials and the women won the team title. Carol and Marty Froelick both qualified for the Olympic Trials 10,000 meters. Carol placed first in the USA Women's 10,000-meter championships and was later named the USA women's team leader for the International Road Relay held in Yokohama, Japan.

One day, I was running on Brays Bayou when this runner approached me and asked me to train him for the Olympic Trials in the 800 meters. I recognized him as Geryl House, who had been a good 800-meter runner while studying at Houston Baptist University.

I asked him what he had been doing in respect to running. He told me had been building his base by running up to eight miles every three days with Fartlek the other days.

I told him that it was six weeks to the trials and to get him in racing shape was going to be a hell of a task. I told him to meet me at the

Houston Baptist University track the next day. I knew he could run around a high 46 seconds for the 400 meters, but I didn't know if he could he run the four 8000-meter races required at the Olympic Trials.

Geryl showed up and I had him warm up with the group. After the warm-up, I told him he needed to run 6x200 with a 30-second rest between and that he would be running by himself, with no help. The goal was 26 seconds per 200.

This was a twofold test. 1. Can he run pace? 2. What was his physical shape? Now the fun would start watching him run 200s in 26 seconds. 1 — 22.8/2 — 23.9/3 — 26.2/4 — 29.8/5. He wanted quit. I told him no. He ran 32.7/6 — 35.8.

After the workout was over, I told him his pace sucked, which was understandable since he had not run on a track in a few years. His determination was good and if he was still willing, I would do my best to get him in shape in six weeks to compete in the Olympic Games Trials.

I put him on a speed strength type workout. His cardiovascular system was good from all the eight-mile runs. What he needed now was to learn how to run a race and get a qualifying time for the trials.

I set a goal of around 1:46, which was achievable in six weeks if he listened. He never shirked any of the workouts and did everything I asked him.

Some of the workouts he attempted and completed:

1	4x500 — going through 400 in 54 then accelerate the final 100 with 8 minutes rest between.
2	400 — 300 — 200 — 100 with 5 minutes rest between. Start at today's pace and work towards goal pace.
3	1000 — 2.30/3 minutes rest/300 — 42/2 minutes rest/200 — 25
4	8x 400 rest 1:45/90/75/60/45/30/15 seconds around 57-58

I entered Geryl in a 1,500-meter race as part of his build-up. Prior to the race, he asked me how many laps it was, as he had never raced further than 800 meters. I thought, "What the hell?" I told him just run second or third until the bell is rung for the last lap and then take off. He stayed behind the leaders until the bell lap, then took the lead and won in 3:48 for his first 1,500-meter race.

I also needed him to run a qualifying time for the Olympic Trials. First, I had him run a time trial with some help from teammates. I set it up for him to run under 2:18 for 1,000 meters, which were 55-second laps. He managed to run 2:17.7.

Next up, he had to obtain a qualifying time for the Trials. I entered him in an 800-meter race at Rice University, where he ran 1:48.7. Now all I had to do was keep him healthy for the Trials.

To reach the final of the 800 meters, an athlete had to compete in three races prior to the finals. I knew Geryl was strong from all the long runs he had done before embarking on strength/speed program.

The 1988 Olympic Trials were held in Indianapolis, where the weather was either hot, windy or raining. In a lot of events, they were wind-assisted, and the tailwind was over the allowable of two meters per second.

I knew Geryl was strong enough to run in wind and rain and could definitely manage four races. In the first heat, with four to qualify to the quarter finals, I told him to get in a good position and finish in the top four. He placed third in 1:48.49. Now to the next round. Same instructions and he placed second in 1:49.3 with four to qualify to the semi-finals.

Now things were beginning to heat up. I told him to let it out a notch when he was 200 meters from the finish. He went on to win the race in 1:46.42 with him in full control.

The final was next and I made one of the biggest mistakes of my life when we were discussing race strategies and I mentioned, "You have an opportunity to make the team for the Olympics as you are stronger than most of the other runners and this is their fourth race in four days."

At the start line, he looked extremely nervous. When the gun went off, he just stood there, frozen to the spot and gave the field ten meters before he started racing. Johnny Gray won the race in 1:43.96, second was Everett 1:46.46, and third was Baskin 1:46.91. Geryl finished last in 1:49.54.

After the race, he thanked me for all the hard work and that was his last race as he was now going to concentrate on his job and family life.

What an adventure it was for both of us the prior six weeks—taking on an athlete I had not seen in years, who approached me with the goal of running in the 800-meter final at the Olympic Games. The mission was completed, but I wondered what would have happened if I had kept my thoughts to myself.

I watched the women's 100-meter race and noticed that the wind gauge official during the 100 meters stood in front of the gauge. Florence Griffith recorded a time of 10.49, where the wind was recorded at 0 mph, whereas one of the other heats recorded 5 mph—the same as the Triple Jumpers. I later looked at the start of the race on You Tube, where you can see the official behind the start line with a white flag standing straight out from the wind. Strange result.

Griffith went on to win the 100 meters at the Olympic Games in Barcelona, Spain, recording 10.54, with Evelyn Ashland second in 10.88 seconds, after Ben Johnson's win was disqualified when he tested positive for taking enhancement drugs. I thought it was strange that Griffith never raced again after the Olympics.

In August, I sustained a stress fracture of the femur, which put me out of commission for 15 months. I have no idea how it happened, but by not running, I had more time to devote to work and coaching.

Michelle Dekkers, Deon's daughter, was originally from South Africa. She attended the University of Houston when she arrived. A few months later, she quit because she was made to run with the slower runners. Deon was not too happy with this process and had her train with me. A few months later, she was able to run for Sam Bell at Indiana University where she went on to win the NCAA cross title in her bare feet.

Chapter 31
1989 — Houston, Texas

The running season started off with a bang when Charlotte Thomas ran 2:38:11 in the Houston Marathon and went on later to represent the USA in the IAAF World Cup marathon in Milan, Italy.

I was named USA women's coach for the Yokohama, Japan international marathon relay. I made a friend with the Russian coach Viktor Bodarenko, who was the husband of Olga Bodarenko, who won the 10,000 meters in the 1988 Olympic Games in Seoul, Korea.

After the race, the Japanese organizers had a banquet on a ship for all the teams. I was following Viktor onto the ship when I landed on my arse. Being over six-feet tall vs. most Japanese, who are around 5'6", I forgot to duck and walked into the top of the door.

I had a gash above my eye, and looked like I had gone a few rounds with Cassius Clay. A couple of beers soon negated the pain. Of course, I received a few strange looks. Just another souvenir.

Carol was the USA team leader for the IAAF World Relay Championships in Barcelona, Spain, where the team came away victorious in a stunning upset. I was asked to place the order of the US team, putting the slowest runner last with the idea that she would have the lead and would run her arse off to preserve the lead. There were quite a few people upset, whose ire soon diminished when the team won.

At work, the new system was working well. Next on my list was to look at replacing some of the handheld meter reading system with an Automatic Meter Reading System (AMR). I phased into production some routes that contained the AMR system. It was a slow process checking out converted programs that would produce the correct results.

We also worked hand-in-hand with the users developing online screens to make their job easier. Our job was to produce as much information as possible that could be accessed on a screen. By doing so, the user could find all the pertinent information about a customer without looking up the information on a paper customer file. The aim was to have a paperless information system.

Over the years, Roy Cullen and I often discussed things outside the world of running. One morning, he telephoned me at work. He wanted to discuss the possibility of hiring a black president for the University of Houston.

The Cullen family had several buildings on the campus named after family members, especially the Ezekiel W. Cullen Building, usually shortened in pronunciation as the E. Cullen Building, which serves as the administrative headquarters of the University of Houston.

I met Roy for a coffee. He said, "I value your advice as you are honest and have never asked me for anything and you even buy me a coffee." He told me what he wanted to accomplish. I told him to go for it, as it was about time a black person was given the opportunity to be president of a major university.

Marguerite Ross Barnett was hired and served as president from 1990 until her death in 1992 from cancer at age 49. A very short life for a promising career.

Chapter 32
1990 — Houston, Texas

In January, Charlotte Thomas finished sixth in the Houston Marathon in a time of 2:41:33 seconds. Later in the year, she and Joy Smith represented the USA in an international road relay held in Yokohama, Japan.

Five Harriers qualified for the National Championships, where Joy ran 16.51 in the 5,000-meter race. She also ran the Chicago marathon in 2:38:22.

Carol, Charlotte, and Joy competed for the South in the Olympic Sports Festival in Minneapolis, MN. Carol won the International Peace Marathon in Kosice, Slovakia in a time of 2:46.0 and later won the San Antonio Marathon in a time of 2:40.32 seconds. The men's winner received a car. Carol's prize was a bed, so she negotiated a deal and exchanged the bed for some spending money. Every winner of the Peace Marathon has their name etched in a stone situated in the city square, and Carol's name was added after her win.

Carol and me in Slovakia for the Peace Marathon.

One day a gentleman showed up at one of our training sessions on the hills and introduced himself as Chris Chaston. He stated that his son Justin was coming from London to live with him in Houston and would it be okay if Justin joined the group. I replied that all he had to do was show up and introduce himself. Justin fit in well with the group and training with faster runners helped his leg speed develop which helped him later in his career.

I upgraded the computer for Public Works from a Honeywell Bull DPS 8/49 to an HW8000/82, which was three times faster than the old system. The systems and programming staff still shared space in the cramped computer room which was not conducive to free thinking.

I was also at looking at the way we did the installation and replacement of water meters. I wanted to create a history for each customer's meter giving us an idea on consumption and repairs. But we needed to get the new system up and running first before we tackled the dream list.

At the end of each shift, we backed up our daily production to tapes. On many occasions, we would have to reload the system from the back-up tapes due to a malfunction. Sometimes, they could not be restored back to the computer, which meant we had to go back to the previous day's back-up tapes and reload the system. If this didn't work, then we would go back one more day to find a good system. We kept three production days of back up. If your third day was in error, you were up shit creek without a paddle.

In one incident, I spent 52 hours trying to restore the database as one of the tapes was corrupt. The third production day's back up didn't work, either. We were in trouble and I had to devise a strategy that I had used 20 years before. On the last back-up tape, there was a record count informing you how many records were on the system. The secret was to find the bad record(s), capture the account number, and record as much information as you could. If you only had one bad record, you changed the count on the last tape, deleted the bad record, and reloaded the data. Once that had been accomplished and all the good data had been loaded onto the computer, we were back in business. The account that was in error was given to the accounting department to be entered into the system. Now we had the same database as we had prior to the malfunction.

When the computer was not working, my phone would ring off the hook, asking, "How long before we get the computer back?" I usually answered, "I don't know as I need to find out what the problem is, and when I do, I will be able to give you an estimate."

When you do not have a back-up system to enter data into a computer, it makes double the work for the user. The accounting department has to record all transactions and write the information on paper to be entered into the computer system at a later date. When the computer becomes available, this data is then entered into the computer. It is very frustrating for the users, as they have to record work twice.

Every year, we would prepare a budget for the department which included labor, material, and overhead expenses. I would put in an order for new tapes with the purchasing agent, who would advertise for bids. Usually you went with the lowest bid. I was so fed up with the tapes he was ordering that I had to contact upper management for help to purchase a better product. I went through the same process with the printer ribbons used to print water bills. In the end, I managed to purchase a better product and all of a sudden, the problems disappeared.

Roy Cullen called me one day at work and asked me to go fishing, and I assumed that meant in Galveston, which was just up the road. Instead, he asked me to meet him at Hobby Airport. I asked, "Where are we going?" "Matagorda," he said. Roy's family owned most of the island. He had a runway built so he could fly his plane from Houston, spend some time on the island, and then return home. Matagorda Island is about 38 miles long and varies in width from less than a mile to about four and a half miles. A great place for a variety of migratory birds, salt-water fishing, hunting (in season), birding, picnicking and historical interpretation.

I met him at Hobby and wandered out to his plane. Roy sat in the front, and I clambered in the seat behind him. I had never traveled in a two-seater plane before. After strapping myself in, we took off. Roy was the pilot with an unlighted cigar in his mouth and me the passenger wondering, "What am I going to do if he has a heart-attack?"

We arrived safely at Matagorda, deplaned, and were met by some of Roy's staff, who helped us onto a boat and we went fishing. I caught my limit and we returned to the shore. We went to his beach home and had a beer while the fish were cleaned and then climbed back onto the plane and returned to Houston. What a way to fish. Boy, did I get spoiled.

Chapter 33
1991 — Houston, Texas

The racing season started out well. The club was growing, with several members competing in international events. We had around 100 members. I was writing schedules for thirty people. The athletes were winning all the road races in the area some represented NIKE TEXAS who competed in all the big events in the States.

The athletes that I coached met twice a week for workouts that I had developed. In the fall I had them run hills every Monday. I had designed several courses along Buffalo Bayou which were very steep but not long. So I would increase the distance by making looped courses up to 400 meters in distance which included several short steep hills. For the steeplechasers I would build some hurdles and would place a few at the top of a hill. When I had them run short reps, the runners wore a backpack which contained 10% of their bodyweight.

In the spring we met at Houston Baptist and later on at Rice University for Monday and Wednesday track sessions. I would split the athletes into groups depending on their ability—females ran with the males. The rest of the week athletes would meet in groups for easy runs. Saturday was usually a race day where everyone tried to beat their fellow competitor.

Zara Hyde came from England and was employed with Exxon in Houston as an engineer. She enjoyed the Harriers team atmosphere because it was based on the British system. We trained hard and afterwards went to the pub for a pint of beer and a good 'natter' (BS session) with the other members of the club. Zara started the season off by winning the Houston Fine Arts Run.

I was selected as the USA Women's Marathon coach for the World Cup Marathon, which was held in London, England. Two Harriers also made the team—Joy Smith ran 2:34:20 and Carol ran 2:46:53 seconds.

My younger daughter, Amy, finished high school and on her achievement, I took her to England along with the team as a reward. After the race, Amy and I did some add-on to the trip. The first day we were in London, Amy wanted to explore the city by herself. Armed with a subway map, she took off on her journey. We had agreed to meet back at the hotel at a certain time. When she arrived, she was confused with the weather situation.

She had left in sunshine, but encountered sun, rain, and sleet. She asked how you were supposed to dress for British weather. I told her to dress for the worst and hope for the best.

Amy and I took a train to Glasgow and I rented a car and we drove to Muirkirk, where I grew up. We stayed with my cousin, and explored the area, with me showing her my old haunts. I took her to Glenbuck, where I spent my first 11 years.

I couldn't believe what had happened in the intervening years. Opencast coal mining had torn the old village to a barren waste. The hills were gone and the only thing I could recognize was the base of the old school. I tried my best to point out places of interest and I was not so sure if she understood. Everything was decimated. It was a sad, sad day. I had a lump in my throat as we drove away.

Remnants of the school.

I drove Amy to the Mull of Kintyre to show her some of the Highlands. Driving in the back roads, she wanted to know where the people were as all she saw were sheep. I had to explain that Scotland is a small country with less than four million people. Hardly anyone lives in the Highlands, which makes it a good place to raise sheep.

I had to laugh when we were driving on a single-lane road and an 18-wheeler was coming the opposite way. She started getting hysterical thinking there was going to be a collision. I told her, "Don't worry, as there will be lay-by for one of us to pull into while the other vehicle drives by." At the end of the trip she asked, "How can anyone live here?" I replied, "If this is all you have while growing up and living here, you get used to it as it is part of your life."

We completed our trip and caught a plane back to the States in time to get her situated before returning to class where she had to take an Algebra course in Deer Park, about 20 miles from Houston, to graduate.

I had given her a Chevy Nova so she could go to class. One day, I got a call from her telling me that her car broke down and it was at a gas station in an unsavory part of Houston. I told her to walk toward the freeway and I would pick her up. I picked her up at the off ramp of the freeway and as we headed down toward the garage where she had left her car, I noticed it was up on blocks. I asked Amy, "Why is your car on blocks?" She replied, "I don't know." I stopped the car at the garage and noticed the car had no wheels. A male who was loitering in the area approached me and said, "For $100, I will tell you who stole the car's wheels." I told him, "No deal."

I called a tow truck to remove the vehicle. When the driver got out of the truck he started laughing and then apologized and said he had never seen anything like this before. He asked what to do with the car. I told him, "It's yours. Do what you want with it." He took off smiling and I took Amy home. On the way, I asked, "When was the last time you put oil in the car?" She said that she didn't know that she had to put oil in the car. Oh boy, lesson learned as I assumed most car drivers know that you have to check the oil occasionally.

Jon Warren broke four minutes for a road mile in the Congress Mile in Austin Texas. Mark Hunter, a 40-year-old, ran 16:10:1 for 5,000 meters on the track.

Jon Warren in the Congress Mile.

After all the hard work that Joy put in training and racing fast, she was selected to represent the States in the IAAF World Championships in the marathon in Tokyo, Japan. She finished 13th in 2:39:16.

Carol and I attended the games. Since I was Joy's coach, my credentials allowed me into the start area to take care of her. I was not allowed credentials for the finish, which was a bummer as I realized that there were already enough personnel available to take care of the finishers.

Tokyo is an enormous city, teeming with people and always a grid lock on the streets. Thank goodness they have one of the best subway systems in the world, which made it easier to get around the city.

We received free passes on the subway, which ran adjacent to the racecourse, so we were able to plan our route. When we thought Joy would be at a certain point of the race, we would get off the subway, rush up to the street level, and watch the race. We did this all the way back to the finish line, which was in the stadium. It was a great way to watch a marathon.

The hotel that where we stayed must have been built for midgets. I am 6'2" and the distance between the top and bottom of the bed was less than six feet, which made sleeping a chore.

One night while getting up for a pee, I fell into the bathtub, which was situated at the same level as the floor. I never switch on the light as I usually take my bearings before I retire to bed. I guess I turned the wrong way and down I went. Lesson learned — turn on a light.

Roy Cullen travelled to Tokyo, as well, and after a couple of days, he said he had to return to Houston as he felt uncomfortable being there. It was still a remnant from World War II, which affected him a lot.

Highlights of the event included:

Carl Lewis won the 100 meters for the third consecutive time in a new world record of 9:96.

Billy Konchellah won his second title in the 800 meters in 1:43.99.

Mike Powell (USA) won the long jump in a new world record in 8.49 meters.

Katrina Krabbe (GER) won the 100 and 200 meters in 10.99 and 22.09.

Liz McColgan (GB) won the 10,000 meters in 31:14.31.

The USA 4x100 team broke a new world record in 37.50.

Carol had turned 40 years old in October and went on to win her first US Masters Title for a 10K. Joy was selected to represent the US in the IAAF World 15K Championships in Holland, where she ran 51:00. I received an award from the USA Women's Track & Field Committee for outstanding services to the sport.

We were bouncing along in the computer room. The new system was running well with little or no problems. I spent time with the users, developing new CRT screens for them to use. We depended on the users to come up with solutions to make their jobs easier. We would look at their ideas and decide if it was worth investigating and what would be involved to start implementation.

Color CRT screens were being introduced into the workplace and I had purchased a few for management. One day, I received a call from a worker wanting to know when she was getting one. I told her, "Probably tomorrow." The next morning, before she arrived for work, I red colored Saran Wrap I had brought from home and placed it around her screen. I returned to my office, fully expecting a call. Sure enough, the phone rang. The lady was agitated. I said, "Good morning, how are you doing? I hope you like your colored screen." Her reply was quite unrecognizable.

Once we designed a new system, we would set up a test system and check results with the user. If acceptable, we would implement. I had very few problems with tapes since purchasing a better-quality tape that solved most of our reload problems.

I decided I needed to purchase more disk space and eliminate backing up the system to tape. I could duplicate customer records on disk and if the production system needed to be restored, I could do so from disk, which would be much faster than restoring from tape.

The City of Houston has a lot of water meters installed in underground vaults in the basements of multi-story buildings. We spent a lot of man-hours reading those meters.

To read a meter underground, the meter-reader had to descend to the basements, slow tedious tasks involving a lot of cost for labor.

We investigated setting up a telephone line which, when dialed, would read the meter and record consumption, which would then be entered into the system to produce a bill. Once operational, it would save a tremendous amount of manpower and time. I was looking forward to this challenge. Once the solution was in place the following year, it saved a tremendous amount on labor and time.

One thing about being in charge of a computer mainframe that produced most of the revenue for the city was that availability was the first priority. Users expected service 24/7 (24 hours per day 7 days a week). There was always something going wrong. My job was to solve the problem as quickly as possible and get the computer running so that the users could get back to work.

To ease the tension, I would go for a 30-minute run every day. I encouraged all my workers to get away from their desk, go for run, walk or do whatever. They needed a break, as I didn't want them tied to their desk when they should have been exercising and giving their brain a rest.

Chapter 34
1992 — Houston, Texas

Heather graduated Cum Laude from the University of Houston with a BA in English Literature and a minor in Radio and TV. Now she had to find a permanent job, even although she had been working since she was 13 years old.

Carol was selected as the USA team coach for the Beijing International Road Relay and Joy was selected as a member of the team. Both stayed for an extra week touring around in Beijing in bicycles checking out the sites, which is one of the best ways to get around as most citizens have bicycles.

It was the Olympic Trials that year and I was busy preparing athletes to make their qualifying times. Two Harriers competed for the USA. Joy finished sixth with a time of 2:35.09 and Carol ran 2:49.60.

Joy Smith at the Olympic Trials

The Olympic Track & Field Trials were held in New Orleans, Louisiana during the end of June in very hot and muggy conditions which was good for swamp rats but a bit tough on the human body. Jon Warren and Noyes Livingston made it to the finals of the 3,000-meter steeplechase, which I considered the toughest event.

They had to run three races in five days. In the first round, Jon finished third in his heat in 8:34.13. Noyes was fourth in his heat in 8:33.86. In the semis, Jon ran 8:35.29 and Noyes 8:32.22. The day of the finals, Noyes admitted that he had made his life-long dream of making a USA Trials final, which was all he had wanted, so he would jog the final race. He hadn't said anything about that before, and I tried to talk him out of it, to no avail. I had to go for a walk to calm down as I was spitting nails. In that final, he finished 11th out of 14 runners in 8:36.40 and Noyes sauntered around in 8:50.12 and then went into retirement.

Joy later competed in the IAAF World Half-Championships in Gateshead, UK, where she finished sixth. Later in the year Joy and Charlotte Thomas represented the USA in the IAAF World Relay Championships held in Madeira, Spain. The Harriers women's team also finished seventh in the USA National Cross-Country Championships in Kenosha, WI.

Carol was voted the USA Masters Runner of the Year, setting USA records in the 20K and 30K. She won the national cross-country title by over three minutes.

Public Works purchased a building across the street from our building on Leeland Street. It had been a restaurant and was going to be converted into a call center and an area for the water bills to be sorted, and inserted into envelopes before being delivered to the post office to be mailed out to customers.

I had to figure out a way to set up communications to the new building so that the telephone call center personnel across the street could gain access to the computer in the main building so they could do their job efficiently.

It was decided that we would run communication lines under the street. We contacted a company that would bore a tunnel under Leeland Street to the new building and then run all the wiring underground. Once we completed that task, we were in a position to start renovating and moving personnel and the mail inserter to the new building. The move went off without a hitch. The only problem I encountered was when I visited my staff—I had to watch myself while crossing the street in case a vehicle took me out.

Robert Stigers, my Computer Manager, decided to go to work for Bill Bulloch, who was my immediate boss, as a consultant on special projects in respect to maintenance. I decided I would not replace him as I could handle any problems.

Chapter 35
1993 — Houston, Texas

The season started out well for the Harriers. Sean Wade finished second in the Houston Marathon, and Jon Warren and Dave Wittman raced in the USA Track Championships.

Carol started the season off with a bang, winning the Masters in the Las Vegas Half-Marathon and Gasparilla 15K road races. She also went on to win the 1,500-meter World Master's in 4:38.70 and 5,000-meter track championships in Myazaki, Japan.

She was named RRCA and Runners World Master Runner of the Year. She was also selected as an Assistant Manager for the IAAF World Track & Field Championships in Stuttgart, Germany.

She raced 29 times that year, winning 26 of them and placing second three times. What a year.

Carol was named as the USA Assistant track coach for the World Championships in Stuttgart. The Chinese caused havoc in every women's race they ran. Seeing was believing as they won the 1,500 meters with Liu Dong running 4:00.50; placing 1, 2, 3 in the 3,000 meters with Qu Yunxia in 8:28.71, Zhang Lili in 8:29.25, and Zhang Lirong in 8:31.95; and 1, 2 in the 10,000 meters with Wang Junxia in 30:49.30 and Zhong Haundi 31:12.55. Viewing how they raced raised a few eyebrows!

At a Friday night open meet at Rice University, Michael Johnson, one of the Harriers idols, showed up to race an open 400-meter race knowing how much it would mean for him to be in the same race with them. I finagled the heats and put Gordon Thomas in lane eight and Michael in lane five. I told Gordon, "I will take a picture right after the start and you will be leading Michael and you can use the picture for bragging rights that you raced Michael Johnson and were beating him."

Heather went to work for Ernst & Young and still had an inkling to go to Hollywood and see if she could obtain a job in the movie industry.

Carol and I travelled to Toronto, Canada for the World Indoor Track Championships and my brother Ian travelled from New Brunswick to visit while we were there. We had a great time both at the meet and visiting sites, but it was bloody cold outside as we were there in March.

One day while watching the meet, I noticed a lady sitting to my left, and I mentioned to Ian, "That lady is from Scotland. I know her from when I trained with Western Women in Glasgow." I went over and asked her if she was Mary Campbell from Glasgow. She said she was, but her married name now was Mary Speedman.

She had married a pole vaulter from Scotland and they had moved to Toronto, where he was a manager with Marks & Spenser. We had a good natter about the old days. It's amazing where I bump into people I know from days old. Sometimes it takes a wee while to realize who it is and when we met.

One morning at work, I received a call from the City of Houston's attorney stating we had to appear in federal court as there was a lawsuit filed against me and the City for $250,000 each. The charge was discrimination.

I knew what it was about and told her I had saved all the documentation from when the person in question worked for me. "You are joking," she said. "Nobody keeps information that long." I said that I had a feeling he would come back and try to bite me.

I showed her the file and she stated, "Good job." We had to appear in court in front of a judge in five days. The judge read the charges, which were that I had dismissed the complainant for not following protocol. He used his daughter, who had just graduated with a law degree, as his lawyer.

The first day, the charges were read and then the judge adjourned until the next day. We showed up in court the next day and I was called to the bench by the judge who told me, "Mr. McLatchie, you have 30 minutes to put on a tie." I explained to the judge I did not wear a tie yesterday. He replied, "Today is a different day."

I never wore a tie, and now I had to find one in 30 minutes. I had a good friend Coy Baskin, who worked at the Police Department, which was located about 10 minutes away. I took off like a bat out of hell to his office. I told him I needed a tie post-haste and would explain later.

I arrived back at the court, wearing Coy's tie, and the bailiff told the judge I had returned. The trial proceeded and I was called to testify. I explained that my staff consisted of a very cosmopolitan group as I had staff from India, Taiwan, Sweden, Iran, and America—a mix of blacks, Mexicans and whites.

The protocol to discipline workers was long and tedious, and many managers just give up and tolerate the worker or try and transfer them. The steps include explaining the nature of the deficiencies and what is expected within a certain timeframe to improve these deficiencies. If there is no improvement, there is a verbal warning followed by letters with one-, three-, and five-day suspensions, and then termination.

The city lawyer displayed the documentation I had, showing several violations against the complainant. I had followed the proper city procedure documenting and warning him of each one. After viewing all the documentation, the judge dismissed the charges.

Aside from the lawsuit, work was going great. All new systems were functioning well and our downtime was minimal, except for scheduled maintenance which was required to keep the computer functional.

Chapter 36
1994 — Houston, Texas

My boss called me into her office one morning and told me that, along with data processing, I would also now be in charge of accounting, cashiers and telephone departments. All of sudden, I would be responsible for over 200 employees instead of 36. I didn't win the lottery; I had the same pay and more headaches.

I spent a lot of time observing how each department operated to try to figure out how to improve production. When working in an environment like the City of Houston, you will find quite a bit of resistance when you try to introduce change. How do you motivate workers if you cannot offer an incentive?

Data processing was not a problem. I gave them an opportunity to pick their start time. The only stipulation was that they had to start before 9 a.m. Each Monday, I would have a staff meeting with the individuals involved in writing programs and the computer operations manager. This meeting started at 8 a.m. sharp, no BS. Each individual had to report on their assignments from the previous week, give me the status of the project, and if they needed me to help, all they had to do was ask. The meetings were beneficial to running a successful operation.

The new departments that I inherited worked a fixed day, which was normally eight hours per day. If they worked overtime, they would be paid for the extra hours worked. The DP personnel that worked for me were on call 24/7 every few weeks. If they worked long hours, and since I could not pay them overtime, I gave them comp time (time off for hours worked).

One day, I received a call from a supervisor in accounting that one of the women under her refused to work and would not listen to her. I went to speak to the employee and asked what the problem was. She told me that she didn't feel like working! So, I told her she could leave the premises and I would pay her a full day's wages. She told me she was not moving. I instructed her that I was going to call the policeman who worked for us in the front lobby and she would have to deal with him.

The officer arrived on the scene and told her that she needed to leave the premises or would be charged with trespassing. She told him, "I am not leaving." When he tried to remove her from her chair, she stabbed him in the hand with her pencil. He then yanked her up from the chair, handcuffed her, and took her to jail.

The department was like a circus, nobody was working as they were all watching the episode. I heard later that a few workers stated, "Don't mess with McLatchie as he will have your ass in jail." That was my baptism in fire working with the accounting department.

Within an hour, I received a call from Congresswoman Sheila Jackson Lee, who was then a member of the Houston city council, asking me, "What did you do to one of my people?" I told her, "I did nothing as it was the police officer who arrested her, not me." Later that day, I received a call from the Public Works director asking me what was going on. I explained the situation and thought that was the end of the incident.

A month later, I received a call from the District Attorney's office asking why the lady who was arrested didn't show up in court for her hearing. I referred him to the police department. Not sure what the outcome was and didn't want to know. She came back to work for me and later I managed to transfer her to another department away from Leeland Street and she was eventually terminated.

The next department I reviewed was the cashiers, in respect to opening mail. I investigated purchasing an envelope-opening machine that would separate the envelope from the check and returned portion of the bill. When this was implemented, it saved a large amount of manual labor.

I also purchased a Pitney Bowes mail inserter, which was used to insert the produced bill and box them for delivery to the post office, where they would be mailed out to customers. It took some trial and error to get the machine running to our expectations.

If we cranked up the speed too much on the inserter, a chain would jump a sprocket, causing the inserter to stop. When we had to call for repairs, the supervising worker and I would watch the repair technician fix the machine, and we decided we could fix it, too. We spent lot of time under the machine putting on the chains that drove it. After a few false starts, we were able to gauge the correct speed with no mishaps, saving us a tremendous amount of time.

We produced approximately 350,000 bills per day, which were done on the night shift. Until we established a transmission line between buildings, the data with all the customer information was hand-carried by tape to produce a water bill at the inserter station. I would eliminate that process once the link was established from the computer to the sorting machine.

If there were any malfunctions on the processing side of the computer, a lot of problems occurred behind it, delaying a multitude of operations, especially inserting bills in envelopes which had to be mailed that day.

Once the communication line was established, the information was sent directly from the computer to the mail inserter system. No more carrying a tape and worrying if the carrier would return safely from crossing the street.

We produced bills on the main computer in mail carrier sequence as determined by the US Postal Service. By doing it this way, we were able to get a postage discount. In fact, we did most of the work. A program was written to produce bills by the criteria laid out by the post office.

With the new machine, bills were folded and then fed into the sorter, which also had a return envelope and a window mail out envelope. At the end of the sorter, a worker placed the sealed envelopes in boxes, which were then delivered to the post office for delivery.

After the incident in accounting, when they called me to take care of the problem because the supervisor and manager couldn't, I approached human resources about having a class for the managers and supervisors who worked for me. The idea was to role play, where the managers became the workers and the supervisors became the managers.

I decided I would be a worker. The task was to get a worker to work via instructions from the supervisor. I was asked by a supervisor to do a task. I told her, "Fuck off, I am not doing anything." The lady was thunderstruck. The rest of the class burst out laughing at the incident. The instructor told her she needed to handle the situation even though I swore at her, which would happen in a real-life situation.

It was an interesting topic, "How do you get someone to work who refuses?"

The Harriers decided that they would have me roasted for the services that I performed for the club. The venue was the Westwood Country Club. Several athletes that I had coached several years earlier made the pilgrimage from all over the country to roast me and give me shit. A couple of reporters were in attendance from the local newspapers. I didn't realize that I had an impact on so many people's lives. It was great for me to listen to their tales of woe.

A great night was had by all. Several athletes stopped at our house later to sample my homemade brew—beer which had a high alcohol content and an effect on how people acted.

One day, Heather stopped by the house asking me to check out her car. While she was sitting on the curb in the shade watching me, I asked if she would like a beer. I gave her one that I had made. After a time, Heather said "I need to go to the bathroom, but my legs won't function." I helped her up and she teetered off for a pee. Ah home brew.

That year, I attended Texas Southern Relays, where I usually entered a men's team in the Distance Medley Relay. While I was watching the meet, the coach from Texas Southern approached me and said, "I would like you to meet Evander Holyfield."

I knew who Holyfield, the world heavyweight boxing champion, was. After introductions, Evander looked at me and said, "I hear you are the toughest coach in America."

I said, "Nope, most other track coaches think that I must be, since most of the athletes I coach win all the races around here and do well nationally."

I said to him, "I bet you train harder than my athletes when you are getting ready for a big fight." He explained that when getting ready for the big dance, it is tough and he has to do a certain amount of running. We enjoyed talking to one another, and before I left, I said, "We could run a celebrity race." He responded, "Forgot my spikes."

Justin Chaston was racing well. He competed in the steeplechase for Great Britain at the European Championships, Goodwill Games, and the Commonwealth Games. He also won the British Steeplechase Championships and raced in Nice, France, where he recorded 8:23.90 for the steeplechase.

Zara Hyde won the British 10,000-meter championships and went on to represent England in the Commonwealth Games. Tommy Harris and I travelled to Victoria, Canada to cheer them on. Justin finished seventh. Zara managed to finish 13th. A Scottish girl, Yvonne Murray, won the race in 31:56.97.

Jon Warren and David Wittman were two of the ten people who broke four minutes for the mile at the Pre-Classic in Eugene, Oregon. Dave ran 3:58.05 and Jon recorded 3:59.30. Dave was also selected to represent the USA in Denmark and Sweden. Joy Smith competed in a 30K road race in Ohme, Japan where she ran 1:49.40.

I was named as USA women's coach for the World Relay Championships in Yokohama, Japan, where I met the temperamental Chinese coach Ma Junren, who trained several world-class middle and long-distance female runners called the Ma Family. They included world-record holders Wang Junxia and Qu Yunxia,

Ma was sitting on a chair smoking and spewing off about turtle soup and his methods that contributed to his athletes' success, which were speed- and stamina-type training and eating soup.

His training regimes were reputed to be tough, involving high mileage. There were suggestions that his athletes were on drugs which contributed to their performances, and there must have been some credence in the allegations as six of his athletes were dropped from the Sydney Olympics after failing blood tests. He had also admitted to physically beating his athletes on occasion and was later fired for many reasons never revealed.

It was strange that there was later only one Chinese woman who competed in the 1995 World Championships, and she dropped out of the race after a few laps.

I played golf a couple of times with Preston Moore, who used to be Assistant Secretary of State for the first President Bush. One day, he invited me to play at Lochinvar, which was a men-only golf club in Houston. Tiger Woods was also there at that time, as he was being coached by Butch Harmon. What a place. There were fans installed near the green. Maybe to keep the mosquitoes away? It sure didn't help my putting. Preston was also involved with Tom Fatjo starting a waste hauling company called Brown & Ferris that later became BFI.

Chapter 37
1995 — Houston, Texas

The Harriers started the season off on a high note. Sean Wade won the Conoco 10K road race. Dave Wittman and Jon Warren competed in the Pre-Classic. Dave ran the mile in 3:57.27 and Jon ran the 3,000-meter steeplechase in 8:30.84.

Carol defended her World Master's 5,000-meter track title for the second time when she won in Buffalo, NY. We competed in the USA Cross Country Championships in Boston where she kicked my butt. Its hell getting old.

Carol and me in Buffalo, NY.

Justin Chaston competed for Great Britain in the steeplechase in the Europa Cup and recorded 8:26.82. Later in the season, he was selected to compete in the IAAF World track & Field Championships in Gothenburg, Sweden where he ran the steeplechase in 8:24.97 in the prelims and 8:38.30 in the semi-finals, which didn't qualify him for the final.

Justin Chaston in the steeplechase.

Highlights:

1500 — Morcelli (ALG) 3:333.78

100 & 200 — Michael Johnson (USA) 9.97 & 19.79

5000 - Sonia O'Sullivan (IRE) 14:46.47

Triple Jump — Jonathan Edwards (GB) 18.29 meters a new world record]

Carol and I went to Gothenburg to watch the Championships and cheer Justin on. It also gave us an opportunity to spend some time with Midde Hamrin, whom I coached while she lived in Texas. It was nice to meet her family and her husband, Andy Sornoski, whom I knew when I lived in Chicago. He moved to Beaumont, where I went to college, and was distance coach at Lamar University. He was responsible for me coaching his wife, which turned out to be a great move.

One morning, we went out for a run through a park which circled a lake. About a half-hour into the run, we came upon an encampment with people and dogs running loose. As I am wary of dogs, I was nervous as all hell, being not so sure if I might get a bite in my arse. Later we found out that we had stumbled upon an encampment of drug users. The city provided tents and free drugs. They had most of the users in one area, which was easier to control.

One night, we were returning from watching the meet when I heard someone shouting, "McLatchie, how is the good doctor doing?" I looked around and saw Brendan Foster sitting outside a pub holding a beer. Naturally we spent some time with him. Brendan was at the meet as a commentator for the BBC (British TV).

We talked for a while, reminiscing about his victory in the Commonwealth Games at Edmonton in the 10,000 meters and how Don Baxter had patched up his feet so he could run the 5,000 meters.

Chapter 38
1996 — Houston, Texas

I was busy at work installing new systems that made it easier to access customer information. We gathered statistics on each account and could track meter information from the time it was placed in the ground to present day. With the new usage information, we could alert the meter reading department that a meter needed maintenance before it broke and set up a maintenance schedule depending on usage. In the old days, you waited until the meter gave erroneous reads before acting.

I was selected to manage the USA Women's international team to compete in a road relay in Seoul, Korea. Seoul is a big city with enormous skyscrapers that house thousands of people. One day while strolling around the neighborhood, I was asked by a citizen if it would be okay if he could practice his English on me. What a laugh as most people shake their head when I am talking, saying "I have no idea what he is talking about, plus he speaks funny." I would just respond, "I understand you, maybe you are listening funny!"

The team was invited to tour Camp Casey, a U.S. military base in Dongducheon, South Korea near the Korean Demilitarized Zone (DMZ) roughly 40 miles north of Seoul, South Korea. We were amazed at how close the North Korean army was to where we were visiting.

The Harriers had a successful year. The Olympic Games were being held in Atlanta, Georgia. Justin Chaston was chosen to represent Great Britain in the steeplechase and Sean Wade ran the marathon for New Zealand. Justin and Sean had trained hard and their reward was being chosen to represent their countries in the Games.

Charlotte Thomas purchased tickets for me so that I could attend the games and be available to Justin and Sean for moral support.

As a coach, training athletes to be fit and fast and race well is usually a challenge, but when they are chosen to represent their country in the Olympics or World Championships, this becomes a whole different ball of wax. Chances are you will mess them up by training them too hard or not training them enough.

I had other problems. Justin's girlfriend was attending the meet and he thought it would be a great idea to get engaged under the flame. I told him this was not the time to worry about getting engaged. The main intent was to concentrate on racing well. I told him, think of all the hard work you have done to get here, don't throw it away before you race." I guess he didn't hear me. He ran 8:28.32 in the heats and made it to semi-finals, where he placed ninth in 8:28.50s. One down.

Sean decided to lead from the gun in the marathon as he wanted to be seen on TV. The race was being televised all over the world and the people in New Zealand would see him leading the pack. The marathon race was an out-and-back course, starting and ending in the stadium. We found a place on the course where the five-mile mark was near a pub. Since the race was being televised live, we moseyed in, bought a drink, and asked for the TV to be tuned to the race.

When the race was approaching the bar, we went outside and watched Sean leading the pack as he intended. We re-entered the bar to watch the race until he returned on the way back to the stadium, which was five miles away.

We stood outside the pub waiting for the runners to return on the way to the finish line. We waited and waited for Sean, wondering what had happened to him. He finally appeared, looking like he was hardly moving. He finished the race in 83rd place with a time of 2:30.35, which was a big difference from his best of 2:10. Two down.

Sean Wade

That was my first and only time attending the Olympic Games. There were just too many people for me in the same area at the same time. It was a nightmare getting out of the stadium, which was right next to the baseball stadium. When both events finished at the same time, all hell broke loose as everyone was trying to get away from the area. What an experience, terrible logistics. I feel more comfortable at the World Championships.

That year was also the end of an era. The Houston Baptist University track was going to be demolished. I received a call from the university president telling me of the plans, and he thanked me for all the work I had done on the track. The Harriers had installed lights and drains, patched the track, and cut the grass. Now I had to find another place to train the club.

I approached Steve Straub, who was the head coach at Rice University. A deal was struck where I could have the track for two hours on Mondays and Wednesdays from 5 to 7 p.m. and in return, I would provide Harriers club members to help officiate Rice's home track meets.

I received another challenge. One of the male runners I coached called me up and said that he had an athlete for me to coach. I asked what he had done and if he was committed. He replied, "I don't think there is anyone more committed than Ramiro Bermudez." I asked, "Why do you think that is the case?" He replied, "He competes in a wheelchair." I said, "You must be joking!" "Nope, you need a challenge."

After he hung up, I said to myself. "I am an unpaid coach who had two athletes compete in the Olympic Games, and I need a challenge— knitting?"

I called Ramiro and set up a meeting with him at Rice, where there was a half-mile blacktop circuit used for cycling in the football parking lot. I decided that I would use that for interval training for him as there was no way he could be on the running track at the same time as the runners.

I had no idea what times I would give him for a workout as I had never coached anyone in a wheelchair before. I decided I would administer the same type of interval workouts that I gave the group and adjust his times as I figured out pace. I asked him if he had raced a 10K. He said he had and gave me his time. I took that and calculated pace for the following workout which I gave him: mile/1320/880/440 with 3 minutes rest.

After the workout, I chatted with him about his life. He said he been born deformed in Columbia. With some help, he moved to the USA. He had some sponsorship to help with his racing and sold papers for the Houston Chronicle for a living.

He won the wheelchair division of the Houston Marathon four times and San Francisco once. He was the Paralympic champion once and the Pan-American Games champion three times.

A great gentleman. A very dedicated man who overcame many obstacles to achieve what he accomplished. There was no way that I could not help him try and achieve his goals.

Ramiro Bermudez

Chapter 39
1997 — Houston, Texas

Since I coached Justin Chaston for Great Britain, I was asked to work with Mark Rowland, who was in charge of the elite middle-distance program in the country. Mark had won a bronze medal for running the steeplechase in 8:07.96 in the 1988 Olympic Games. I attended steeplechase training camps and helped Mark devise workouts to improve athletes' hurdling technique over the water jump.

We filmed a lot of athletes as they went over the water, and then we would spend time critiquing the athlete's form with the athlete and his/her coach, if they were in attendance. We offered suggestions on how to improve and wrote some schedules for those who asked and helped in any way that we could to get the athlete to improve.

At the 1998 general convention in December I approached the USATF about having the Women's Cross-Country trials to select the USA team for the IAAF World Championships in Houston, to which they said, "Yes." The problems that were lurking around the corner soon appeared.

Mike Krakower approached a local bank seeking financial aid. They said they would give me some money if the Harriers would have a race for children under 15 years old. Mike told them that would not be a problem and we would have the kids run with the number one, their logo, on their shirts. The bank thought that was a great idea and funded the championships.

A company from San Diego who filmed road races for ESPN contacted me a week before the race and said they could televise the event if we paid them $10,000. I told them it was not going to happen. Every week, ESPN televised the race of the week and was supposed to televise the San Blas race from Puerto Rico which was cancelled because of weather. I knew they had been paid to provide a service. They did not have a back-up and probably thought they could get the trials. I think someone forget to tell them they were dealing with a Scotsman.

I told them, "You are welcome, but I cannot pay you a fee. We will give you hotel rooms for the crew and provide you with platforms for your stationary cameras to film the race," and they accepted.

The Wednesday before race day, Houston had one of its torrential rainstorms, which left about 20 feet of water on the cross-country course. The course ran alongside Buffalo Bayou, and when there was heavy rain, the bayou backed up from the Gulf, creating a mess with tremendous flooding.

One of the Harriers who worked near the course on the 10th floor of an office building called me and said, "I am looking out the window of my office, and there is about 15 feet of water on the course. What is plan B?" I told him I didn't have one, and hoped that since there was no more rain forecasted, the water would recede and the race would proceed.

The Friday before the race, I was clearing debris and marking the course and came across a dead possum. I didn't lift the animal. I just ran the chalk marker over its body. The next day, prior to the race, Toni Reavis and Ed Eyestone, who would be commentating, walked the course and came across the dead possum.

When they bumped into me afterward, they said there was a dead animal on the course with a white stripe on its back. I replied, "Yup, I guess the poor bugger is dead, and I didn't have time to move it."

The race started off with the kids, which was funny and exciting as they headed to the first hill where there was a two-foot-wide ditch filled with water. Most of the kids fell in the ditch, and after scrambling out, they still had to negotiate a muddy hill. I tried to help some kids navigate the ditch and was told, "Leave me alone, I can do it." The kids loved the race; they were soaking wet and covered in mud. I believe the parents didn't care for me too much. The junior race went off with a couple of mishaps except for two runners who lost their shoes in the mud.

Lynn Jennings was the starter for the senior women's race and told Carol that she couldn't fire a starting pistol. Carol had to high-tail it home and brought back a bell that she had won at the Bonne Bell race. She gave the bell to Lynn who started the race with, "On your marks, set..." and a ting-a-ling of the bell. The race was won by Nnena Lynch, with a time of 20:17 over Amy Rudolph on a hilly, muddy 6K course. Reavis loved the course in Houston as he said it was tough and a true cross-country course.

ESPN showed 30 minutes of the race the following Tuesday, which was a great viewing spectacle. All it cost the club was a couple of rooms and meals. A great bargain for the club and I am sure the company that was working for ESPN took a financial hit, but that's just business.

Jon Warren and Patty Valadka represented the USA in Athens, Greece, competing in the World Marathon Cup. The race started in the town of Marathon and finished in Athens. Patty remembers it as being hot and dusty and she, like a lot of competitors, was tired and thirsty.

After about 20 miles, she stopped at the side of the road and was sitting down when a farmer approached her and told her if she made it to the top of the hill, she could see Athens and she would make the finish line as it was all downhill from there. Patty, like 20 other runners, never made it to the finish line.

Jon Warren suffered in the same conditions, which he termed a 'death' march, finishing 63rd in a time of 2:45.56. 41 other athletes called it quits along the route. It was a great experience for both, but a tough way to see the sights of Greece.

Highlights — Maurice Greene (US) won the 100 in 9.86.

Gebrselassie (ETH) won the 10,000 over Tergat (KEN) by 1 sec in a time of 27:24.58

4x400 won by Great Britain — USA disqualified

Szabo (ROU) 5000 — 14:57.68. Brunet (ITA) 14:58.29, Ribeiro (POR) 14:58.85. A race towards the finish line.

Carol was selected as the USA Team Manager for the IAAF World Half-Marathon Championships held in Kosice, Slovakia.

There was nothing exciting at work as I had a good staff and everything was running smoothly with few hiccups, so one day I decided to create some. I gave them a task and let them solve the problem. There was a meeting in the conference room and I set off a stink bomb outside the door and watched the pandemonium erupt. The person in charge of maintenance was running up the hall with a toilet plunger. After a few minutes, he came out the bathroom shaking his head and stating that he could not find any blockage. The smell finally dissipated and work resumed as normal. I laughed all the way to my office. They never figured out the cause of the smell.

Chapter 40
1998 — Houston, Texas

City of Houston meter readers were allowed to finish their shift early if they completed all the work that was installed on their ITRON handheld meter readers. Most of the old houses had meters installed in backyards, which were a pain to access. Since the incentive was to go home early if the work was completed, a lot of the younger meter readers would climb over customer fences to read the meter, which saved a lot of time.

The older meter readers would open the gate, read the meter, then close the gate and walk to the next house. We asked customers who kept dogs in their backyard to notify us so we could take precautions, which usually meant asking the customer to have the dog tethered the day that their meter would be read.

We investigated purchasing a meter that could transmit a signal that could be read without the meter reader climbing fences, and could be read in water. Houston gets a lot of rain, and on many occasions, the meter box in the ground is filled with water. If the meter head was not properly sealed, it could not transmit a signal. By eliminating manual meter readers, we could save money on labor.

Once again, the Harriers were showing their colors nationwide. Mack Stewart won three USA Masters Track titles, and was later voted the USA 60-64 Athlete of The Year. He is one of the few runners who has been able to run 400 meters faster than his age. Mack won several world titles. Mack is now in his mid-eighties.

Mack Stewart

Patty Valadka won the USA Half-Marathon Championships and was later voted USA Master's Runner of the Year.

Joy Smith was selected as the USA leader for the Women's IAAF Half-Marathon Championships in Zurich, Switzerland. Later, she and Joe Flores represented Houston in the Athens Marathon, which Joy won and where Joe placed seventh.

Charlotte Thomas and I travelled with the USA Road Relay Team to Beijing, China as team manager and coach. As we were departing the airport in Beijing, I could hardly see for the smog. I thought, "This is going to be tough on the runners."

On one of our excursions, we had to visit the Forbidden City as part of their "We will show you what we want to see" PR. I wandered off by myself and lo and behold, I was lost. I thought, "Not to panic, just head back to the start and the Chinese tour leaders will find me." On arrival at the entrance gates, a Chinese lady approached me and said, "You lost the group, just stay here. They will come back here, as they don't like to lose anyone." Sure enough, a bus with the USA team and Chinese tour guides showed up. I played dumb, which I thought was funny as I was supposed to be taking care of the team.

At one of the Friday evening meets held at Rice University, Shynae Godfrey ran a great 800 meters in 2:04.98s.

Chapter 41
1999 — Houston, Texas

We had a few problems during installation of the automatic meter reading system. If an installed meter was near a chain linked fence or an aluminum boat, the metal bounced the signals around erratically, and they could not be interpreted by the computer. After much testing, we finally figured out how to deal with that problem.

It took a little trial and error to determine the range that we could pick up a signal. An automated reader was housed inside a van and was programmed to pick up reads in a 360-degree circumference. Once the range was plotted, we were able to read meters at a considerable faster rate than someone walking the route. Meters that were not detected were noted and read manually.

The next year, 2000, or Y2K, was when all computer programs and computers were expected to stop functioning. Fly by night companies were appearing all over the place preaching the doomsday message that anything that used a date as a calculation would fail and the program would have to be rewritten.

These companies were offering fantastic salaries to programmers to go work for them, and in the process, I lost a few of my staff. I approached my manager and asked for a meeting with the mayor or his staff to explain that if I did not get some help, we were doomed for failure.

A meeting was arranged with the mayor's office, controller, treasurer, finance director, and my boss. At the meeting, my boss started talking and was abruptly told to shut up as he was told, "Only one person in this room tells the truth and that is Jim McLatchie." The others in the room were a bit shocked, but the person who made the statement, Don Hollingsworth, had hired me when I worked for him in the police department. He knew I told the truth and irrespective of how it was accepted, you knew what you were dealing with. In a lot of cases, the truth hurts, but if you lie, you are going to get tripped up.

The mayor at that time was Lee Brown, who had served as the Police Chief of Houston from 1982 to 1990. Don had worked for Lee when he had hired me.

Prior to Brown being the mayor, there was a movement in 1997 by several prominent people to hire him and I was privy to some of that information.

One evening, Carol and I were having a meal at a barbeque place when in walked Don, Lee and another gentleman. Don had moved to Chicago after leaving the police department. He and I talked for a while and during the conversation, I asked "Are you moving back to Houston?" He replied, "It's possible."

Shortly after the meeting, Lee Brown was nominated to run for mayor of Houston with the backing of the financial sector, which once again proved that money talks.

Back in the Y2K meeting, I explained to the group that Don Hollingsworth had invited me so they could hear of our situation. I told them that we processed approximately 3.5 to 4 million dollars a day on a system that used the date field to calculate bills and invoices so that bills can be paid on a timely basis. I explained that I had lost several programmers to other companies paying big salaries and I needed four programmers to replace the ones that I lost, along with an increase in salary for my staff.

The doomsday message floating around was telling companies they were all heading towards the end of the world and nothing would work unless you rewrote computer systems, which cost a lot of money. People were scared and believed these scary messages. My solution was simple—other than needing replacements for my lost workers and paying a competitive salary, the problem would be fixed at a minimum cost.

I explained that a few lines of code would fix the problem as I had dealt with a similar situation years earlier when the date field in a computer program was set at five digits (y/mm/dd) 9/01/01and all programs today were set at six digits (yy/mm/dd) 99/01/01

To save space within records the date field was set to receive 5 digits for the year. Hardly anyone thought about when the decade arrived there would be a problem. When that was discovered all companies changed the date field to contain 6 digits — yy/mm/dd knowing that it would cause a problem in 2000. The premise within companies was that all programs containing a date field would be rewritten prior to 2000 which in many cases did not happen

With no changes to the programs which calculated day payments prior to 2000, programs would calculate a negative number. Example -

How many days between December 12, 1999 and January 2, 2000?

	Date	Working Storage
Original	99/12/12	1999/12/12
New	00/01/01	2000/01/01

Set up the Working Storage area to accept the four- digit year. Test the year field. If yy = 99, add 19, move 19 and 99 along with the information to the month and day fields in working storage field, 'ELSE' move 20 and current year to working storage.

Julian Date converter was used in COBOL programs to calculate days.

Original	y/mm/dd	6/12/01
Newer	yy/mm/dd	99/12/12
2000	yyyy/mm/dd	2000/01/01

Year 2000 - 000101 minus old year - 991212 you would end up with a negative number, but if you increased the date field from six characters to eight with the year becoming four, Old - yy/mm/dd, New — yyyy/mm/dd.

If you wanted to know how many days there are between December 12 and January 2, with no changes the computer using 'Julian Date' would calculate a negative number as follows:

Present system — new year - 000102 minus old year - 991212

After program changes - 200000102 minus - 19991212

Now your date field looks like this for calculation purposes: 20000101 minus 19991212, you get 20 days.

The Finance Director was told to start the ball rolling, issuing the necessary paperwork to hire four programmers and give salary increases to the computer staff with the understanding to meet again in four weeks.

I hired four programmers from India on a temporary status. I informed them that if they wanted to stay in the country after four years, they had to apply for a green card.

I met with the mayor's department four weeks later informing them that I had hired four programmers. We had completed the necessary changes to programs that had dates embedded and computed calculations of days and it was working. In the process, I leased another computer that was used to test the system with the new changes without disrupting daily production. I was now ready when the year changed from 1999 to 2000. A job well done.

I told them all of my staff were happy with the salary increase, except the captain of the ship. They wanted to know what I was talking about. I informed them that I was the only one that didn't get a salary increase, which was soon rectified with my salary being backdated to reflect the increase.

It was a quite year for most of the runners. A mixed Harrier team represented Galveston in a road race in Niiagata, Japan against other sister cities from across the world. It was great experience for a few that had never participated in an international competition. I was the coach, which was an easy task as I had done several trips abroad with a USA team before. And I knew all the runners on this trip, so it was a breeze. I was allowed to pick a mixed team of three men and three women running various distances which totaled 42 kilometers.

We were up against local teams from all over the world. The idea was to pick athletes that you thought could run a good 5K or 10K. In most cases, the legs consisted of men 6.195 km + women 4 km + men 10 km + women 8 km + women 6 km + men 8 km.

Usually after the race, there was a banquet for all the teams and officials that competed. When a Kenyan team showed up, it was usually curtains for the rest of the teams. Interesting note was that the next morning on an easy run, all of the Kenyan team ran together at the women's pace.

I coached several Houston high school athletes. Normally, a parent or high school coach would approach me and ask if I could coach their athlete.

I would check out the athlete and then decide. I remember Chris Hickman's dad approached me about coaching him and Shelton Ervin. Chris attended Westbury, which was one of the top schools for producing good hurdlers.

I told his dad that if the Westbury coach agreed to the set up, then I would coach Chris and Shelton. The coach agreed and I started the process of getting them in shape to compete well in the Texas State Championships.

To reach the finals of any Texas high school championship, an athlete has to compete in Districts and Regionals before reaching the State Championships, which is a tough chore for all athletes.

I coached Chris as an 800-meter runner, namely to build strength and let 'Big" John Eder coach him on hurdling techniques. John had coached Sheryl Dickey, who finished third in the 1996 Olympic Trials in the 100-meter hurdles, where she went on to finish fifth in the Quarter

Finals and third in the 1997 World 60 Hurdles Final.

The day of the State Finals, the rain was coming down in buckets. I took Chris aside and told him there was no way he could get beat. I had him run hard into the rain and make the hurdlers hurt. Chris carried out the plan to a T and came home the winner in 36:97. Shelton made the final of the 800 meters where he finished sixth in 1:54.35.

Both boys went on to run in the 4x400, where Westbury finished fifth in 3:15.90, which was less than a second in finishing second.

It was a great performance from the two boys who had to endure prelims and finals in the rain.

Later on, Shelton attended Kansas University. One day, he called me to tell me he was coming home as Lawrence, as Kansas was too cold for him.

After graduation, Chris attended Barton College, and while there, he made the USA World Junior Championships team in Santiago, Chile, competing in the 400-meter hurdles.

That year, Simon McNamee, one of the original Harriers, died. Simon was attending Lamar University when I went to school there. He and his wife Susan helped a lot as they gave me a place to visit and have a cup of tea.

Simon had a bout of Hodgkin's Lymphoma, which he managed to beat twice, but he later succumbed to a heart attack. After the funeral, Carol and I had a chat with Len Hilton, who had a run in the 1972 Olympics and was also a founding member of the Harriers.

Walking away, Len said, "I'm next." I ran after him and asked what he meant but he wouldn't say. When I returned home after the funeral, I called Al Lawrence, who had coached Len while he attended the University of Houston. Al told me that when Len had a medical exam for a new job, the medical staff had noticed something wrong and told him to report to MD Anderson Hospital immediately, where he was diagnosed with pancreatic cancer.

The Harriers had a "White Horse" cross country race where each runner brought a wrapped gift which was placed on a table and the last person selected the first gift, which they unwrapped. This process went all the way backward to the winner, who could either keep the last gift or select any gift that a previous runner had unwrapped.

I managed to get Len to attend and be part of the celebration. Finally, we had a talk and he told me his dilemma, which was no good. I promised him I would there for him.

My younger daughter, Amy, was married to Chris Mace. The

wedding was held in the Wimberley, Texas area. It was bloody hot. Here I was dressed up like a "flea hook," wearing a suit and a tie with the sweat pouring out of me. I thought I would be walking my daughter up the aisle, which happened to be some roll of cloth leading to a tree where they were married. I was wrong. Guess I must be getting old.

Chapter 42
2000 — Houston, Texas

At work, we ran the system as normal and had no trouble processing from the year 1999 to 2000. Now my next objective was to convert all programs running on a Honeywell computer to an IBM machine.

I started contacting IBM, telling them what my plans were, and asked if they would be able to support us in our task. Knowing full-well when dollars are involved, one has some leverage. Multiple meetings were held to determine the scope and how long it would take. Once I received the information I was looking for, a plan was laid out and off we went.

I had a good staff and broke up the system into blocks. Each programmer was responsible for converting a Honeywell program to an IBM program, testing the validity, and then moving on to the next program.

On the running front, I was contacted by Peter Thompson telling me that Scotland was looking to hire a distance coach to be in charge of their program. I put together my resume with my past history of originally being from Scotland and representing them several times in international track meets.

I was told to report for an interview and prepare a Power Point presentation of what I would do to improve Scottish participation in worldwide events. I flew to Glasgow, where I rented a car and drove to Edinburgh for an interview the next day. As I had a whole day to kill, I walked around the neighborhood where I was staying, checking on prices of furniture and houses. I was quite amazed to find out that some things were more expensive than in America.

The next day, I had an interview with a panel that consisted of Meg Ritchie, who won several NCAA discus titles while attending university in America, and Olympian Frank Clements, who was the head of Scottish athletics.

I thought the interview went well but was informed that they had chosen someone else, an Englishman. Later I was told that I was the best candidate for the job, but politics played its part.

Justin Chaston was chosen to represent Great Britain in the Olympic Games steeplechase, which was held in Sydney, Australia. He placed 7th in the heats in 8:31.01.

The Harriers had three women—Karen Killeen, Patty Valadka, and Joy Smith—and Jon Warren qualify for the Olympic Marathon Trials. Karen came down with a stress fracture prior to the race and did not want to compete. I told her she was going to the trials and would line up at the start line with the rest of the runners and drop out of the race after the start. I explained that she had earned her spot to be there with all the women who had qualified.

When Len was admitted to hospital, Al Lawrence called me up and said he could not visit him as it was too emotional. I promised that I would visit him as much as I could.

Len at that time had been living with a lady he met while working at Enron. She had made a rule that she would decide who would be allowed to visit. I ignored her and visited. On one of the visits I told Len what she was doing. He told her, "He will visit me anytime he wants."

Len was an original Harrier. We had been good friends since 1975. I paced him to the first four-minute mile in Texas. We spent lots of time together. We helped each other install fences and re-roofed our homes. We ran together, drank beer, and stayed out of trouble. When I visited Len, I would look at him and see my brother David, knowing full well he was going to die.

Len had an idea where his cancer had come from. When he was working in South America, some rebels blew up a pipeline. Since Len was in charge of the project, his job was to stop the oil from leaking. He would jump into the hole with his workers to stop the flow of oil. Most of the time, while working in that environment, he would be covered with oil, which probably contributed to his cancer.

I would visit Len once or twice per week, sit and chat, and talk about some of our escapades. I used to get upset when his partner would discharge him from the hospital and have him taken home. A few times when I would visit, the bed would be empty. I thought that he had passed on. I would approach the nurse's station and ask where Len was. I was told that his partner had him moved him home. The house was surrounded by a fence which had cameras installed. I am not so sure they were installed for safety or to observe who was at the fence door. Len's partner informed the maid that under no circumstance was I to be allowed into the house.

Len was still friendly with his first wife, Donna, who was Canadian.

She flew down from Winnipeg and was not permitted by his partner to visit him. When a few of his friends knew his partner would be working, they would sneak Donna into the hospital to visit him.

Len and I had a mutual friend, Barbara, who experienced the same welcome when she tried to visit. I would tell her when I was visiting so that she could come with me. I always wanted the partner to be around when I was taking Barbara to visit. It would be an interesting situation. I was sure the sparks would be flying.

When his health deteriorated, he was taken back to the hospital. I would visit him nearly every day. Once again, I was not notified that his partner moved him back to his house, where he died shortly after at the age of 52.

I am sure his partner was upset when she was informed that Len made sure I was one of the main speakers at his service prior to his burial. I spoke about our friendship, the fun, and the hard times. I left out a lot of escapades that he and our other good friend, Don Baxter (we were the three musketeers) indulged in while we were together. He died too young. I enjoyed all our time together. The ups and downs are what life is all about. I will surely miss him!!

Len's partner/wife was a high-powered lawyer for Enron and was used to getting her own way. She met a stumbling block in me as I never backed off.

My good friend, John Egan, played in the NBA for 11 years and coached the Houston Rockets from 1973-75. His wife, Joan, was a local runner who would always give me stick about being Scottish and coaching all the good runners. We had some great discussions with banter going back and forth.

Joan died in 1998 from ovarian cancer. Prior to the service and burial, John called me on the phone and said Joan had told him before dying to make sure I would be in attendance.

I showed up at the church as the service was starting and sat in the back behind two ladies, when one turned around and asked, "What are you doing here?" I thought, "Who the hell is she?" as I did not know her. I replied, "I am fulfilling a dying wish."

Two years later, when visiting Len in hospital, I saw his partner in the room talking to him and at once recognized her as the woman in the church.

The Harriers were approaching 25 years of existence and a momentous occasion was being organized. Harriers that had left Houston to seek their fame and fortunes attended. The organizers had a race on the bayou, a get together at a pub, and a great reception in a hotel. Many tales were told, some true and some questionable. I think a lot had to do with how much one drank. The sad part was that Len was dying and could not attend. I am sure he would have had a lot to reminisce about as he was one of the founding members.

I was awarded the keys to the City of Houston for services towards the community and a plaque, which said, "Committed to fair play and good sportsmanship, having devoted countless hours to practice and training which has led to many outstanding accomplishments." I don't remember ever getting a key!

Chapter 43
2001 — Houston, Texas

Carol kept asking me when I was going to retire from work. I told her after I implemented all the programs on the present system and converted them successfully to operate on an IBM computer.

I purchased an IBM computer and after having the programmers trained in an IBM format, we started the task of converting programs from the Honeywell computer. The programmers I had from India were very smart and didn't need much prompting.

Carol and I attended the IAAF World Track Championships in Edmonton, Canada. It brought back old memories from when Don Baxter and I travelled for the Commonwealth Games in 1978.

One night on that trip, we were having a meal with Tony Simmons, Nick Rose, Tony Staynings, and Steve Jones when Don said to me, "Let's tell the guys to run the bill." After the bill was paid, Don said, "Let's run the bill." The guys took off like a shot out of a gun. Hitting the street, some ran left, some ran right. Don and I nearly pissed ourselves laughing.

One night while walking after the meet had finished, we heard this shouting, "McLatchies, over here!" Carol and I looked around and couldn't see anyone. Once again, "McLatchies, over here!" Finally, we located the voices of Jim O'Brien and Pat Butcher sitting outside a pub. Jim wrote several articles for various running magazines and is now the Director of Communications for New York Athletic Club. Pat wrote for the London Times and wrote several books, notably Quicksilver about Emil Zatopek and The Perfect Distance about Seb Coe and Steve Ovett.

We moseyed on over to where they were and had a beer or two with them and reminisced about past and present running. It was great night, getting to talk to writers who had seen a lot in the field of track and pick their brains.

Highlights of the meet:

1500 — El Guerrouj (MAR) beat Bernard Lagat (KEN) in a mad dash to the tape in 3:30.68 to 3:31.10. El Guerrouj defended his title form 1999.

10,000 meters — Kamathi (KEN) 27:53.25, Mezgebu (ETH) 27:53.97,

Gebrselassie (ETH) 27:54.41 which was a real dust up the last 800 meters.
 Men 4x100 South Africa were first as the USA was disqualified.
 800 Mutola (MOZ) 1:57.17
 1500 Szabo (ROU) 4:00.57 — she won the 5000 in the 1991 championships
 10,000 — What a battle to the tape with 3 Ethiopians. Tulu 31:48.81, Adere 31:48.85 Wami 31:49.98.
 4x100 Germany won the title as the USA was once again disqualified.

Carol and I were in Oregon during the month of July at a track meet in Eugene. After the meet, we travelled to the coast, then over to Crater Lake and up to Bend, where we were spending the night before driving to Portland to catch a plane to Houston.

While in Bend, we were in the downtown Starbucks when I heard this Scottish accent. Looking around, I zeroed in on a lady talking to a man. When the man departed, I walked over to her and said, "What the hell are ye daen in Bend?" She replied, "I could ask you the same question."

Her name was Glenda and she sold real estate. When she graduated from Edinburgh University, she moved to Hawaii, where she met her husband, who was a builder. When Bend started booming, they moved to Bend.

She wanted to know if we were looking for a house. Carol jumped in and said, "He will be retiring shortly, and sure, we could look." Anyway, the lady and Carol exchanged information.

During the month of November, Carol told me she was going to Bend to check some properties. I didn't say much, as I thought since all of Carol's good friends lived on the east coast and my brother lived in New Brunswick, Canada, we would be heading east. How wrong I was.

Carol flew to Bend and checked out the properties that Glenda suggested. She found one she liked, knowing what I was prepared to pay. Then I heard what the asking price was, which was twice the price of our house in Houston. The seller and we settled on a price and I flew to Bend in December to meet with the house inspector and check out the house.

When I arrived in Bend, I was greeted with snow, which I hadn't seen since I lived in Chicago in 1975. The inspector and I met at the house, which looked okay inside, but on the outside, I couldn't see much for the snow.

I was a bit worried about the roof as it was covered in snow. The inspector said he had crawled in the attic and found no leaks. The house was smaller than the one we had in Houston. Since there were only two of us, and we had three bedrooms, there wouldn't be a problem.

Chapter 44
2002 — Heading to Bend

Having purchased a home in Bend, Oregon, I had to sell our house in Houston and decide when I was going to quit my job. We located a moving company to move our furniture and my MGB car to Bend. We kept a bed settee as I need someplace to sleep, and some eating utensils.

After the furniture was removed, I did some paint touch up and repainted the inside of the garage. When I completed these tasks, I put our house on the market to sell as-is. I had a lot of fly by night people trying to get me to lower the price. My retort was always the same: "Look somewhere else." After five days, I had a buyer, and after several weeks hassling with his bank, the deal was finally sealed.

I stayed with Sean Wade and his wife while the banks were sorting out the loans. I was very grateful for them putting up with me and taking care of my needs until I left for Bend.

My boss was gracious enough to let me work until the house sale was complete. My staff gave me a going away party, which was very emotional. After many years together, we shared many ups and downs, working long hours and weekends to take care of problems and install new systems.

I made sure that Robert Stigers replaced me when I left. I had many discussions with personnel, who told me he was not qualified as he did not have a college degree. After many arguments telling them that he was working on his degree and had over 15 years' experience working in the environment, they relented and promised me he would take over when I left.

I spent some time with my daughter, Heather, before I left. I had checked the weather and it was reported that there was going to be a lot of snow up in the Colorado area, so I decided to travel Interstate 10.

I loaded up my Subaru and headed west for a new life. I took off early in the morning and headed west. I had a cell phone and a road atlas to help me in my journey. No GPS systems back in those days. The first day, I drove to Horizon City, Texas, which is a straight drive on Interstate 10 and a very boring trip. After getting checked into a hotel, I had something to eat and then a hot bath and went to bed. Too tired to watch TV, I left early the next morning with the intent of driving as far as I could manage from Horizon City. When I arrived in Bishop, California, I was greeted with snow, which was going to be interesting since I hadn't driven a vehicle in 'white stuff' since 1975. I had a good night's sleep. In the morning, I filled the car with gas and was ready for the journey to Bend. I was okay until I saw a car heading downhill begin to slide, hit a snowbank, and land on its side. I thought, "What do I now?"

I had to make a decision whether to head towards Interstate 5 or continue on 365. I decided to brave the elements and head towards Mammoth Lakes and Reno. What an experience, driving white-knuckled. In the previous few years, I had experienced incidents that I managed to survive, so I thought, "Another life's experience." It took me four hours to drive to Reno. I never saw another car for three hours. I don't think I left a brown streak in my shorts, but on many occasions, I was scared shitless.

Finally, I made it to Reno. I did not stop as I was trying to get to Bend ASAP. My only stop was to fill up and use the bathroom somewhere just past it. I continued on Highway 365 until Lakeview in Oregon, and then turned onto Highway 31 to Highway 97 and headed north to Bend.

Outside of Bend, it started snowing and I was tired. Believe it or not, I was lost after travelling nearly 2,200 miles. I had bypassed the exit I was supposed to take. I stopped at Cooley Road and called Carol. I gave her my location and asked how to navigate to the new address.

She gave me the instructions and shortly after I finally made it to the house, frazzled out. I didn't even unpack the car. I wanted a beer, a kiss, and a good night's sleep, as tomorrow was another day.

Chapter 45
2002 — Early Days in Bend

I had worked nearly all my life and was used to getting out of bed around 6:30 a.m., working to 4:30 p.m., going to track practice on Monday and Wednesday, and returning home around 7 p.m. I missed the regime of going to work and facing another unexpected day. I had hired all the staff that worked for me. We were like a family, and saying goodbye to people I had known and worked with for nearly 20 years was going to leave a big void in my life.

The first few weeks, I was like a lost soul wandering around trying to figure out the neighborhood. Most days, I would put on a pair of running shoes and go for a run. I managed to get lost a few times, but I always returned home after a six-mile run that ended up being around ten miles instead. I guess I wasn't in the early stages of dementia yet.

Some days running along the Deschutes River, I would stop, take off my shoes, and wade out into the river until I found a rock where I could sit. I am sure many people that saw me sitting on a rock in the river thought that I was getting ready to commit suicide. Nah, just resting and trying to figure out what I was going to do in Bend.

After getting situated, I got more familiar with Bend. Since I had been involved in running all my life, I thought I had a lot to offer in respect to coaching.

One evening, Carol and I attended a local running club meeting when an elderly lady approached me and said, "You are going to coach me." I replied, "I have no idea who you are, and how do you know I coached people?" She replied, "My name is Suzy MacLeod, and a friend in Houston told me that you were moving to Bend." I went on to coach Suzy for several years and we became great friends. She later broke the world age group record for 400 meters.

One morning, Carol and I decided to attend "The Chain Breaker," which is a bike race held on some trails in Bend. After parking our car and heading towards the race, we heard this shrill voice, which I recognized as coming from Priscilla Welch. I thought, "This is strange as the they live in Colorado." Sure enough, around the corner, there stood

Priscilla waving a flag and directing cyclists.

When we saw each other, we both said at the same time, "What the hell are you doing here?" We found out that they had moved to Bend one month before us. We had known each other since the eighties, when Carol and Priscilla used to race one another.

Priscilla twice broke the British record for the marathon. She finished sixth at the 1984 Olympic marathon in 2:28:54 and second at the 1987 London Marathon in 2:26:51. The latter time stood as the W40 World Masters record for over 20 years. She also won the 1987 New York City Marathon.

During the 'Eighties' Priscilla was stationed in the Shetland Islands, which is a very remote part of Scotland that sticks out on the North Atlantic and has observation posts for monitoring Russian activity and others.

She would always good naturedly give me hell about me being Scottish and telling me how she had to suffer the terrible weather while stationed up in the sticks. I used to tell her, "Buy a coat."

Priscilla had a most unlikely career in international athletics, having been a smoker of a pack a day until she began running competitively at age 35. An officer in the British Army, she met her husband, Dave Welch, while serving in Norway. She quit smoking, and under his tutelage, ran in the 1981 London Marathon at age 36, running 2:59:00.

Priscilla, Carol, and I still meet for a chat and reminisce about the old days. Priscilla volunteers at St. Charles Hospital, where she helps people find the right location and helps out where she can.

One weekend, Carol and I drove to Portland, where I had entered a master's 800-meter race. What a disaster. I ran 2:59, and said to Carol, "That's it, no more racing." I never raced again, as I felt I'd had enough. I was 61 years old and I had been racing since I was 13.

I had great career and travelled to several countries to compete. I received a scholarship to the States, which was a blessing in disguise as it got me out of the Scottish weather, with an opportunity to get an education and live a better life.

Chapter 46
2003

In 2003, I sent a letter to the Athletic Director at Summit High School telling him that I would like to help with their running program. I was later informed that there a female coach working with the distance kids who stated that as long as she was there, "Jim McLatchie will never coach at Summit." I never even received an interview. One down.

I thought, "Jeez, who have I pissed off?" I found out later that I was coaching one of the local runners who used to be her boyfriend. Oh boy.

I was informed later that Bend High School needed a cross country coach. I sent in my application with my resume. I had an interview and was rejected. I asked why, and was informed that they had hired a math teacher. I replied that was funny as there was no mention during the interview process about me teaching. I had taught at college level but never was asked the question. Two down.

A couple of weeks later, I was informed that Mountain View High School was looking for a coach. I sent in my application. I had an interview with a panel that included the Athletic Director, a parent, a coach, and an athlete. At the end of the interview, I was informed they were hiring someone younger. I informed them that they had crossed the age discrimination line. The Athletic Director said he didn't mean to say what he did. I was not one for not holding a grudge and said, "Okay, I will coach the young coach." He said he didn't understand. I left thinking, "This is ridiculous. I am 61 years old and I am too old." Three down.

Later that day, I went for a run at Pilot Butte Middle School and while there, I was asked by the Athletic Director to help him install the safety net for the discus circle. While I helped him with the net, he asked me if I would like to help coach his kids. I said, "Sure. Can my wife, Carol, come along also and help the kids?" He said, "Sure." Carol and I coached hurdles for him for five years.

During that time, I noticed that Pilot Butte did not have a fence surrounding the track to keep people out that did not belong on the premises. I contacted management and told them I was writing a letter to the local The Bulletin newspaper about the situation about people destroying the facilities. They were using the premises for a dog park and setting off fireworks during July 4th.

The Bulletin contacted me and asked if I wanted them to print the letter I had written. I replied, "Sure, as something needs to be done about this situation." Within a month of publishing the letter, a fence was installed around the perimeter of the track. I guess I upset a few people who no longer could walk their dogs or set fireworks on the track. What a shame!

I needed something to keep me occupied other than coaching hurdles at Pilot Butte, so I decided to re-upholster my 1973 MGB. I contacted my younger daughter, Amy, whom I'd promised the car to several years earlier. I told her about my project and asked what color she would like the car to be painted before I started the task. She wanted maroon.

The car was repainted from a blue color to maroon. I ordered all the parts I needed to complete the project. I had never done any re-upholstering in my life but was looking forward to replacing the seats, carpets, and interior. This kept me busy for a few weeks.

Restored 1973 MGB

Another project was to build a couple of garden plots so that I could grow vegetables. The soil that was there at present wouldn't grow anything. I had to have soil and mulch delivered and installed in the vegetable beds. It took several years of mulching before I could grow anything worthwhile.

I was also asked to write the certification program for Level 3 and 4 coaches associated with British Athletics. I spent a week in Birmingham, England, obtaining as much information as possible to compete the task. I was surprised there was a lack of information. Seemingly, in the past, the people involved in coaching the steeplechase kept the information to themselves. I thought, "If we do not share information, how will future coaches learn?"

When I felt I had enough information, I set forth on the task of producing the information required for coaches to be certified in the field of steeplechase. The tests were a success and helped coaches climb the ladder to another level.

Chapter 47
2004

In 2004, I was chosen as the USA women's coach for the IAAF World Half-Marathon Championships to be held in New Delhi, India. At the same time, I was asked to travel to Stirling, Scotland, as a candidate for the position of High-Performance Manager.

I decided I would go to New Delhi with the USA team. When we arrived at the airport, we were met by the Indian delegation. After flying 16 hours from the States, we were kept waiting at the airport to be picked up and bussed to our hotel. After about an hour, I was losing my patience as we were all tired and needed a bath and a good night's sleep. All I received from my protests was, "Be patient." There is no such thing as being punctual in India, as there is always tomorrow. What an experience. I think I aged a few years.

New Delhi is big, dusty, and poor. I had never seen an elephant walk down the street before, or cows lying all over the place. Of course, in India, a cow is a sacred animal. I never saw so many people begging, and with a part of an arm or foot missing. I guess that people would have more sympathy for deformed beggars.

While I was there with the USA team, I was contacted by a lady who was one of the leading doctors in stem cell research and had visited the States for seminars on the subject. She said she would like me to meet her daughter and talk to her about running training. I said, "Sure." Carol and I were invited to her house to meet her daughter. She said she would pick us up at the hotel and drive us to her home.

This was an eye-opener. As we approached the house, there was a 12-foot fence surrounding it with an armed guard stationed outside the entrance.

Inside the grounds, there was a tennis court, an area where she bred dogs, and about two acres of gardens. The house was immaculate, about 5,000 square feet of space. I asked if this was normal for people of her status. She replied that she was just middle class.

Her daughter and I walked around the property, with her showing me her running trail that was about a half-mile in distance. During the walk, I figured out she that she did not want to train too hard to reach the next level. Her main sport was tennis. "It's easier than running," she said.

Her mother informed me that the tennis coach would be attending dinner and he and I should have something in common as he also was from Scotland. During our introduction, I asked how he ended up with this gig. He informed me that when he lived in Glasgow, Scotland, he had married a lady from India and later moved to India.

On his arrival, he figured out with all the new money finding its way to families who all of a sudden were wealthy, it was a status symbol to attend the best schools, hire coaches for their children, and claim they were middle-class. Tennis seemed to be at the top of the heap.

He decided that he needed to teach tennis, and to accomplish that, he had to have a coaching certificate, so he attended certification seminars in Florida. Then he returned to New Delhi and coached tennis. His name was Andy Murray.

The evening prior to the half-marathon, I had the 'Delhi belly' and was sick with diarrhea. I was very careful as I only drank bottled water and used the same to clean my teeth. Seemingly I consumed something that caused the sickness. I think what caused the problem was steamed vegetables. Being sick, I missed the reception and meeting the Premier of India. I was given a handful of pills and sent to bed, puking.

Earlier that day, women were painting the road barriers alongside the route white. The blue line marking the route was hand painted. The method was mind-boggling, involving two pieces of string about 50 feet long and two sticks about ten inches long. One woman tied the string to the sticks, which had a gap around nine inches wide. This was used to mark the course. Two people carried the marker, which was then placed on the road, and a third person painted a blue line between the strings. I guess it was a way to use your surplus people.

The course was a ten-kilometer loop which started and finished on the track. I noticed that when the runners left the track to race on the road, they were having to navigate some electric junction blocks sticking about three inches above the ground, which I thought was dangerous. I approached the race management about my concerns, and within ten minutes, I was told to leave the stadium. I guess they are not used to complaints.

As the race was nearing the end, with the finish inside the stadium, Carol and I were standing outside the venue. Along comes Hugh Jones, who had certified the course. He was shouting, "Somebody has moved the cones directing the runners to the finish." Carol and I helped Hugh put the cones in the correct position before the runners appeared. Phew!

Back in Bend, I started coaching a few local runners, whom I would meet a couple of times a week. We did track workouts at Pilot Butte Middle School and hill workouts on Mount Washington on a path next to the road. Max King, Jeannette Groesz, and Suzi MacLeod were a few of the runners I coached who went on to perform on the national scene. Max competed for the USA cross country team twice in the World Championships and Jeannie won several USA titles. Both are still competing today.

Chapter 48
2005

The 2005 IAAF World Championships were held in Helsinki, Finland, where Carol and I had travelled to the first championships. Helsinki is a beautiful city, easy to navigate, and everyone speaks English. We would explore the city by putting on running shoes and hitting the trails. We visited some of the places we had seen in 1983 and were amazed at the changes that had occurred since then.

A couple of times, we were invited to the meet headquarters by Zara Peters, whom I coached earlier and was now was working for UK Athletics. All the dignitaries, along with some coaches, would congregate to talk about past events or gossip. We met several coaches whom we knew and others who were trying to figure out what we were doing there.

We bumped into Robert Weir from England, who was playing dominoes with some Jamaican coaches. Jamaicans love to play dominoes. I don't know if Robert won any games.

The meet was a great success, even when we were caught in a violent rainstorm. Spectators who had no overhead coverage were trying to crowd into the areas that had coverage. People who were under cover moved closer together to allow others some shelter. The meet carried on regardless of the weather, which is usual in Europe.

We were not allowed into the stadium with caps on water bottles. The security staff made us take the caps off and dispose them in a waste bin. Seemingly, at soccer matches, people threw caps at the referee or players. I have attended track meets all over the world and have never seen spectators throw anything at the runners. Maybe we are a bit more civilized than soccer spectators.

Highlights of the meet were Justin Gatlin won both 100 and 200 meters. Rashid Ramez (Bahrain won both 800- and 1500-meter races. Tirunesh Dibaba (Ethiopia) won both 5000- and 10000-meter races.

Chapter 49
2006

Health-wise, 2006 was a tough year for me as I was diagnosed with prostate cancer in March. I decided I would wait until I was 65 years old and covered by Medicare to have cryotherapy surgery to get rid of the cancer. Seemingly, as men get older, chances are they will get prostate cancer, which is one of the slowest growing cancers.

When I was diagnosed, my doctor stated that I would probably die from something else. Chances are that it would be heart-related as my Dad and his brothers all died with heart problems. Genetically, it was likely that I was going to have heart issues, which later proved true. The operation was successful, and after a few weeks, I was able to get back into jogging and walking.

The doctors I saw would ask about my family history. The response was always the same. I told them my mother and brother died from cancer, my dad's side of the family died from heart ailments. The response from the doctor was, "Did the medical staff perform post mortems to determine cause of death?" I would reply, "No. In Scotland most people died from cancer, heart problems or were killed in the coal mine. Unless it was a murder, there was no need for an autopsy."

In the fifties and sixties, the death rate from cancer in Scotland was 400 per 1,000. While the total number of cancer deaths have reached the highest for 25 years, the overall mortality rates from the disease have fallen by 10% in the last decade, going from 358 deaths per 100,000 people in 2007 to 321 deaths per 100,000 in 2017.

I spent a lot of time gardening and trying to figure out the short growing season. It was not unusual to have frost or snow in the month of May. I had a small greenhouse built so that I could start seeds in a warmer environment before transplanting them outside to my garden.

I decided to visit Australia and attend the Commonwealth Games in Melbourne.

While at the games, I met John Landy and spent a few minutes talking with him. John raced Roger Bannister in the epic mile in the 1954 Commonwealth Games. I visited the gravel track where he trained. It was worse than some of the tracks that I raced on in the fifties and sixties.

John told the story of when he was running with Percy Cerutty's group. He said Percy had them run like horses and carry a bamboo stick. John taught at Melbourne University and one morning, one of his students approached him and asked, "Sir, did I see you running through the trees carrying a stick and chanting?" John said he had to tell a lie. "No, that wasn't me."

When John was a 4:43-miler, he was talked into training with Cerutty. After four months of coaching, he ran 4:17. John was always uncomfortable working with Cerutty, and later broke with him and trained alone with his own system.

John Landy

Runners running up a dune.

After the games, I decided to visit a friend in Wangaratta, which is north of Melbourne. I travelled there by train, which was a nice relaxing journey.

My friend's neighbor was a horse jockey and raced at the local track. I attended the races one day while he was riding but didn't make any money. I just donated it to the horse racing establishment.

I played golf one day with my host and his wife. There were quite a few birds on the course feeding on the grass. At one tee, my host's wife drove her ball up the fairway and got a birdie, but it was the wrong kind. Her ball struck a bird stone dead.

Priscilla Welch's husband Dave, a great friend of mine, who died whilst having breakfast outside Geneva with a group of friends from Bend, Oregon. Each year this group would ride some of the Tour de France. Dave was conversing with the others on his cycle tour about having a very easy ride that day, so that he would be healthy for the flight home the next day. While eating with the group at breakfast, Dave succumbed to a heart attack.

The people that he was travelling with called his wife Priscilla and told her of his demise. She called Carol and me and told us what happened, and said I was responsible for getting the body back to Bend.

What a chore that was. She contacted Mark, Dave's son, who was in the British army and stationed in Belfast and told him what had happened. Mark said he would fly to Geneva to claim the body. I tried to explain the situation to the airline. I asked if it would be possible for Mark to travel to Bend on his dad's ticket and ship the body freight.

The first thing the agent asked was, "What flight was he was on and do you have the ticket number?" Oh boy. I was dealing with a dumb shit! After fuming at the mouth for a few moments, I told her she could look up the passenger list and should be able to get all the information. That didn't work. Once again, I told her Dave was dead and I did not have a copy of his ticket and I wished to speak to her supervisor, as I was not getting through to her of the situation at hand.

The supervisor came on the phone, and once again I explained the situation. The lady responded that there would be no problem and that Mark should contact the airline when he arrived in Geneva and all would be sorted out.

I talked to Priscilla and told her that Mark could fly home with the body to Portland and then take the puddle-jumper to Bend. It didn't work out as the coffin was too big for the second plane, so the body was transported from Portland to Bend via a hearse.

Priscilla decided to have Dave cremated. While at the funeral home, Mark told the funeral director that he wanted to see the body being cremated. He was told that was an unusual request, but he would grant it. We were told to meet the body in a building which looked like a big warehouse, where the oven was situated for the cremations.

Walking into the building with Mark, we noticed a stack of cardboard coffins leaning against the wall. At the same time, we said, "Um, nice business."

The body arrived on a gurney and was pushed in front of the oven door. Mark said, "You and I are pushing the body into the oven for finality." I thought, "Another chapter in my life."

We had to pick up the coffin a couple inches off the gurney to get it inside the oven. When we set it down, my fingers were stuck under the coffin. Mark kept saying, "Push!" I replied, "I cannot, your dad is having the last laugh as my fingers are wedged between the coffin and the gurney and I cannot push." Mark lifted up the coffin and freed my fingers and we proceeded to push the coffin into the oven. "Bye, Dave you old bugger!"

Chapter 50
2007-2009

During the next couple of years, nothing much exciting happened. Carol and I were still coaching hurdles at Pilot Butte. No kids wanted to train for distance events. The most popular event was the pole vault. Depending on how many poles were available, there was usually one kid for each pole. They would stand on the runway area holding a pole until they had to vault, complete the task, and then return to the end of the line and wait for their next turn. Lazy buggers.

We would get about four or five kids showing up for hurdles. We emphasized a lot on technique and starting out of the blocks. After a few weeks, we managed to develop a couple of good hurdlers.

Of the runners I was training personally, Max King secured his place on the USA cross country team for the second time.

I "wogged" (walk-jogged) most days, usually on the trails, where I fell a couple of times. I guess I wasn't picking up my feet. I did track workouts with Jeannie Groesz to encourage her.

I was asked if I would like to be the 2008 Olympic Trials Coordinator for special events, which included 400 meters for high school boys and girls, 3,000 meters masters, 100 meters for Special Olympians, and 100 meters for athletes with prosthetic legs. What a challenge. I had never done anything like this in my life before.

My task was corralling the athletes in the warm-up area, checking in with the clerk of the course, making sure they received a number, and escorting them to the holding area and then to the start line.

The first event was the masters, which went without a hitch as all of the athletes were used to the procedure. I thought, "This is a good start," indicating that things would go great. How wrong I was.

The second event was the 100 meters for the Special Olympians. On the way to the start line, I noticed there was a giant TV screen past the finish line which a runner could glance up at as they approached the finish to check their competition. I thought, "Oh my, a disaster waiting to happen," knowing full well that if these athletes look up at the screen, they will be running all over the place rather in their lanes towards the finish.

At the start line, I never mentioned the TV. I told the athletes, "Stay in your lane through the finish line." I turned it over to starters and headed to the finish line. The gun went off and all athletes managed to stay in their lanes to the finish. After the race, one athlete asked if he could do it again as it had been so much fun.

Two down, three to go. The next event was the 100 meters for athletes with prosthetic limbs. I went through the same procedure getting them to the start line. At the start, one athlete approached me and told me he would need extra time as he had to take off one of his artificial limbs and replace it with another which contained running spikes. He said when the starter gives the "On your marks" command, he needed some time to pump air into his artificial leg. I went to the starter and explained the situation and then headed to the finish line. Whew! I had never seen an athlete take off a limb, put on another, and then have to insert air which only lasted 30 seconds before it expired.

The last event was the girls and boys 400 meters, which I thought would be a piece of cake. How wrong I was. I would corral eight runners from the warm-up area and head to the check-in tent, where you had to check-in as a group. At the check-in, I only had six runners. I asked where the other two had disappeared to. I was informed the bathroom. When the other two arrived, we checked in. Then I was leading the runners to the holding area, and once again I was missing runners, again to the bathroom. Finally, I had eight runners head into the holding area, where I turned them over to the clerk of the course. Then I headed to the finish line to watch the race.

I went through the same procedure with boys. After they completed their race, I escorted them back to the warm-up area to cool down. I was frazzled. I thought this would be an easy task. Time for a beer and to move on.

Carol and I travelled to Berlin for the 2009 IAAF World Championships. The last time I was in Berlin was 1961 which was a stop-over on my way to compete in Leipzig. I remember the Berlin wall which was built to separate the people living in the eastern portion of Berlin from the western section.

Part of the original wall is still standing and is used today by artists from all over the world to paint murals or express themselves.

We travelled on the river Spree and were amazed to see so many bullet holes on the western side of the river. The soldiers on the eastern side were shooting at people who were trying to swim across the river and escape to the west.

One evening, on the train heading to the World Championship track meet, we were sitting a couple of seats away from the BBC television commentators, which included Steve Cram. They were discussing a female 800-meter runner who was going to raise some eyebrows.

Entering the stadium, we bumped into Peter Thompson, who was working for the IAAF in Monte Carlo. He mentioned that Caster Semenya, the South African runner, would probably raise some questions about her validity as a female. We thought she must be the same runner the BBC commentators were discussing.

Sitting in the stadium, the women's 800-meter field was announced, and as they headed towards the start line, you could hear the crown murmuring. Semenya was walking and flexing her arm muscles. I thought, "What a show person." She went on to win the title by over two seconds with a winning time of 1:55.45.

Later, Carol was having a tough time walking as she had severe pains in the small of her back. I was not so sure whether to call for medical help and find out what was going on. She told me wait a bit and see what happens. After a few minutes, the pain subsided, and she was okay. When we returned home, she went to the doctors and was diagnosed as having gallstones, which were surgically removed. Below is a picture of her with them.

Carol holding her gallstones.

Chapter 51
2010 — Summit High School

One day in 2010, I received a phone call informing me that Summit High School had an opening for a distance coach and telling me that I should call them up. I was flabbergasted, as eight years earlier, they would not entertain the thought of hiring me. I met with Dave Turnbull and Lisa Zimmerman, who hired me on the spot. I could hardly believe it. I had finally landed a job coaching.

The first week was an eye-opener when a girl told me that I needed to talk to her old coach about the training I prescribed. I told her that would never happen, and that if she had a problem with my training, and we couldn't come to a consensus that she liked my approach, then she needed to leave.

I had a fair idea what type of training to prescribe. I had coached several athletes in Texas who won state championships at sea-level, but now I was confronted with running at 3600 feet. Another challenge!

The first year, I had 18 athletes to coach. It took me a while to find out who could handle my workouts. Since I didn't coach them in the fall, I was not so sure how much work they had done before spring. After a few days, it was obvious which ones had done some running and were in reasonable shape and the others that had done little or nothing.

I started to map out a program to get some of them to qualify for the state championships. I was fortunate to have three athletes who were able to compete. One girl won the 3,000-meter race and was named state champion, which was a good start to the program.

Separately, I was still doing my private coaching, and one client in Austin, Texas, called and asked if I knew a lady called Maton whom I used to coach in Houston. I told her, "I never knew a Maton." She said, "Her name used to be Michelle Dekkers," which rang a bell. I replied, "Yes, I did coach her, along with her father, mother and brother." She informed me that Michelle wanted to talk to me about her daughter, Ashley.

One thing led to another, and she found out I would be around for a wee while. Michelle told me she would be heading to Bend in the next few weeks. When she was due to visit, I was already planning to be in Eugene for the state track championships. Michelle showed up at the stadium and watched Megan Fristoe win the 3,000 meters by five seconds.

After a short visit, she said she was heading to Bend to check it out and would get back to me. In July, Carol and I were on holiday with some friends in Yosemite National Park when I received a call from Michelle that she and her family were on their way to Bend— permanently. What a surprise as I had not heard from her in several weeks.

I was looking forward to meeting her family as I knew Michelle's family well and we all got on together. I thought if Ashley is as good as her mother it was going to be scary good. As time went on, things began to change.

Carol and I were selected to officiate at the Masters World Track & Field Championships in Sacramento, California. What an experience. Some days, the temperature recorded 114 degrees on the track, which was hot enough to fry an egg.

I had never seen a "sighted" (near-blind) person run a steeplechase before. Watching her race as she approached a barrier, she would slow down and climb over the barrier. We were also informed that if an athlete was bleeding, we had to escort them off the track. Well this lady's nose started bleeding, and we had to tell her what the rule was in respect to blood. So, each time she climbed over the water jump she would wipe the blood from her nose and continue to the end of the race. amazing!!

Suzi MacLeod, whom I had been coaching since 2002, was very fit and at the start of the season, with the intent to win the 75 to 79 age group in the 400 meters and break the world record, which was 87.17 seconds.

Eight weeks before her race, I zeroed in on her running 21.5 seconds for each 100 meters and planned her training accordingly. The first week, she would start off running:

12x50 meters in 10.8 with 1minute rest
6x100 - 21.5 with 2 minutes rest
4x150 — 32.2 with 4MR
3x200 — 43 with 6MR
3x250 — 54 with 8MR
1x300 — 65 with 10MR
1x350 — 75

Prior to the race, Suzi approached us on the back straight of the track, where Carol and I were officiating, and complained about a wasp biting her on the 'arse'. She proceeded to show us her butt, but we couldn't see any bites other than aged skin. We believe that she was so nervous about the race that she had to think of something to get her mind in the right frame of mind. It must have worked because she set a new world record of 85.40 seconds.

Chapter 52
2011 — Summit High School

In 2011, I had a good bunch of kids and started planning an assault on Jesuit High School in the girl's relays. I normally studied other team's athletes who are running the same distances as they relay. Then I juggle the team around to put athletes where they will perform better.

Ashley Maton had finished fourth in the invitational 1,500 meters, so I decided to run her last on the 4x800-meter relay so she could get extra rest. I put our second-slowest girl on the first leg with instructions to stay up with the leaders. She came in third, running five seconds faster than she had ever done before. I knew then that we would probably win. Ashley anchored the team to an eight-second victory over Jesuit.

The girls also managed to win the distance medley relay. I put our fastest 1500-meter runner on the lead-off leg, giving us a sizeable lead, which we held to the finish, beating Jesuit by three seconds. This was a great achievement for Summit against bigger schools.

To compete in the Track State Championships (State), an athlete has to place in the top two at District Championships (Districts), with a third place given to the next two top times statewide in that event. Summit went 1, 2, 3 at Districts and achieved the same at State, with only 1.5 seconds separating the top three for Summit. This was the first time any coach had ever coached the top three in a distance event at State.

I made a mistake by entering Ashley in the 800 meters in the Districts as she had to run both 800 meters and 1,500 meters at State. She finished second in the 800 meters, getting beat by 0.11. Two distance races on the same day with a short rest is a no-no! Megan won the 3,000 meters for the second consecutive year by 24 seconds.

The Summit team concluded with a good track season, especially the girls, who won several major events. I still had some work to accomplish with the boy's team.

Chapter 53
2012 — Summit High School

At the start of the 2012 season I had to hope that the athletes who competed well in the fall did some sort of running during the winter months so that when they showed up for track in the spring, they were fit. That season, I increased the volume of work for those I had coached the previous year, with the intent that they would compete better and be able to race faster.

I always made a point to enter the best available teams in the Oregon Relays and Jesuit Relays. The competition at these meets are the best in Oregon, with teams competing from California, Idaho, Oregon, and Washington.

Summit had a group of sprinters that year and I talked to Dave Turnbull about entering a Sprint Medley Team (200, 200, 400, 800) in the Oregon Relays as I had decent 800-meter runner in Sam Naffziger, who with a dive at the tape, won the race for Summit by a scant .02 in a time of 3:38.64 to the second place time of 3:38.68.

Ashley Maton won the invitational 800 meters in 2:16.57, and her brother, Matthew, won the freshman 3,000 meters in 9.09. The boys finished second in the distance medley relay — (1200/400/800/1600 legs) in 10:31.5, getting beat by two seconds.

At the Jesuit Relays, I entered a girl's 4x800 meters, and once again, we scraped out a victory of 9:18.81 to 9:18.83. How lucky can you get? We were fortunate to have good anchor runners who would not give up until they raced past the tape.

At Districts, I got into a conflict with an athlete as I did not enter him in the 3,000 meters due to injury. He told me he was faster than the athletes that I had chosen. I informed him that he was recovering from an injury and I was not going to risk more damage.

One thing led to another and his dad requested a meeting with the head coach and assistant principals of Summit. This meeting was held and he started ranting and raving about my method of coaching. He was so hot at one time he threw a book at me, saying, "This is how my son should be coached." The book was by Arthur Lydiard. I informed him, "I coach high school kids, not world-class adults, and if you ever throw a book at me again, I will knock you on your ass." The meeting was adjourned and he was told to go home and cool down and we could discuss his problem at a later date.

At State, Ashley Maton won her second consecutive 1,500-meter title in 4:37.57, with our other two girls finishing fourth and fifth. Ashley tried to come back and race the 800 meters, where she finished fourth. Two races back-to-back don't work. Eric Alldritt won the 3,000 meters in 8:44.38 by .5 seconds. He came back the next day to finish second in the 1,500 meters with a time of 4:02.60, losing out by one second.

After the 3,000 meters, I could not get Eric to cool down. He told me it wasn't every day that he won a state championship and being interviewed by ESPN was more important than cooling down.

I was officiating at a track meet in Hayward Field and one of my assignments was to be stationed at the first exchange zone for the women's 4x100-meter relay. Lo and behold, Oregon ran past the exchange zone and up goes my yellow flag. Next thing I knew, masses of people were shouting at me, "Do you know what you have done?" "Nothing," I said, and moved on.

At the Prefontaine Track Meet, I was once again officiating in the same area where the relay incident happened earlier. Dan O'Brien, who won the Gold medal for the decathlon in the 1996 Olympics, approached me. He said, "McLatchie, I will give you $100 if you keep your flag down." Dan said it was terrible how the fans were berating me for doing my job. I replied, "I follow the rules. If there's a rule violation in my area, up goes the yellow flag!"

Later, I was selected to officiate the 2012 Olympic Trials at Hayward Field. A couple of incidents stand out. In the first, during the final of the women's 1,500 meters, a TV camera man was at the start line filming. After 800 meters of the race, the camera team was heading towards the finish line to capture the finish. I was officiating on the curve of the track, which was 50-60 meters past the finish line, when I noticed that about 20 feet of cable that the camera man was dragging behind him was on the track. Looking up, I saw that the runners were approaching the bell lap with 400 meters to the finish. I had to sprint, bend over to pick up the cable, and throw it clear of the track, which avoided a disaster. Afterward, I heard a voice from the crowd shouting, "McLatchie, I didn't think you could move that fast!"

Later on, during the meet as I was heading to my position on the track near the finish line, I heard someone shout, "McLatchie, don't mess up!" Looking up to the stands, I noticed a gentleman standing up and pointing at me. It was Rick Breidenbach, whom I used to coach in Houston. I replied, "Fuck off!" Later, Rick told me that the people sitting next to him asked, "Was he swearing at you?" He replied, "Yup, he always swears."

In the second incident, I was stationed on the inside of the track near the take-off board for the long jump. People who probably never had attended a track meet were shouting at me to move because they could not see the board.

I never swore, I sat down on a stool in the middle of some potted plants that had been placed near the jump area for display. I wasn't a wallflower, but a long jump flower.

I was later approached by the school principal to be the head cross country coach. I told her, "I cannot take that job as you would probably fire me in the first couple of weeks." She asked why and I said, "As soon as one parent starts asking why their kid is not on the team or whatever, I would tell them to fuck off and leave me alone."

I suggested she instead hire Carol, who is a really a good organizer and can handle parents, and I would work for her and do the coaching. The principal was in agreement with that suggestion and told me to tell Carol to apply for the job, which she did.

 Carol told the principal that we would be in Canada with the grandkids on holiday. The principal said she would interview her on the phone. While we were in Victoria, Canada, the principal called and conducted the interview and Carol was offered the job.

The training regime was revamped at Summit. We started out in July meeting with the runners and had them running three days a week, which was mostly running on the grass and trail. On Mondays, we started out with a warm-up run, followed by core, then a relay or a light workout. Wednesdays were 45-60 minutes easy runs on the trail followed by core exercises. Friday was the same as Monday.

The first thing I did during the second week of August was to have all the kids run a 4K time trial at Drake Park on the grass. I would examine the results and then break the kids into groups depending on how they performed in the time trial. We broke the kids into three groups: Black, which contained the athletes who could make varsity or JV; Silver, those who could step up to the Black group if their race times improved; and Green, the kids who were out of shape or just wanted to belong.

When the official season started, I introduced the group to hill workouts which several had never done before. There are a lot of dirt trails in the Summit area, with a few hills not too far from the school. I measured out several courses. One was approximately 1,200 meters. I could stand up on one of the hills and watch all the runners. They were great courses which are no longer there. The area was sold to build houses. The area is now called Discovery Park. Progress, my butt!

At State Championships, Travis Neuman won in 15:29, with Matthew Maton second in 15:42. The boys won the team race by 28 points. The girls won the team race by a slim margin of eight points. Carol recorded her first State Championship.

Then, I had a health scare! On September 26, I told Carol that I would work on our fence and meet her and the Summit principal for dinner and she could handle the workout. While I was trying to remove a post embedded in concrete, I started sweating and not feeling good. I thought, "I wonder if I am having a heart-attack?"

I went upstairs and swallowed two aspirin and drank a glass of water, then I went back downstairs and sat on the bottom steps, still feeling woozy. By that time, Jesse Fortier showed up to help me rebuild the fence. I called out to him and said, "You need to call an ambulance, as I think I am having a heart-attack." He responded, "Don't give me any of your bullshit." I said, "No, this is for real."

He walked out towards the street, a very flustered man. My neighbor saw him and asked, "What is going on?" He replied, "Jim thinks he is having a heart attack." Jesse finally called 911 and explained the situation.

As I was late for the dinner, Carol called and asked, "Where are you?" I responded, "I am busy right now having a heart attack, and waiting for an ambulance." I thought I could swear, but she had me beat.

Deb, my neighbor who is in the medical field, came to where I was sitting. She was fiddling around trying to find my pulse and said, "I cannot find anything, but keep talking even though I don't understand you." She was sponging me down and kept telling me to hang on and keep talking as help was on the way.

An ambulance finally showed up, and the EMTs stuck an IV in my arm. Carol showed up as they were wheeling me up the driveway to the ambulance, and let out another stream of oaths. I just smiled. "That's my girl," as they carted me of to St. Charles Hospital.

On arrival, I heard one of the attendants say, "We need to wait ten minutes as there is not an operating theater available." I was still conscious and responded, "I don't think I have ten minutes to spare."

The next thing I knew, I was lying on a table in the operating theatre, and when I came to, I was lying in bed with tubes sticking in my body. I was informed I was lucky as I had a blockage of the left anterior descending (LAD) artery, the main artery down the front of the heart. When it's totally blocked or has a critical blockage, right at the beginning of the vessel, it is known as the Widow Maker. That's what I had survived. The heart specialist inserted a stent and I felt great. Thankfully, when it happened, I was probably in much better health than I had been for several years. After a few days in the hospital, I was discharged and ambled out to meet the kids for a workout. Therapy!

A couple of months after my heart attack, I was approached by Dave Turnbull, the head track and field coach who also taught sports management, asking if I would talk to some of his classes about surviving a heart attack.

He lined me up to talk to three classes. During the introduction, Dave warned the class that I have a tendency to swear. During one of the classes, a young boy asked, "When you were going to heaven, did you see any angels?" I replied, "No, I was going down into the black depths and when I saw this fire that started to burn me on the ass, I decided, I have to get to hell out of here." Here I am today! What an experience.

Chapter 54
2013

Carol was chosen as the women's distance coach for the 2013 IAAF World Championships in Moscow. As I knew she would be busy with the team and would have no time to watch the meet or do some sightseeing with me, I invited my brother, Ian to come meet me.

Ian was flying from Canada to Moscow and we decided we would meet at the hotel where we were staying. During our off time from spectating, he and I would tour the city and on occasion, we got lost. Moscow is a hard place to get information as all signs are in Russian and very few people speak English. I am sure none spoke with a Scottish dialect.

One night after the Championships had finished, we followed the masses to the subway station, and jumped on a train. We both knew that it was seven stops to Red Square. I kept looking at the stations, and after a while decided we were on the wrong train. We disembarked at a station, and went upstairs and outside. We had no idea where we were. We started walking and after a while found someone who spoke limited English, who directed us to a hotel where someone would be able to help us to get back to Red Square.

There, someone who could speak English told us we were 10 kilometers from where we wanted to be. The person summoned a taxi driver who said he could drive us to Red Square. When hearing the price, we thought, "He must think he is dealing with a couple of Scottish bumpkins." We decided to hoof it back to the subway station and catch a train back into the city.

At the train station, we met a lady who looked Mongolian. She spoke excellent English and said she would tell us when to get off the train. The big problem in Moscow is that all trains on the subway system stop running at 1:30 a.m. The train would proceed to the nearest station at that time and tell all passengers to get off. As it was nearing 1 a.m., we were sweating a bit. Not from the heat, but from being kicked off the train in a city where all the signs were in Russian and few people spoke English. Lesson learned — pay attention.

Red Square

My brother Ian with some Old Russian effigy.

The Moskva River that runs through Moscow.

Summit's track season did not go off without a hitch. One of our runners was injured quite a lot during the season. He had some leg problems and the doctor had him wear a walking boot. I learned later that he was seen running in Drake Park. I met with him and decided we needed to visit the orthopedic doctor whom we had seen earlier to determine whether he was fit enough to train.

After the examination, the doctor said, "No. He cannot run." I asked the doctor to put his leg in a plaster cast, knowing that he couldn't take it off to go for a run. He did, and the athlete was not a happy camper.

Later on, after he was recovered, that same athlete entered a University of Oregon track meet. The school principal asked me if it was permissible for a high school athlete still attending high school to compete in a college meet. She asked if this would be a problem as she didn't want any repercussions at a later date which might affect his college career. I told her that I did not know and would contact some people who should.

I contacted several friends who coach college athletes and they stated they would not let a high school athlete compete in a college event. My next move was to contact the Compliance Board at the University of Oregon. Several weeks later, I received a letter stating there was no problem. I informed the school principal and showed her the letter from the Board. We determined the issue was closed.

Not so. I was at the Oregon Relays with the Summit athletes when one of their "yes men" informed me that I needed to go talk to Robert Johnson, the head coach at the University of Oregon. I told him, "If he wants to talk to me, I will be over at the start of the 3,000 meters." Needless to say, he never showed up.

Several weeks later at State, I was told I was banned from being on the track for accusing U of O for violating the rules concerning high school athletes.

After Matthew Maton won the 5A state 3,000-meter race. I climbed over the fence at the start and walked up the track to present Matthew with his medal. No one kicked me off the track.

Summit runners were competing well and winning their fair share of races.

Hannah Gindlesperger won the Freshman 3,000 meters at the Oregon Relays by nine seconds in a time of 10:16.27.

At the State championships, Matthew Maton won the boys 1,500 meters in 3:55.12 and 3,000 meters in 8:28.62. Eric Alldritt finished third in the 1,500 meters in 3:59.66 and second in the 3,000 meters in 8:35.78.

Hannah went on to win the 3,000-meter title in 10:09.79 by nine seconds. Luke Hinz finished third in the 800 meters with a time of 1:56.76. It was a great meet as we recorded three state championships.

At State, Maton was so far ahead of the field that they forgot to take down a barrier, which misdirected him off course by at least 50 yards. He had to backtrack and climb under a rope to get back on the course and went on to win by nearly a minute in 14:59. The team finished first by a score of 38 to 64.

In the girl's race, Summit finished 1,2,4. Hannah won the race in 17:53, freshman Olivia Brooks ran second in 18:37, and Kaely Gordon ran fourth in 18:54. The team won the title by 47 points. It was a nice double and Carol's second State title.

At the NXN regionals in Boise, Hannah finished fourth and was chosen to represent the Northwest Region in the Nike Nationals, and that team won the regional team race.

The athletes had great season both on the track and over country. I could see that what I was prescribing was working—keeping the kids off concrete and doing most of their training on dirt and grass. Hill workouts and weight training were paying dividends.

Chapter 55
2014

The track season started off with a bang. At the 2014 Oregon Relays, Matthew Maton won the 1,500 meters in 3:55.85 and Sarah Reeves ran the 800-meter leg in the sprint medley to victory.

At the Jesuit Relays, Maton won the invitational 1,500 meters by over four seconds with a time of 3:49. Freshman Olivia Brooks won the open 3,000 meters in 10:30.11 with Piper McDonald third in 10:41.34. The girls finished fourth in the DMR.

At the State championships, Maton won the 1,500 meters in 3:53.08 by six seconds, his second consecutive title. He also won the 3,000 meters in 8:29.87 by ten seconds with 91-second last 600 meters. He followed the race plan to perfection, running behind the leaders until 600 meters from the finish and then hitting it. He just destroyed the field as no one could match his speed over the last 400 meters.

Sarah Reeves won the 800 meters in 2:13.60, which was Summit's third state title for the championships.

I was selected to officiate the 2014 IAAF World Junior Championships at Hayward Field. The coaches at the University did not want me on the track as they had banned me prior. They were informed by the USATF official's management that I would be officiating irrespective of what they thought about me.

It was a great experience working with young athletes from all over the world, helping them solve some of their questions and making it easier for them on the world stage.

The Summit cross-country teams were competing well and won both boys and girls cross country State Championships. Olivia Brooks won the first of three consecutive state titles with a time of 18:10. Hannah Tobiason finished third in 18:16 and the girls won the State title by 49 points, giving Carol her third state title and Summit its seventh straight title. Matthew Maton won his second state title running 14:45 sec, which broke Galan Rupp's course record. The boys placed 1, 2, 4, 6, and 7. The boys won the State title with a score of 19 points, 42 ahead of the next team.

I was surprised to see Alberto Salazar, who came to me for help before the 1984 Olympics, was coaching several athletes for NIKE. It was called the Oregon Project, and meant a graduate of U of O hanging around the finish line. When the winning teams were told to stand on the awards stand, Salazar had a microphone and you could hear him calling Galen Rupp on the phone telling him he was talking to Maton. "The crown here Rupp congratulating Maton on breaking his record." I thought, "This is a ploy for Salazar to brag about the University of Oregon."

After the race, Salazar approached me and said, "Matthew must go to Oregon and not anywhere else." I told him to back off and let him enjoy the win.

Since I was banned from being on their track, I thought it funny when Andy Powell, the distance coach for the University of Oregon, visited Maton about attending Oregon. I also attended the meeting where we discussed a scholarship. Later on, an offer in writing was made to Matthew to attend Oregon, which he signed.

Normally when the team does well at State, I ask if they want to go to Boise to race in the NXN Regional Championships. Maton said no and I asked him why. He informed me that his mother said it was in his best interest to compete in the Footlocker cross-country race instead. I approached his mother and asked her about the team concept, and she informed me she didn't care about the team.

I told the boys he wasn't running and to prove a point they should go out and qualify for Nationals, which they did in grand style. The boys finished second in the NXN Regionals in Boise, getting beat for first place by four points, which qualified them to compete in the Nike Nationals Cross Country Meet. The girls missed qualifying by eight seconds, finishing a creditable third.

At Nationals, the boys ran a great race, finishing 17th out of 22 teams without their number one runner. Once again, if a team is motivated and believe in themselves, then anything is possible.

Chapter 56
2015

The 2015 season started off well. At the Oregon Relays, we put together a good girls Distance Medley group, winning the race by eight seconds in 12:09.95. The next day, Summit won the Sprint Medley with Kaely Gordon running the 800-meter leg.

At the Jesuit Relays, Summit produced some good results with Tyler Jones winning the 1,500 meters in 4:04.27 and Alex Martin winning the 3,000 meters in 8:40.48. Both won by less than one second. The girls finished third in the DMR with 12:19.7; Jesuit won in 12:14.9.

At State, Olivia Brooks starting Summit's winning ways when she won the 3,000 meters in 9:53.59 with Hannah Tobiason finishing third in 10:12.91. Olivia came back the next day and won the 1,500 meters in a time of 4:37.70. Kaely won the 800 meters in a time of 2:18.35. On the boy's side, Alex Martin finished second in the 3,000 meters by the narrow margin of 8:37.95 to 8:37.37. Tyler had the same experience in the 1,500 meters with a mad rush to the tape where he finished fourth in 4:00.18, which was less than one second behind the winner.

Prior to Oregon Relays, Matthew Maton was removed from the Summit Track Team by the head coach for his refusal to follow school policy. This move caused a lot of friction within the team, but you cannot have one individual dictating his own policy. His mother, Michelle, went ballistic: Below is an excerpt from Michelle.

From Texas Running Post

Michelle Maton believes that the school coaches held a "grudge" against Matthew for his decision to run Foot Locker last fall, rather than the Nike meet. She attended a meeting with the coaches last week, who according to her, said Matthew was being kicked off the team because he was warming up on his own on an optional practice day during spring break and "because he does jumping-jacks in a manner that draws attention to himself." Michelle Maton added, "Anyone who knows Matthew knows that he can be funny, especially when it comes to things like jumping jacks."

I was not involved in the meeting she describes. I believe she threw me under the bus, blaming me for being involved in the decision to remove Matthew from the team. I was in Corvallis at a track meet when I was informed by the head coach that Matthew refused to warm up with the team which was not optional, but a necessity as part of team building. When he refused, he was told he was no longer part of the team. Matthew was told he could rejoin the team if he followed team policy and he refused.

There were some nasty comments about me being a bully, and that I should be fired and not allowed to coach kids. Of course, when you coach one of the best high school runners in the States and he's removed from the team, someone, according to the general public, should accept the blame. In this case, it was the athlete who was at fault, not the coach, but I was crucified.

NXR (NIKE cross-country regionals) is not a high school event and if an athlete doesn't want to run in this event, that is okay. The normal process is that the coach will ask the athletes if they want to compete in the regional race to be held in Boise, Idaho. A sign-up sheet is presented, explaining costs per athlete, and if they would like to attend, they can sign up and the coaches will look at the events and decide where they will compete, and enter a team or individuals. Normally the team that does well at state championships would like to compete in the regionals. No attempt is made to coerce the athlete to compete. Summit does not have athletes only compete in the championship races. Past results speak for themselves.

While coaching in high school you hear about helicopter parents, which evolved to "dive bomber" and now is referred to as "snow-plow" parents. I have talked to several coaches, many like me who volunteer their time and do not get paid to coach basketball, football, track, soccer and volleyball. They've chosen to give up coaching. The main reason they do so is that they do not want deal with parents. They cannot be bothered listening to parents rant and rave about how and where their child should participate. Who wants to deal with irate parents? Many parents believe they know more than the coach. It's an experience in human nature.

Later in the year, Carol and I took a trip to Scotland to visit the Outer Hebrides and the Isle of Skye in the northern part of Scotland. I had never visited either of these places while living in Scotland and decided I needed to pay a visit and get an idea what it is like to live in a remote part of the country.

We travelled with a tourist group of ten people, including us, from

Australia, Canada, Germany, and the USA. We integrated well and shared stories. Of course, if there was something questionable, I was blunt with my query. Luckily, I was rescued several times by the tour guide, who was also the bus driver.

The scenery was spectacular but desolate in many places. People lived right on the coast in small dwellings which were built with rocks and sod. I don't know how they survived the winters with winds howling in from the Atlantic. They must have been a tough bunch of people. Their longevity was very short as they spent most of their time trying to survive on food they grew or fished from the sea. They didn't spend their evenings watching TV

Scotland: The Outer Hebrides and the Isle of Skye

Returning from Scotland, Carol and I devised a plan to try to get the kids to perform well in cross country. We entered them in all the big races in the area. We wanted other schools to be aware that Summit was

a force to be reckoned with as we felt the team was going give a good account of themselves in all the big races.

Our first big race was in Portland, where Olivia Brooks finished third in the Danner Invitational. The boys finished third in the team race.

At the George Fox Invitational, our JV boys team won the team race by 29 points, with Camden Hammer winning from Cole Rene by less than one second. The varsity boys won the team race by 77 points. Alex Martin was the first finisher in fifth place. Olivia was first overall with a time of 17:45, leading the team to second place. The JV girls won the team race by three points, with our girls placing 2, 3, 4, 10, and 14.

At State, the girls won their eighth consecutive championship. Olivia won in a time of 17:46, Hannah Tobiason was second in 18:23, and Taylor Vandenborn was third in 18:25. The team scored 23 points, winning by 26 points. The boys won the team race by four points scoring 32. Alex Martin finished second.

Chapter 57
2016

The 2016 season at Oregon Relays started out with Olivia Brooks winning the 1,500 meters in 4:41.73 and the girl's relays finished second in the 4x800-meters and DMR with times of 9:28.08 and 12:09.21.

At the Jesuit Relays, Alex Martin won the 3,000-meter race in 8:31.26 by four seconds. The girls finished third in the DMR in a time of 12:29.97.

At the State track championships, I had three girls qualify in the 800 and 1,500 meters. Sarah Reeves won the 800 in 2:14.90, with the other two girls placing third and seventh. In the girls 1,500, Olivia won in 4:38.23 with Hannah Tobiason second in 4:39.24, and Taylor Vandenborn fourth in 4:39.67. What a battle to the finish line. Olivia also won the 3,000 in 10:10.17, ahead of Hannah, who ran 10:12.46.

On the boy's side, we had three qualifiers who finished eighth in the 800, fourth in the 1,500, and third in the 3,000.

Training went well for the track runners and I was looking forward to the cross-country season.

In the Nike Classic, the girls finished third in the team race with Hannah the highest placing individual, in 14th place. The JV girls placed fourth with Stella Skovborg placing tenth overall. The boys placed fourth.

Olivia won the George Fox Invitational in 18:08, with the team placing second. JV girls won the team race by ten points with a score of 30. Stella Skovborg placed second and Anna Hinz was third. The boy's JV won the team race by 26 points with a score of 24. Connor Steele was first with Andy Jones second and Zack Weber third.

At the District Conference meet, the girls placed 1, 2, 3, 6, 7 and 8. The boys placed 1, 2, 3, 6, 7, and 9. Both teams were on their way to State.

At the State Cross-Country Championships, Olivia won her third state title by 53 seconds with a time of 17:45, Taylor and Hannah finished second and third, and the rest of the team placed 11th and 12th. They won the team race with a score of 23 points to 104 for the second-finishing team. Summit Girls won the cross-country title for the ninth consecutive time.

Olivia Brooks, six times state champion

The boys finished second behind Crater with a score of 32 to 41. Nic Sjogren led the boys with a second-place finish in 15:46, which was 25 seconds behind the winner.

At the regional meet in Boise, the top two teams would qualify for the National Championships. The girls and boys both finished second. They were on their way to the National Championships, and we knew full well that the Thanksgiving holiday with their parents would take precedence over training for the race.

Stela Skovborg won the Emerging Elite race at the regional meet by eleven seconds, which was a great performance for freshman.

In the National Championships, the girls had a terrible day, finishing 22nd, last place in the team race. The boys fared a wee bit better, finishing in 20th place. Like I said, Thanksgiving plays havoc with trying to keep a team training together. The kids will tell you they were training, but looking at them when they return, their physical condition said something else.

I was running out of places to conduct hill-running as houses were being built where I had been training the kids around the area of the school.

I mentioned the predicament to one of the coaches, and he said he would talk to one of the local companies and asked if they would donate a couple of truck-loads of gravel to be delivered to the dirt trail alongside the road on Skyline Ranch Road, which they did.

Several parents showed up with wheelbarrows, rakes, and shovels, and Brendan, one of our coaches, came with a front-end loader. After several hours of grunt work, we had a trail that I could make 400 meters uphill for training. I measured every 100 meters and drove a stake to be used as a marker. I ended up with a measured course where I could run any combination from 100 to 400 meters.

I had another health scare on New Year's Eve. While I was watching TV, suddenly I lost the use of my right arm. I would raise it up and it would just fall down. I had no power. I called Carol, who was next door with our neighbor, to return to the house and take me to the hospital as I believed I was having a stroke.

She rushed me to the hospital, where they performed some tests and decided I had a small stroke called a transient ischemic attack (TIA) which is like a stroke, producing similar symptoms, but usually lasting only a few minutes and causing no permanent damage. Often called a mini-stroke, a transient ischemic attack may be a warning for bigger things to come.

During the examination, one of the nurses told me that the platelets in my blood were high and I needed an oncologist to determine what was causing that. I recovered fairly quickly and was discharged but was worried about the platelet count.

Chapter 58
2017

2017 was a trying year for me when I was diagnosed with a blood disorder. My body was producing too many blood platelets, which meant I had to take a drug to reduce the numbers. As I am not too keen on taking pills, I had to succumb to taking them anyway to keep the numbers in control.

At the Oregon Relays, the girls distance medley team were beaten by less than a second by Mountain View from Idaho — 11:59.98 to 12:00.58. What a race. Later, Olivia Brooks finished third in the 1,500 meters in a time of 4:28.42.

At the Jesuit Relay, Olivia finished third in the invitation mile in 4:51.16. In the DMR, girls won in 12:07.66 by four seconds. Scott Kinkade won the 1,500 meters in a time of 4:02.66. Nic Sjogren finished third in the 3,000 meters with a time of 8:50.13 and the boys finished fourth in the 4x800 meters.

At State, Emma Stevenson won the 800 meters from Isabel Max in a time of 2:17.55. Olivia won her third 1,500-meter title by 11 seconds from Fiona Max in a time of 4:30.71. Olivia also won her third consecutive 3,000-meter title from Fiona by 19 seconds in a time of 9:50.94. Nic finished second in the 3,000 meters by less than one second in a time of 8:38.26.

Carol and I attended the IAAF World Championships in London. Prior to that, we took a side trip to Iceland, where I had competed twice, back when the roads outside Reykjavik were all dirt. The terrain looked like something from the moon with barren landscape and few trees.

We took a couple of tours and walked all over the city, exploring sights. Noticeably, the price of a beer was pretty steep. It would be expensive to get drunk in this city. After four days, we headed to London.

As usual in England, it rained. Especially when we visited Windsor Castle along with half of China. I was amazed at how many Chinese were standing in line along with us, all under umbrellas trying to shield the body from the rain.

Another day, we visited Hampton Court and enjoyed walking amongst the plants and flowers. No, I didn't pick any flowers.

The greatest moment for the Brits was when Mo Farrah won 10,000 meters and was pipped in the 5000 meters. We saw Usain Bolt getting beat in the 100 by Justin Gatlin and then in the 4x100 where he pulled up lame with 50 meters to the finish. Great Britain won the 4x100 meter relay.

After the games we spent some time with our friends, the Peters, relaxing, playing golf, ten-pin bowling and sipping a few beers. Then we had to get back on a plane and head to the States and start getting the kids ready for cross country.

The cross-country season started off slowly. At the Nike Classic in Portland, Summit girls finished fourth with Fiona Max our highest individual finisher in 11th place. The girls finished second in the JV team race with Jasper Fievet our highest finisher in fourth place. The boys got crucified, finishing in 11th place.

At the George Fox Invitational, the girls had started to improve, winning the team title by 30 points with a score of 73. Fiona led the charge, finishing second with Taylor in fourth and Isabel Max in sixth place.

The State Cross Country Championships would be the last time for Summit to compete at this level for the year, which I considered pretty easy since we had raced all the top teams at other events. The girls crushed it, recording the lowest score possible with 15 points. Taylor won convincingly by seven seconds over Fiona, with Isabel in third. The team won its tenth consecutive state championship and Carol's seventh title. We were looking forward to the next year, when Summit would be competing in Division six.

At the Nike Cross Country Regional (NXR) championships in Boise, the girls finished third and missed being selected for the National championships. Fiona was the top finisher in 19th place. In the Emerging Elite race, the girls ran well with Jasper winning by 15 seconds with a time of 20:11, and Elie Skjersaa finished tenth

At the beginning of the year, Taylor Vandenborn was having a tough time with her feet. She was diagnosed as having a neuroma in her left foot, which necessitated surgery. She was moral support for me and I was for her. When we met, it was always, "How are you doing?" I attended the hospital with her and family. The surgery was a success. Now was the hard part—get her back to running.

I had her walking, riding a bike, and swimming; then she started jogging when able. I developed a schedule for her with an eye on getting her fit enough to win the state cross country championships. I am sure she thought I was drunk, crazy or had completely lost it.

I presented my plan to Taylor and off we went. Starting in July with easy running, the goal was to be ready to roll in November at State.

The week workout for Taylor went something like this:

Sunday: Easy bike or swim

Monday: Running — started on grass and progressed to hills

Tuesday: Easy swim or bike up to 45 minutes easy

Wednesday: Grass work

Thursday: Easy run, swim or bike for 45 minutes

Friday: Warm up 30 minutes with a few strides.

Saturday: Race

In total, Taylor was probably lucky if she was running 15 miles per week. Monday and Wednesday workouts became a bit more intense as we sauntered on to the State Championships.

On the day of the event, I walked the course as usual and when I came back, I talked to the runners. At the end of the talk, I took Taylor aside and told her she could win. She looked at me and said, "Give me my 800-meter split and I will take it from there." I responded that I would. I knew there was a 1K marker split and I would have to measure backwards to get 800 meters.

I took off, found the 1K mark and proceeded to step back to get approximately 800 meters. As I was walking back, several people wanted to talk to me. I had to tell them, "Sorry," as I was on a mission. I drew a line across the trail and decided this was the 800-meter mark.

The race started and Taylor was setting off the pace with the lead group. As she approached the 800-meter mark I shouted, "3.03," and she gave me a smile and headed to the front, never to relinquish the lead. She won the race in 18:28 by seven seconds. At the end of the race, we both had tears of joy after a year of missteps. Summit went on to win their tenth consecutive state title.

Taylor Vandenborn on her way to winning the title in a time of 18:28

The girls won the team title with a score of 15 points, which was the lowest score a team could possibly score. The girls ran 1, 2, 3, 5, and 6.

The fourth finisher did not score as she did not have team.

This is what Taylor wrote for an English class:

A Smart Old Fart with a Heart

A high school student with a 17:56 five-kilometer personal record and a 10th-, 3rd-, 2nd, and 1st-place finish in the Oregon women's 5A state cross-country race; these accomplishments describe me. A coach to seven World Championship athletes and three Olympians; these much more impressive stats describe somebody that has taught me so much about life. He also pulled me through four demanding but rewarding years of high school running. His name is Jim McLatchie.

Picture a tall, white-haired Scotsman in a green rain jacket and baseball cap. His huge Hoka running shoes round out his determined walk across the football field. His wristwatch can be seen through the little clear patch in his jacket sleeve. A black cord hangs out of his pocket, attached to a yellow stopwatch, swinging as he walks. He calls splits to packs of young runners just ahead of me as they cross the 200-meter line on the track, letting their limbs flail about after they hit the mark. "Good workout, gang," he calls as we all catch our breath on the grass. To my knowledge, every cross-country athlete, despite the pain of how much or how fast they just ran, feels accomplished because of these three little words. Jim's approval of your running is more than anyone could ever ask for.

Lesson #1: Genuine praise is monumentally meaningful. It takes effort and shows true character. Jim has just quietly watched us exhaust ourselves around the track, maybe yelling at us if we took off "like a bat outta hell" or needed to "pick it up a bit," but otherwise an observer. I slowly jog my post-workout cool down lap with the girls, feeling accomplished. When we round the corner of the track, Jim is standing there next to his famous red clipboard on the bench. He claims it is thirty years old, and every timed workout I've ever run with him has been recorded in that thing for the past four years. "It can last thirty more," he tells the freshman.

Lesson #2: Treasure old things: the folder and the man. Old things have been in the world longer, and have had more time to develop a thick skin, but they are softer on the inside. "How'd it feel sweetie?" he asks me, motioning to my feet. With that little question you can tell he cares so much.

Lesson #3: Asking people how they are and really meaning it works wonders. I have tried this many times, and I've found when people see you actually care, they react much more openly to you. Sometimes they even tell you how they really are! Jim showed me this kindness in really asking how I was, and now I can do the same for others. When Jim asks how I'm doing, he doesn't really want to know how my feet feel—they hurt every time I run—but really, he wonders what I'm thinking. Am I still mentally tough? Is the pain too much to race on Saturday? The answer is rarely different than this: "Good, thanks Jim," or maybe "Fine, thanks Jim." With this response, he knows exactly where my head's at, and that no matter how bad my feet are actually hurting that I will be giving it my all at the weekend competition. I have modeled my perceived strength after Jim's. When he had health issues this year and had to go to the doctor many times, he would act normal. He would tell you straight up what was happening if you asked. He would not complain, would not exaggerate, and would not show any break in his composure.

Lesson #4: Act tough and you are tough. If you are strong enough to ignore it, nobody else knows it's there, and it goes away in a sense. Running is such a mental sport, you would completely fail without the will to do it, and so it is hugely important to have your head in the game. Sometimes, I lose focus and my mind wanders. This man I admire and rely on so much has seen me in my weakest mental state. Jim watched me cry at the doctor's office when I had a shock nerve test done on my feet. Jim watched me cry when the anesthesiologist explained how I would pass out, and then again when I went into surgery for my foot. He has seen me almost cry a million times. I get so emotional and want to hold it back, but when I get close my voice cracks. Jim knows this but never mentions it. He lets me get away with my pride still intact.

Lesson #5: "Everyone needs a shoulder to cry on," as said by Jim himself. Jim has been my shoulder. As a kid, he lived in Scotland with his many siblings, and went to work in the coal mines when he was only fifteen years old. There is no lack of hardship or toughness in this man, yet he shows tenderness and lends a hand in any way he can. Sometimes the best relationships in life are the unexpected ones. I never really thought I could be friends with somebody more than fifty years older than me, but I am so glad I am.

I have learned a lot about myself as both a person and runner, as well as life in general from Jim McLatchie. He was just the old fart that yelled at us when I met him freshman year, but now I look forward to everything he has to say. He knows what he's talking about: I might as well listen. For some reason I keep on running, year after year, even though it hurts. Maybe that's because it means I get to see Jim. So much of my identity is embedded in being a runner, and I owe the proudest moments of my life to this sport. Still, it may not be part of my life without him. Thank goodness for that crazy Scotsman.

Chapter 59
2018 Stroke

At the Oregon Relays, the girls won the 4x800 meters in a time of 9:35.45 and finished second in the DMR. At the Jesuit Relays, Olivia Brooks finished third in the mile with a time of 4:51.16 and the girls won the DMR by four seconds with a time of 12:07.66.

While attending the Jesuit Relays with the Summit team, I bumped into Daniel Maton, who is Matthew's younger brother. He told me he enjoyed doing my workouts. I said, "That is not possible as I live in Bend and you live in Washington State." He replied that his mother had most of the workouts that I gave Matthew and she was giving them to him. It seemed to me that Michelle was telling the coach how to coach her son. Daniel said his favorite workout was: 8x400 meters with decreasing rest of 1:45, 90, 75, 60, 45, 30, and 15 seconds.

At the State track championships, Isabel Max won the 800 by eight seconds with a time of 2:14.76 with Azza Borovicka-Swanson in third in 2:22.32. Fiona Max won the 3,000 meters over Kelsey Gripekoven by 0.1 with a time of 10:00.66 and finished second in the 1,500 meters with Taylor Vandenborn finishing third.

Training the cross-country team was interesting as we had a bunch of kids who wanted to train hard and listen to what the coaches were telling them. We started out well. At the Nike Invitational, the girls won convincingly, scoring 38 points and winning by 63. Fiona finished second, getting beat by four seconds in 17:36. The other girls did well with Teaghan Knox in sixth, Kelsey Gripekoven in 11th, Isabel in 14th and Azza in 15th. Great running by the girls.

In the girl's JV race, the team absolutely dominated the opposition, taking the top five places with 15 points and winning by 50 points. Maggie Williams was the overall winner with a time of 19:24, followed one second later by Ashley Boone, then Liv Downing, Elie Skjersaa, and Jorun Downing. It was bloody amazing and looked good for the future.

I raced the boys in lower classifications, where they performed well.

The next big race was Warner Pacific, where the girls were finally showing that they belong on the big stage, winning the team race by 119 points. Fiona finished second in 17:28, losing by four seconds. Teaghan finished third, Kelsey sixth, Isabel seventh, and Azza ninth. In the JV race, Jorun won, Ashley was second, and Elie ran third, yet we only finished third in the team race.

A few weeks before State, the varsity girls approached Carol and me, asking why Summit never performed well at Nationals. We told them that most of the kids take off on Thanksgiving vacation to Hawaii, Mexico or skiing, and when they return to school they are out of shape.

We told them that if they wanted to perform well at Nationals, providing they qualify, they needed to ask their parents to postpone their vacations and stay in Bend and train. We gave them a few days to come back with an answer. All the girls informed us that they would be in Bend during the holidays and wanted to train for Nationals.

I was a having a tough time at some of the cross-country races, where my pulse would be racing even when I was sitting down. I knew I had Atrial Fibrillation, which usually happens as one gets older. I would wait until my pulse (heartbeat) would subside, then I would move on. I never really worried about it, but later I talked to my heart doctor, who put me on a heart monitor for two weeks to record my heart to find out what was really happening.

A few weeks after that, I had another health scare where I nearly kicked the bucket. On October 16, I was watching TV, when all of a sudden, the room started spinning and I couldn't see. I thought, "Oh, shit…here comes the big one." Carol was playing bunco with friends at another location. I managed to find my phone, called Carol, and it went to her voicemail. I then tried to call my next-door neighbor, to no avail, as I couldn't see his number. I knew where 911 was on the phone, which I called, and told the dispatcher where I lived and thought I was having a stroke. While talking to the lady, I started feeling sick and made a beeline for the kitchen to throw up in the sink. As I could not see, I ran into the kitchen table, which knocked me on my arse. I managed to get up and make it to the sink. While throwing up, I could hear the ambulance's siren in the distance. I was still throwing up when help arrived. They put me on a gurney, asked me some questions, gave me an IV and whipped my butt to hospital.

The next thing I knew, I was in hospital and a doctor asked if he had permission to give me a clot buster, which he told me could be fatal. I said, "Yes." Carol was at the hospital by the time I got there. When my neighbor, Fred, saw the ambulance at the door, he called his wife, who was with Carol, and told her to get home immediately. Seemingly when

I tried to call, she had turned off her phone because she was having a night out and didn't want to talk to the parents calling about their kids.

The next thing I remembered was my friend, Anne Sjogren, with me in the Intensive Care Unit. She said if asked, I was to say she was my niece. I guess I was in ER Care for three days before being transferred to Intensive Care. I had suffered a massive cerebral hemorrhage on the right side of the brain, where the clot was lodged.

One evening, while in Intensive Care, I had to go to the bathroom. After I finished, I tried to stand up and down I went, hitting my head on the wall. I called for help and my daughter, Amy, opened the door and went running for a nurse. Between the two of them they managed to get me back into bed. Apparently, I was not to be left alone, but when the nurse stepped out for something, down I went. I was rushed to have a brain scan, and when the results came back, the bleeding in my brain had stopped. Being me, I said to the doctor that hitting one's head on a wall might be part of the recovery process.

The first week, I had to attend rehab and could hardly do anything. I couldn't walk up or down four stairs without help. I was on a tether attached to the therapist when they had me walking. I was helpless without aid. Looking at other stroke victims, I made my mind up. "I have to get out of this place." Each day, I was getting stronger and the medical staff kept asking what I wanted to do. I replied it was simple, "Get me out of here."

The District Cross Country Championships were being held in Bend. On the Wednesday before the race, I told the medical staff it was imperative that I be allowed to attend. I wanted to be in attendance to cheer our kids to victory.

On Thursday, they had me walking outside on the grass with a walker to see how I could navigate grass and obstacles. I passed with flying colors. The staff had a meeting and decided to give me a pass to attend as long as I had someone keep their eye on me.

I was picked up from the hospital by a good friend, Aaron Gordon, who took me to the Championships. When I arrived, I was happy to see Olivia Brooks, whom I coached and now attends the University of Colorado. It was great day as Summit won all four races. Being there watching the kids perform really helped me mentally, which gave me the satisfaction that the training plan was working.

Aaron took me back to the hospital, where I had to have a nap. The next day, I retook a battery of tests which I had failed seven days earlier. This time, I passed with flying colors, scoring 35 out of 36. One of the tests was to stand on one leg, then repeat with eyes closed. I never ever thought I would be standing with my eyes closed on one leg, and I wasn't even drunk.

After the tests, there was a meeting with the doctors and the physical therapy staff, who came back to my room and told me that I could home tomorrow. Thank goodness. I was out of there. Hospitals are great for taking care of you and getting you back on your feet. I like my own bed and surroundings and really dislike the hospital regime of being wakened up every hour. I know it is a necessity, but if you don't get sufficient sleep, you are no use to anyone.

Even though I was delirious at times when Carol asked what the workout was for the runners, I could always come up with a workout that the team had to do. Most times, I don't remember Carol asking, but what I said was documented and the kids did the workout.

I really have to thank several people for helping me through this ordeal while in hospital. Carol was there every day helping me get around, cajoling me to behave myself and slow down. My daughter, Amy, drove from Portland, offering moral support and attending to my needs. Heather, my daughter in Houston, called every day and gave me words of encouragement. I would not let Heather fly up from Houston as I told her I would be up and about as I was going to beat this thing. I told her to visit when I was out of hospital, which she did. Ian, my brother, called Carol every day to get a status of my condition.

Carol, my wife.

Heather, my eldest daughter.

Amy, my youngest daughter.

My two grandkids — Simone and Isabel.

I must thank all the people that showed up at the hospital to give me hell and good wishes, and the physical therapy staff that brought me back from a physical wreck to near normal. Some people tell me that this will never happen as I don't know what normal is, but the medical staff missed the results of me wearing the heart monitor for two weeks prior to the stroke. Seemingly, the report was not read until I was in the hospital. I am not so sure that it would have made a difference, but it was overlooked and did cause some concern with the medical staff.

I was discharged around lunch time on a Monday and showed up at the hills later to watch the team do the workout I had prescribed earlier. It was an emotional moment for all and reminded them to focus on the task at hand which was to qualify and place at nationals. I wasn't too worried about winning State as we had Jesuit's number.

When I got sick John Platt contacted me and said he was sending me a book written by a co-founder of a company John was instrumental in establishing. The book was called *tPA for Stroke*, which is the story of a controversial drug. John and I have remained good friends to this day. What a man.

Chapter 60
2018 — National Champions

The night before State, Carol invited Peter Thompson to give the runners a motivational speech. It was a hit, and even today, some of the team talk about the inspiration that they received.

I kept the level of workouts high and only eased up the week of nationals. I didn't change the training protocol at all. Damian Olsen was in charge of taking care of developing the runner's body strength through a regime of exercises that developed their core. Carol took care of the logistics. Dave Sjogren and Brendan Layden helped me monitor the workouts that I had developed. We had a good support team, which one needs on the journey to compete well at a national level.

We had been looking forward to the State 6A Championships, and Fiona won the title in 17:29 and probably would have broken the course record if she didn't have a hiccup the last 300 meters. Teaghan Knox, our precocious freshman, finished fifth, leading to the team taking the title over Jesuit by 39 to 68 points.

The following week, we headed to Boise for the Regional Championships, where the top two finishing teams get to attend the National Championships. I told the girls, "Run as a team, and we will be going to the National Championships." The girls won fairly easy with a score of 54 to 106 over Jesuit. I entered Ashley Boone and Jorun Downing in the Rising Stars race, and they finished first and second with Ashley running 19:19 and finishing 25 seconds ahead of Jorun. It was the third consecutive time that our young girls excelled against teams from the Northwest Region, including Alaska.

I entered the boys in the open race, where Sam Hatfield finished second by 0.5 seconds, with Zach Weber finishing third. In the Rising Stars race, the team finished second, getting beat by nine points.

Carol and I asked Stacey Hager, one of our assistant coaches, if she would be in charge of the team at Nationals, and she accepted. Carol had to attend the USATF national convention in Indianapolis, so she was not available. At my age, I am not too keen on following the regimented procedure of the event, and I did not have the energy required to keep the kids occupied and enforcing Nike's protocol. I couldn't handle another championship where you are dictated as to where to go and what time you had to be there.

I told Stacey that I would show up the night prior to the race and would be there for the team on race day. I received a ride to Portland with Dave Sjogren, who dropped me off at the hotel. I met up with Stacey and discussed the plans for the race.

A cold damp day in Portland, Oregon on Saturday, December 1, 2018 was the site for the Nike Cross National (NXN) Championship—a 5k race on the Glendoveer Golf Course. 22 teams were competing, along with the Summit High School girls running under the Central Oregon name. I rode the bus with the teams. When we arrived at the racecourse, as usual, I went and walked the course noting where the water and mud were on the course. I then returned to the holding area and spent some time with the team. Before the start, I explained where all the tough parts were on the course and said, "Run your usual race, and with one kilometer from the finish, hit it, and you will win this thing." On leaving, I looked at their faces and could see they were ready.

At the two-mile mark it was announced Summit was leading by 16 points. When I heard we were the leading team, I said to myself, "There is no way we can lose this race. Our team doesn't start racing until one kilometer to the finish." I headed towards the finish and stood at the bottom of the hill, about 300 yards from the finish. As one of our runners approached the hill, I would shout out, "150s!" as we do 150s every workout. Watching them take off, I knew we had it in the bag.

After the race, I sought out the kids, rounded them up, and told them job well done. I was approached by an official who told us to head to the awards stage as a team. The girls asked me, "Well, how do you think we finished?" I replied, "We won the fucking championship." The organizers had three teams on the stage, and they went through the drama of introducing the third-place team, and then the second-place team, and when that is done, everyone knows who won.

We were announced as the winners with 120 points; North Naperville was second with 186 points. We went from leading by 16 points to 66 over the last mile. We were the first team from west of the Mississippi to win the nationals with a team that would be back the next year to defend.

I was tired and emotionally drained and told Stacey and Dave I was going home and they could attend the awards ceremony for Carol and me. Later we found out that we were also announced as coaches of the meet.

It was amazing how many coaches would ask me, "How many miles are the kids running?" I'd tell them, "I don't know. We run for minutes, not miles." Or the question, "How far are your tempo runs?" My response, "We don't do any as we are only racing 5000 meters, and there is no need for them."

Dave Turnbull, who is Summit's head track coach, gave me a ride home. When I entered the house, I opened a beer and smiled, saying out loud, "We did it."

2018 NXN Champion, Central Oregon, Summit High School.

Athletes	Coaches	
Fiona Max	Carol McLatchie (head coach)	
Teaghan Knox (FR)	Jim McLatchie	
Kelsey Gripekoven (JR)	Dave Sjogren	Stacey Hager
Isabel Max (JR)	Kari Strang	Damian Olson
Azza Borovicka-Swanson (JR)	Brendan Layden	Carrie Carney
Stella Skovborg (JR)	Chris Shunk	J.D. Downing
Jasper Fievet (SO)		

Summit Girls with their trophy

During my 9 years at Summit High School as the Distance Coach I have coached the following State Champions:

YEAR	800	1500	3000
2018	Isabel Max		Fiona Max
2017	Emma Stevenson	Olivia Brooks	Olivia Brooks
2016	Sarah Reeves	Olivia Brooks	Olivia Brooks
2015	Kaely Gordon	Olivia Brooks	Olivia Brooks
2014	Sarah Reeves	Matthew Maton	Matthew Maton
2013		Matthew Maton	Matthew Maton Hannah Gindelsperger
2012		Ashley Maton	Eric Aldritt
2011		Ashley Maton	Megan Fristoe
2010			Megan Fristoe

In cross-country since 2012, Carol and I have coached the following State Champions and won 7 consecutive girls team titles for a total of 11 consecutive titles for Summit girls:

YEAR	Girls	Boys
2018	Fiona Max	

2017	Taylor Vandenborn	
2016	Olivia Brooks	
2015	Olivia Brooks	
2014	Olivia Brooks	Matthew Maton
2013	Hannah Gindelsperger	Matthew Maton
2012		Travis Neuman

I believe that if I had proper feeding when I was growing up and not going to bed hungry, I would have broken 4 minutes for the mile. Lack of nutrition is like not putting enough gas in a car. You will drive along for a bit before you run out of fuel.

Appendix
Training Schedules

1. JIM McLATCHIE — SCOTLAND
2. JIM McLATCHIE - TEXAS
3. HARRIERS — HOUSTON, TEXAS
4. RENEE ODOM
5. CAROL McLATCHIE
6. MILERS IN TEXAS
7. MARATHON TRAINING
8. MARTY FROELICK
9. SYLVIA MOSQUEDA
10. SUMMIT HIGH SCHOOL
11. STEEPLECHASE PROGRAM
12. JUSTIN CHASTON
13. SUMMIT HIGH SCHOOL
14. TRAINING SCHEDULES THAT I HAVE DEVELOPED

Jim McLatchie — Scotland

Growing up in Muirkirk, there was no track to run on. I did most of my running in the hills, and for strength work, I would run up a "slag bing," created from stones and dirt that were the residue from the coal dug underground. It was over 200 feet tall and I would run to the summit wearing coal miner's boots, which weighed about four pounds. Each boot had steel heel and toe plates studs in the soles. I would run as many as 20 repetitions. Other days, I would run in the hills and visit the local soccer pitch twice a week for speed work. It was a grass surface and I could get about 200 meters around the pitch.

When I moved to Glasgow, I was able to train on a 440-yard cinder track and started working on pace. Along with track workouts, I'd run on a golf course at lunch time, most of the time in my bare feet. There was nothing like feeling the grass as you ran.

I was probably running about 50-60 mile per week but didn't really count miles. Time on my legs was more important. Some days, due to the weather, I would do circuit training indoors. It was an effort on many days to open the door and go for a run. We had no indoor running facilities, so I was used to running in all weather: rain, snow, slush, and wind.

Living in a remote village in Scotland. I enjoyed getting out in the fresh air and nature and just running along without a care in the world. I fell down a lot running in the snow. Because of the snow, I would miss a turn on a road or trail and end up in a six-foot drift. I never panicked. I just lay down and rolled out until I could walk out of the drift and then continue my run.

My schedule was as follows if I was not racing:

Day	Activity
Sunday	Long easy run anywhere from 10 to 15 miles
Monday	Track workout
Tuesday	Easy run — if weather was bad in the winter, I did circuit training
Wednesday	Track workout
Thursday	Easy run — if weather was bad in the winter, I did circuit training
Friday	3-4 miles, if racing. 30-minute warm-up then strides
Saturday	Race or one hour easy

Below is what I did for 28 days before I ran a 4:8.3 mile. I ran most days at lunch time on the golf course, usually around three miles to loosen up — nice and easy.

Days out from race	Activity
28	Warm up/10x300 with 2-minute rest/jog 10 minutes/6x70/walk back
27	4x880 in 2:10 with 3-minute rest/jog 10 minutes/2x 440 in 60-62/3-minute rest
26	Rest day
25	Race — 3 miles in 14:46 — warmed up and cooled down
24	Easy run followed by 6x100 and 2x400; no times
23	Rest day
22	Won ¾-mile race on grass track in 3:02.5
21	Easy run with 6x220 with one-minute rest/jog 5 minutes/6x140 with 45 seconds rest between each
20	Won a 3000-meters steeplechase in 9:21.7
19	Easy one hour with 10x220; no time/one-minute rest between
18	Won a handicap (30 yards short) mile in 4:03.
17	Easy warm up on grass/8x400 yards in 54-55 with 2-minutes rest between each
16	Rest day
15	Track meet. Ran 880 heats in 1: 52.9. Final 1:53 off 10 yards (raced 870 yards)
14	Easy run with 6x100 with one-minute rest/jog 5 minutes/6x140 JB
13	Easy run with 2 miles Fartlek
12	Warmed up/ran easy mile in 4:13/cooled down
11	Ran 20x200 with 45 seconds rest at lunch/ran 6x440 in 58 2 min rest in evening
10	20x110 bends on track/45 seconds between each
9	Rest day
8	Warmed up/easy 880 in 1:57
7	Rest day
6	30 minutes easy with a few strides
5	3 miles Fartlek then 4x220 around 30 sec with 220 jog
4	Rest day

3	Rest day
2	Scottish Championships heats — jogged mile in 4:25.8
1	Scottish Champs Final — finished second in 4:8.3

Jim McLatchie — Spring – Summer – USA - 1963

Training in Texas was completely different, as now I had to deal with heat and humidity, whereas in Scotland it was always cold, wet, and windy. I arrived in Beaumont at the end of January, which was not too bad for running and reminded me of our best days in Scotland. As the months progressed, I had a tough time with the conditions. When it got too hot, I trained around 9 p.m. at night some days. Every morning around 6:30 a.m., before classes, I would jog to South Park High School and run in my bare feet for 30 minutes with a few strides. I enjoyed that a great deal as it was much cooler than in the afternoon.

The fall was not too bad as it was much cooler and I got more running under my belt. The following is what I did when I beat Jim Ryun over a mile in Houston. Ryun went on to run in the Olympics and record 3:51.1 for the mile.

Days From race
28 — Rest day
27 — 1 ½ miles of sprint jogs then 2x220 around 27 seconds
26 — Warm up 6x220 averaging 26 seconds with 1 minute rest/jog 10 minutes/440 — 53.5 seconds
25 - 5 miles easy run
24 — Warm Up raced 880 in 1:53.2sec cooled down
23 — 6 miles Fartlek
22 — Easy run then 20x110 around bends jog back/5MR 440- 54.4s
21 - Rest day
20 — Warm up Time Trial ¾ mile — 3:04/15 MR/220 — 25.3 seconds/15 MR/440 54.4 seconds
19 — Easy run with 3-mile Fartlek
18 — Easy run with 3-mile Fartlek
17 — 6 mile run with 1-mile Fartlek then 2x200 25-26/jog 440 between
16 — Travel to Brownswood, TX for Conference
15 — Temperature was 107, which was bloody awful. Won mile in 4:23.7 and 20 minutes later had to run 880, where I finished 4th in 1:57.
14 — Travel back to Beaumont
13 — Easy 5 miles followed with 16x140 jogged 300 between/easy 5 minutes then 2x220 around 27 seconds
12 — Warm up — 10x220 around 30 with 220 jog between

11 — Warm up — 4x 440 around 60 with 110 jog between
10 — Easy 2 miles — 4x880 - 2:08 with 440 walk/jog between
9 — Rest day
8 — Warm up then ¾ mile time trial — 3:00.3.3 (58/67/58.3) testing kick
7 — Easy 2-mile run in 9:41
6 — 8x 220 29-30 with 220 jog between
5 — Easy 5 miles followed with 10x150 pick-ups jog back
4 — Jogged 3 miles with a few strides
3 — Rest day
2 — Rest day
1 — Mile race led from start to finish first in 4:7.9 (62,63/63/59.9)

The following week, I finished first in the Texas National Championships in Dallas. I jogged easy most of the week with a few 150s and 220s. Nothing strenuous. This time I held back until the last 660 and ran 4:10.7. (65, 67, 60, 58.7)

Jim McLatchie — Fall — USA - 1963

The weather was conducive to getting some decent workouts under my belt. I had decided to arrange my class schedule so that I had time to get in an easy run before lunch. That, along with my morning escapades on the grass and what I was doing in the afternoon helped me improve in my racing.

When I raced cross country in Scotland, I went several years without getting beat and managed to win the National Title as a junior. All the time I spent running in the hills and up and down coal tips made me nearly unbeatable. As there were no hills in Beaumont, I was hoping that with some extra mileage and better weather, I would be hard to beat.

Most days, I was running three times a day. I jogged every morning and at lunch time, I ran about five miles easy. In the evenings on Mondays and Wednesdays, I'd do a track-type workout. The rest of the week was easy running up to ten miles. If I was racing on Saturday, Friday would be one workout of 30 minutes easy with a few strides. I warmed up and cooled down after a workout.

26 days before the USA National 10K Cross Country Championships, I didn't do the 30-minute easy jogs before class.

DAYS from National Cross-Country Championships

26 - 20x220 with 30 seconds rest between average 30+
25 - a.m. 5 miles easy/PM — 4x mile average 5:10s with 440 jog between
24 — a.m. — 4 miles Fartlek/PM 9 miles easy
23 - a.m. — 4 miles Fartlek/PM — 4x440 with 440 jog 1-5 average 57s last — 54.5s
22 - p.m. — easy 40 minutes with mile in 5 minutes/10 minutes easy — mile in 5 minutes in rain-cooled 59 degrees
21 - Race Gulf Federation 4 miles XC; finished third in 19:46 seconds; it was rainy and 60 degrees
20 - a.m. - 9 miles easy — recovery run
19 - a.m. - long easy run of 17 miles
18 - a.m. — 35 minutes easy/PM 5x mile average 4:55 seconds with 440 walk between
17 - a.m. — 4 miles Fartlek/PM 9 miles easy

16 - a.m. — 30 minutes easy with 6x150 easy/8x880 with 440 walk average 2:11.5s
15 - 30 minutes easy with a few strides
14 - Race Houston 10K Trials for Nationals — finished second in 30:42
13 - 9 miles easy/legs sore — felt tired
12 - Went to beach and ran around 1 hour — legs still sore — stood in water
11 - 1 run around 30 minutes — Achilles aching
10 - Day off
9 - Tough workout — 4x440 with 110 jog — 58.6,59.0,58.4,58.0/10 minutes easy/6x110 run bends/jogged 10 minutes/440 — 54/felt good
8 - a.m. - 4x mile with 220 walk between — 4:58/4:48/4:49/4:44/Later in day left for East Lansing Michigan with team from Houston — Driving
7- The day President Kennedy was killed. Warm-up indoors/3 miles fast/slow/cool down
6 - 4:45pm East Lansing Michigan — 40 degrees — 10 miles easy with some strides
5 - 9 miles easy with some strides
4 - NCAA Championships — could not run because of freshman rule; ran 4 miles easy with some strides
3 - 4 miles with some easy hills
2 - Chicago 4 miles easy with a few strides — sore throat
1 - National 10,000 meters cross country championships in 48 degrees; finished second to Tom O'Hara 30:12 to 30:17. I made a move with a mile to go and picked up the pace. I was still leading with 200 from finish and just fell apart. Jeff Fishback was third in 30:22.

Harriers - Houston, Texas

Most of the Harriers followed a general schedule each season. 70 percent of the Harriers were average, dedicated runners all trying to improve and achieve the best they could in competition. Rice University held track meets on Friday evenings for all runners that were interested in running races. I had several athletes who competed in the USA championships, Olympics and World Championships. Those athletes followed the general schedule and an individual track workout schedule would be designed for them.

FALL

Sun - 9 — 18 miles easy — depends on the individual
Mon - Hill work — done on the Bayou which was short and steep. I would make a 200 circuit. Each runner wore a backpack which contained sand equal to 10% of body weight.
Tue - 6-8 miles easy
Wed - Track workouts plus circuit training
Thu - 8 miles easy
Fri - 6 miles — if Sat. race — 30 minutes easy with a few strides
Sat - Race or 8 miles easy

SPRING

Sun - 12 - 15 miles easy
Mon - Track — speed workout
Tue — 1-hour easy running
Wed - Track
Thu — 1-hour easy running
Fri - 6 miles — if Sat. race — 30 minutes easy with a few strides
Sat - Race or 8 miles easy

Track Workouts:	
1	10x400 at mile pace with 3 minutes rest between
2	6x300 with 100-walk between at mile pace less 2 sec/400
3	200/200 jog/200/400 jog/400 50-yard walk/400/mile at pace 5 sec per 400/jog 400/REPEAT
4	4x (400 walk 100 — 300) 4 min sets

5	Check Summit HS for more workouts

SUMMER

Sun	6 to 8 miles easy
Mon	Track — speed workout
Tue	1-hour easy running
Wed	Track
Thu	1-hour easy running
Fri	6 miles or track meet at Rice University
Sat	1-hour easy jogging

Renee Odom — Texas

Renee is Carol's sister and my sister-in-law. She ran for Kansas State in college, but was burned out by graduation and did not want to race again. She moved to Houston a few years later and I spent a considerable amount of time cajoling her to start training again. It took me about four years for her to change her mind.

Renee was a tough cookie, but easy to train. She would run through a wall if I told her. She recorded 2:05.52 for 800 meters, 4:09.42 for 1,500 meters, and ran an outdoor street mile in 4:28.

She followed what most of the Harriers were doing on the track and I had her train with Mack Stewart, a master runner who was running the same times as she was. She did long, easy runs during the week except during track season. Depending on where and when she was racing, her program would be adjusted with a combination of recovery runs, Fartlek or rest. Below is what she did when she ran 4:09.42 in 1985.

Days from race	
29	9 miles easy
28	3x330 with 110 walk - 45.1, 45.2/jog 10 minutes/440 - 60.8s
27	45 minutes with 10 minutes sprint jogs
26	4x 110 jog back/5 minutes rest/440 - 57.9s/5 minutes rest/4x110 jog back
25	45 minutes easy
24	20 minutes easy with a few strides
23	Race 1,500 meters in 4:17.3s finished first
22	9 miles easy
21	440 — 68/660 - 1.40/440 - 64/220 29/2 minutes rest between
20	45 minutes easy run
19	Mile - 5:05s/10 minutes jog/2x440 with 50 yard walk 62.6 - 62.9
18	45 minutes easy
17	20 minutes easy few strides
16	Time trial ¾ mile - 3.23 (65, 67, 71)
15	9 miles easy
14	330 — 46/660 — 1.37/330 - 45/220 - 27.6 with 4 minutes rest

13	45 minutes with 12 minutes of sprint jogs
12	Tough workout — 660 - 1:41s/440 - 70/330 - 51/220 - 32/110 - 17 all with 1-minute rest between
11	45 minutes easy with strides
10	20 minutes easy
9	880-time trial 2:05.1 (62.5, 62.6)
8	9 miles easy
7	45 minutes easy grass with 6x 175 1-minute rest
6	Easy 30 minutes 440 in 57.7s with 1-minute rest 220 — 28.7s
5	20 minutes easy with 440 in 60
4	20 minutes easy with a few strides
3	1500-meter heats ran 4:14.75 to qualify for the final
2	20 minutes run with a few strides
1	1500 — meter-race in 4:09.42

Carol McLatchie — Texas

Carol was unique. Growing up in Kansas prior to Title 9, there were no track programs for girls in high school and college. She moved to Houston in 1973 to attend Rice University to work on her Master's degree in Geology. While attending Rice, she got in involved with several women who ran and started jogging with the group.

The track coaches at Rice University held a summer track program with races on Friday evenings. I had moved to Houston in 1975 and formed the Houston Harriers. One of the founding members, Len Hilton, who competed in the 1972 Olympic Games, was getting back into shape.

Carol had heard about the race where Len broke four minutes for the mile. She was hooked and joined the Harriers. When she started, she could hardly break 40 minutes for 10K. Slowly, she began to improve, and in the eighties, she was a force to be reckoned with in the women's racing circle.

Carol followed the basic training schedules, but when training for a major race, the schedule was tailored for her needs.

Her personal bests:

TRACK			ROADS	
1500	4:28.00		10K	32.41
3000	9:19.50		15K	51.22
5000	15:45.10		10 Miles	55.15
10000	33:03.10		20K	1:13.28
			½ Marathon	1:14.50
			25K	1:34.30
			30K	1:53.30
			Marathon	2:35.09

The following is what she did when running 32:41 for a 10K and 51.29 for a 15K.

1. All 30-minute morning runs were on grass. She usually ran around four miles, some days two miles. I did not care about distance covered.
2. AM. 18 miles easy
3. PM. 880 — 2.36 440 jog/mile — 5.17 880 jog/2 mile 10.54
4. AM. 4 mile easy/PM. 9 miles grass — weights
5. AM. 4 miles easy/PM. Mile — 5.02/1320- 3.53/880 — 2.32/440- 66/440 jog between
6. AM. 4 miles easy/PM. 6 miles easy
7. AM. Travel to Jacksonville, Florida — 3 miles easy with strides

8. Jacksonville 15K River run — 1st — 51.22
9. AM. 72 minutes easy run
10. AM. 4 miles easy/PM.2x2 miles 11.06 11.02 with 5 minutes rest between
11. AM. 4 miles easy/PM. 12 miles easy
12. AM. 4 miles easy/PM. Mile — 4.56 lap jog/4x220 32/220 jog between/lap jog/mile — 5.13
13. AM. 4 miles easy/PM. 9 miles easy
14. AM. 4 miles easy/PM. 6 miles grass
15. Bayou Classic 10K — first 34.52 — won 6 consecutive years
16. AM. 21 mile run nice and easy — Olympic Marathon trials 6 weeks away
17. AM. 4 miles easy/PM. 3x mile 5.07/5.09/5.10 3 minutes rest between
18. AM. 4 miles easy/PM. 9 miles grass
19. AM. 4 miles easy/PM. 440-73 880 jog/880- 2.32/mile jog/mile 5.21
20. AM. 4 miles easy/PM. 9 miles grass
21. AM. 6 miles grass/PM. Fly to New Orleans
22. AM. Run last 4 miles of Crescent City course
23. Crescent City 10K race placed second in 32.41
24. AM. 4 miles easy/PM. 6 miles grass
25. AM. 4 miles easy/PM. 8 miles grass
26. AM. 4 miles easy/3x440 — 70 -2 minutes rest/880 jog/1320- 3.44/880 jog/3x440 — 70 ,70,69 with 2 minutes rest
27. AM. 4 miles easy/PM. 10 miles easy
28. AM. 6 miles easy/PM. 4 miles grass/Fly to San Francisco
29. PM. Jogged 30 minutes over course
30. Avon 15K finished first in 51.29/Dietz 2nd in 52.14

Carol's marathon training followed what I designed for the general marathon schedule, except the last few weeks were tailored for Carol. Morning runs were on the bayou which was all grass. The workouts below were done two weeks after she won Avon 15K in San Francisco.

Days before marathon:

Beach — supposed to run 15 miles — knees sore running on sand; ran 20 minutes
AM — 4 miles easy/PM. — 3x mile 5.07/5.08/5.06 with 440 jog/Jog 880 then 2 times circuit course.
AM. 4 miles easy/PM. - 15 miles easy

AM. 4 miles easy/PM. - 4x440 — 76/74/74/74 /2 miles 10.47/440-67/all with 3 minutes rest
AM. 4 miles easy/PM. - 1 ½ hour easy run
AM. 4 miles easy/PM. — fly to New York — 30 minutes easy
Trevira Twosome 10-mile race placed first in 55:15
AM. Easy run around reservoir. Travel to Houston
AM. 21 miles easy
AM. 4 miles easy/PM. 12 miles easy
AM. 4 miles easy/4x 880 2.34/2.35/2.35/2.36 with 4 minutes rest
AM. 4 miles easy/ 1 hour easy run
AM. 4 miles easy/6 miles easy
5K GAC champs — first — 17.41
AM. 15-mile easy run
PM. 2x 2mile 11.20 11.28 4 minutes rest
PM. 6 miles easy — grass
PM. Fly to Seattle — 6 miles easy
Drove Olympic Marathon Trials course — massage — no run
Jim drove course I jogged miles 20-23 get and an idea last part of race
First Women's Olympic Marathon Trials — finished 12th in PR of 2:35.09

In 1981, Carol went to New York to compete in   which was a 10K road race. Very few people knew her name outside Texas. Greta Waitz, Patty Catalano, and Jacqueline Gareau were in the race. Carol's instructions were simple—run with the leaders. As the race progressed, Carol was still with the leaders. As no one knew who she was, they were getting a bit worried. A dark horse! Carol went on to finish second behind Greta. Now they knew who she was.

Milers

The athletes that raced the mile race followed the general plan during the track season except when getting ready to compete in a major mile race. The Harriers had a couple of athletes who competed in the mile. Jon Warren ran 3:59.30 for the mile at the 1994 Prefontaine Classic and 2:15 for the marathon in a period of less than four months. David Wittman was the other athlete who ran under four minutes when he recorded 3:57.47 in the same Prefontaine.

They were two different type of athletes. Jon was the strength runner whereas David was the speedster. Jon had recorded 8:30 for the steeplechase while David was a sub-1:50 800-meter runner and a member of the Clemson University team that won the NCAA Indoor 4x800 meter relay title.

Most of the coaches welcomed the Harrier athletes with open arms, even though we beat their athletes. I would put together a Distance Medley team which won most of the Relay meets in Texas. The team included David and Jon. Getting an athlete to run the 400 leg was a challenge. On a few occasions, a college coach would let me borrow a 400-meter runner. The rules were different then.

These are a few of the sessions that David and Jon did prior to a big race. Morning runs were usually 30 minutes easy.

Sunday -   Easy 1 hour
Monday -   5x 500 with 6 minutes rest. 400 at 57-58 then sprint last 100 meters
Tuesday -   Easy 1 hour with a few strides
Wednesday — 1600 - 4.16/1200 — 3.09/800 - 2.04/400 - 58/3 minutes rest between
Thursday -   Easy 1 hour with strides
Friday -3(400 2MR 300) 4 minutes sets/jog 10 minutes- 400
        Dave — 55.5 - 42/ 56.5 - 41.4/ 56.4 - 44.4/ 54.9
        Jon - 57.1 - 43/ 57.2 - 42.1/ 57.8 - 46.0/ 56.5
Saturday -   Easy run or rest day
Sunday -   Easy 1 hour
Monday -   Jon — 400-60.1/1200- 3:04/400-56.4 all with 5 minutes rest//
        Dave — 200-24.9/200 jog/200— 25.4/jog 800/200 — 24.6/300 walk/300-37.5
Tuesday -   Easy 1 hour
Wednesday — 2x200 with 30 sec rest/Dave — 24.8/25.6//Jon — 28.1, 27.7
Thursday -   40 minutes easy with a few strides

Friday — Travel to Eugene — 30 minutes easy run with strides
Saturday - Mile race — David 3:57.47 and Jon — 3:59.30
At that time, I had a great bunch of distance runners. David, Jon, Justin Chaston (4:04), and Sean Murray, who ran a 4:03 mile. They were an easy bunch of men to coach who helped each other achieve their goals.

Marathon

When deciding to train for a marathon you must determine feasible goals for the race, then figure out marathon pace per mile.

Eg: Marathon in 3:03.3 is 7 minutes race pace

7 minutes = 420 seconds. Race pace less 10 seconds = 420-10 = 410 = 6:50

Predicted time for 800 with 20 seconds less per mile = 420-20 400=/2 = 200= 3:20

The schedule below was developed for athletes that wanted to run a marathon with no aspirations of being world-class. Most of the people who attempted the schedule worked for a living and running a marathon was on their bucket-list.

Workout

- Saturday runs should be run at 10 seconds per mile faster than race pace

- Try and run at least 30 minutes each morning Mon — Fri — don't worry about distance.

10-WEEK PROGRAM

WEEK 1	
1	10 mile easy
2	6x 1600 — race pace less 10 seconds per mile with 200 jog between
3	6 Miles easy
4	20 x 200 with 100 walk between run how you feel
5	6 Miles easy
6	10 Miles easy
7	Race or 8 miles easy

WEEK 2	
1	12 miles easy
2	3x3200 race pace less 10 seconds per mile with 600 jog between
3	6 miles easy
4	20x300 with 100 walk between run how you feel
5	10 miles easy

6	6 miles easy
7	Race or 8 miles hard

WEEK 3	
1	15 miles easy
2	6x1600 — race pace less 15 seconds per mile with 200 jog-between
3	8 miles easy
4	10x800 race pace less 20 seconds per mile with 200 jog-between
5	8 miles easy
6	8 miles easy
7	Race or 6 miles hard

WEEK 4	
1	15 miles easy
2	2 x 3 miles race pace less 15 sec per mile with 800 jog between
3	8 miles easy
4	20x 200 with 100-walk between — race pace
5	10 miles easy
6	6 miles easy
7	Race or 8 miles hard

WEEK 5	
1	15 miles easy
2	3 x 2 miles race pace less 15 sec with 600 jog-between
3	8 miles easy
4	12 x 800 race pace less 25 sec with 200 jog-between
5	8 miles easy
6	8 miles easy
7	Race or 15 miles easy

WEEK 6	
1	18 miles easy
2	6 x1600 race pace less 20 seconds — 200 jog between
3	8 miles easy
4	20x 300 with 100 walk between race pace
5	8 miles easy
6	6 miles easy

7	Race or 3 miles easy

WEEK 7	
1	20 miles easy
2	2x 3 miles race pace less 15 seconds — 200 jog between
3	8 miles easy
4	20x 400 with 200 jog between — race pace
5	8 miles easy
6	8 miles easy
7	Race or 10 miles easy

WEEK 8	
1	20 miles easy
2	12x 800 race pace less 30 seconds — 200 jog between
3	8 miles easy
4	6x 1600 race pace less 20 seconds — with 200 jog
5	8 miles easy
6	8 miles easy
7	10 miles easy

WEEK 9	
1	15 miles easy
2	3x3200 race pace less 20 seconds with 600 jog- between
3	8 miles easy
4	20x300 with 100 easy walk between
5	5 miles easy
6	5 miles easy
7	8 miles easy

WEEK 10	
1	8 miles easy
2	3x1600 race pace with 100 jog between
3	6 miles easy
4	40 minutes easy
5	30 minutes easy with a few strides
6	30 minutes with a few strides
7	RACE

Marty Froelick — Marathon in 2:10.59

Marty graduated from Rice University in 1981 and contacted me shortly after about coaching him. I decided that his best event would be the marathon. Marty followed the basic plan that I had developed for the marathon. One of the integral parts of his training was a 30-mile run about 3-4 weeks before the race. I would ride alongside him on a bicycle for company and during one of these escapades, I had a flat tire with about four miles to the end of the run. I told him to finish the run and I would catch up with him at the finish. It was raining and windy. I left my bike at the side of the road and ran to where my car was parked and returned to pick up my bike and meet Marty at the finish. I was knackered and Marty looked like he had been out for a jog.

A couple of workouts that Marty did prior to the Twin Cities Marathon were the repeat miles shown below and running 40x200 with a jog across the middle of the track around 35 seconds.

He ran 2:12 in his first marathon in 1983 in Houston. Two years later, he won the Houston Tenneco Marathon in a time of 2:11. That same year, he was selected to run in the Cross-Country World Championships as a member of the U.S. national team. In 1987, he ran an exceptional race to win the Twin Cities Marathon in a personal best of 2:10.59. I remember telling him that when he crossed the Mississippi Bridge to hit it and keep it going. He took off on the bridge and the announcer for the race said," An unknown runner has taken the lead." After a few minutes, they figured out that the unknown runner was Marty, who went on to win.

29 Days before Twin Cities Marathon. Most days, Marty also did morning runs 30-45 minutes easy

29	30-mile run around 6 minutes pace
28	1 hour easy
27	40x200 jog across middle
26	1-hour run
25	10-mile run - 2 @ 6.00/2@ 5.00/2@ 6.00/1@ 4.40/3@ 6.00
24	45 minutes easy with a few strides
23	10K road race 30:20
22	20-mile run around 6-minute pace
21	10x1K — 3.00 — 200 jog-between
20	1 hour easy
19	2 @ 6.00/2@ 5.00/2@ 6.00/1@ 4.40/3@ 6.00
18	1 ¼ hours easy
17	30-mile run around 6-minute pace

16	1 ½ hours easy run
15	1 hour easy
14	6x mile 4.40 with 1 minute-rest
13	1 hour easy
12	2 miles — 10.00/5MR/2X1 — 4.40 3MR/4X880 — 2.16 — 1MR
11	1 hour easy
10	1 hour easy
9	15 miles around 6 minute-pace
8	1 hour easy
7	4x mile pace with 1 minute-rest between
6	1 hour easy
5	2x 2 miles pace 1 minute-rest between
4	45 minutes with 5 minutes pick up
3	30 minutes easy with a few strides
2	30 minutes easy with a few strides
1	Twin Cities 1st place 2:10.59

Sylvia Mosqueda

Who is Sylvia and what is she?

Sylvia won the 1987 NCAA cross country championships in 1988 and also won the 10,000-meter title on the track in a time of 32:28.57, which stood for 30 years before it was broken.

Carol was the Team Manager for the USA in the IAAF World Half-Marathon Championships held in Bristol England on October 7, 2001. Sylvia was a member of the team and told Carol that she did not have a coach. Carol suggested me and that is how we became coach and athlete.

Sylvia contacted me on November 15th, giving me an outline of what she had been doing in respect to training. I told her I would prepare a schedule for her for the month of December, which I am sure was a wake-up call:

6 x mile with 1 minute-rest around 5:10.

8x 800 with 45 seconds rest around 2:32.

Based on how the workout went, we decided to have her first race on January 20, 2002, the San Diego Half-Marathon, which she won in 1:12.37.

The next race planned was a half-marathon in Austin, Texas, on February 2, 2002. Ten days prior to the race, I had Sylvia do the "Ball-Buster" workout:

2x mile with 30 secs between jog 400 after set	5:12/ 5:09
2x800 with 30 secs between jog 400 after set	2:29/ 2:30
2x400 with 30 secs between jog 5min after set	74/ 74
2x mile with 30 secs between jog 400 after set	5:06/ 5:08

2x800 with 30 secs between jog 400 after set	2:29/ 2:29
2x400 with 30 secs between	74/ 74

After that workout, I had a good idea that she was ready to run a fast time.

Carol and I drove over to Austin from Houston to watch the race. Sylvia and I had spoken several times on the phone, but had never met face to face as she lived in Los Angeles. Driving to the start of the race in the dark at 6 a.m., Carol spotted Sylvia running up the street. I stopped the car, jumped out, and ran towards her. She began shouting, "Who the hell are you?" I said, "I'm Jim McLatchie, your coach, you silly bugger."

I gave her a hug and told her to go "kick some ass" and that Carol and I would be out on the course cheering her. The rest is history. She set a new course record of 1:10.46. She went on to break that record again in 2004 with 1:09.52, which ranked her eighth in the USA at that distance.

Sylvia ran the New York Marathon in 2002 and finished 13th in a time of 2:33.47. In 2003, she finished 10th overall in a time of 2:33.10. She was the first American to finish the race, and was on the podium with the other top nine women. Alberto Salazar was presenting the prizes, and had to ask Sylvia her name.

Here is the last 21 days of training she accomplished leading up to the race. Monday through Friday, she ran 30 minutes in the morning.

1	2x mile- 5:08 - 1 min rest/jog 400/2x800 230 -1 MR/ jog 400/2x400 —70 / jog 5 minutes then REPEAT
2	1 hour run
3	8 mile run as follows: 1 — 5k pace/2 — 10k pace plus 1 minutes/2 — 10 k pace/ 3 — 10k pace plus 1 minutes
4	1 hour easy
5	45 minutes easy with a few strides
6	18 miles easy
7	1 hour easy
8	3x 3 miles at 10k pace with 4 minutes rest between
9	1 ¼ hour with 4x 3 minutes pick-ups in middle
10	4x mile 452 with 2 minutes rest between
11	1 hour easy
12	45 minutes with a few strides
13	15 miles easy
14	1 hour easy
15	2x 2mile at 10k pace with 2 minutes rest
16	1 Hour easy
17	45 minutes with a few strides

18	45 minutes with a few strides
19	20 minutes easy with a few strides
20	20 minutes easy with strides
21	New York Marathon 10th place in 2:33.10

In 2004, Sylvia had her best opportunity to make the Olympic team. She was fit and probably in the best shape of her life. At the marathon trials in St. Louis, she was in second place with three miles to go and ran out of steam. Everything had seized up. She could not walk and I had to carry her to the finish area. Luckily, it was about a mile across the park. Four weeks later, she ran a 10,000-meter race in the Mt. Sac relays to try and obtain a qualifying time for the Olympics. I explained to her that no one would run under the qualifier at the trials, which were to be held later in Sacramento, because it would be too hot. So, she needed to get a qualifying time at Mt. Sac.

Sylvia ran with a woman from Germany until the last mile and coasted to the finish line, which was a mistake, in 31:57.64. She missed the Olympic qualifying by six seconds.

During the 2004, season she recorded her fastest 5,000 meters in 15:33.38; 15K in 50:08, and half-marathon in 1:09.52

My only regret about coaching Sylvia is that if I'd had the opportunity to coach her when she was in her mid-twenties and not in her late thirties I believe she would have raced faster. All in all, we had a great journey.

Steeplechase Program

As mentioned in chapter 39, I was engaged by United Kingdom Athletics to work with Mark Rowland (present coach for Oregon Track Club) to develop men and women steeplechasers in Great Britain. I travelled to England several times a year and Mark and I would try to improve the athletes and educate the coaches. I designed the coaching exams for Level 3 and Level 4 certification.

Workouts described below are for steeplechasers with examples using 3K and 5K as the base for establishing workout times.

8 Weeks Build-Up (September — October)

1 hour easy run

Hill work — short hills plenty of reps with short rest

10 x short loop (150 meters with 2 hills) 30 sec rest/jog 5 minutes/repeat

Build up to 8 x 450 meters with 90 sec rest

1 hour easy

Tempo runs e.g. 2 miles easy/1 — 5k pace/1 — 10k + 20 seconds/mile/1 — 10k pace/1 — 5k/

Cool down. Note any combination to equal 8 miles of continuous running.

1 hour easy

45 minutes easy

Long run start at 1¼ hours add 15 minutes every 2 weeks until 2 hours is reached

November — December

2 hours easy

Track work — Long repeats: 2 x mile 30 seconds rest between/jog 5 minutes/4 x 800 30 sec rest

4 (mile 1 MR 200 quick) 3 minutes between sets

2 x 3000M 4MR   Try and do

3 x 2000M 3MR   at today's

4 x 1500M 3 MR   5K pace

6 x 1000M 2 MR

1 hour easy with 2 x 5 minutes pick-ups during the run

10-mile Tempo run.   Any combination of pace per mile to equal 10 miles

warm up/2 miles — 10k pace/1 mile 10k pace + 20 seconds/1 mile — 5k pace

1 mile 10k pace + 20 sec/1 — 5k pace/cool down

1-hour easy run
30 minutes easy if racing tomorrow else 45 minutes easy
Race or hill/grass work — long reps e.g. 3 x mile 3 minutes rest/or 6 x 800
3 minutes rest/
　　or mile: 2 x 800: mile 3 minutes rest between

January — February

2 hours easy
2.　　Track work — Variable repeats: 16 x 200 30 SR between/Jog 5
minutes/800
　　　　　　　　　　　　　　or　　　10 x 300 30 SR between/jog 5
minutes/800
or　　　6 x 400 30 SR between/jog 5 minutes/800
or　　2 ml/2 MR/2 x mile 1MR/4 x 800 30 SR
or　　　3 x 1000 30SR/J 400/2 x 1000 30SR/j 400/1000
1 hour easy with 3 x 4 minutes pickups during the run
10-mile tempo run.
Any combination of pace per mile to equal 10 miles
　　warm up/2 mile — 10k pace/1-mile 10k pace + 20 sec/1 mile — 5k
pace
　　1-mile 10k pace + 20 sec/1 — 5k pace/cool down
1-hour easy run
30 minutes easy if racing tomorrow else 45 minutes easy
Race or hill/grass work over hurdles.
　E.g.　1000M 3MR/2 x 500 90SR/1000M
　　　　Or 3 x 1000M 3 MR
　　　　Or 500M 90SR/1000M 3MR/1000 3MR/500

March — April

　2 hours easy
　Track work — Long repeats:
　　　　4 x mile 2MR
　　　　　　　　　　　　or　　　3000M/2 x 1000/2 x 600/3 MR
between
or　　　2000/5MR/1000/3MR/500
or　　　4 x 800 2MR/jog 5 minutes/4 x 800 1M
　3. 1 hour easy with 4 x 3 minutes pick-ups during run
　4. Track work- short reps　　200:400:600:400:200 3MR between
Or　　10 x 200 200 jog between
Or　　2x(4 x 400 2 MR) 5 minutes between sets

Or   4 x 400 rest = 3M/2M/1M/jog 5 minutes/repeat
1 hour easy run
30 minutes easy if racing tomorrow else 45 minutes easy
Race or hurdle work on track. E.g.
                Water jump drills
Hurdle drills
Flexibility

May - June
1 hour easy
2.   Track work — emphasis on pace:
        2 x mile 8 MR over hurdles
        or   1600/1200/800/400 3MR over water
        or   6x 800 3MR change up: 2 @ 2.12:2.04/2.10 no hurdles
3. 1 hour easy
4. Track work- variable reps
        400:1200:400 4MR over hurdles no water
        Or   1600:800:1600 4MR over hurdles every 2nd lap
        Or   400/60SR/800/2MR/400? Jog 10M/400 fast. No hurdles
        Or   1000/1MR/500 3MR/500/1MR/1000 over hurdles
5. 1 hour easy run
6. 30 minutes easy if racing tomorrow else 45 minutes easy
7. Race or Hurdle work on track. E.g. Water jump drills
Hurdle drills
Flexibility

10 Day — Pre-Big Race
1 hour easy
1500-meter race
10 miles easy
1600:1200:800:400 3MR over water only
1 hour easy run with a 5 minutes pick up in middle
400:1200:400 4MR over hurdles no water at race pace
1 hour easy
30 — 40 minutes easy with a few strides
Heats - 3000M S/C
Final - 3000M S/C.

Justin Chaston — Steeplechase

Justin competed in three Olympic Games for Great Britain: 1996, 2000, and 2004. His dad was working in Houston and when he graduated from London University in 1990, he moved to Houston to join him. Justin improved leaps and bounds. A lot of it had to do with the training group, plus he was a hard worker. No short cuts for him.

When he moved to Colorado Springs in 2003, it took me several weeks to figure out new workouts for him at that altitude. After a while, I decided there was not much difference between training in the heat in Houston and running at 6,000 feet in Colorado Springs.

One spring morning, I received a call from Justin wanting to know about a workout I had given him. It was 800s over hurdles including a water jump. He said, "We have a problem as there is ice in the water pit." I started to laugh before it sunk in, that at that altitude in May, frost is definitely on the calendar. We modified the workout and he was off and running.

Justin followed the regular Harriers schedule with modifications depending on his race schedule. Below is a 28-day schedule that Justin completed before the Stanford Invitational.

Days from Race	
•28	1 hour easy
•27	14 — 16 miles easy
•26	1 hour with 2x 4 min pick ups
•25	1k — 2.50/500 — 85/1k — 2.48/500 — 84/3 minutes rest
•24	1 hour easy with drills
•23	1500m time trial —
•22	20 — 30-nminutes warm up with a few strides
•21	Hills
•20	10 — 12 miles
•19	3x 1k with 2 minutes rest — 2.47/2.49/2.45
•18	1 hour easy
•17	4x 400 — 68 pace with 400 jog
•16	20 —30 min warm up with a few strides
•15	Mt. Sac Relays — 3,000 meters - 8:36.29 (third)
•14	Hills
•13	10-12 miles easy
•12	1 hour easy
•11	1600 — 4.35/ 1200 — 3.25/ 800 — 2.14/ 400 — 60 3 min rest over 2 hurdles

•10	1 hour easy with drills
•9	20 x 200 with 30 sec rest 32-33 seconds
•8	45 minutes easy
•7	Hills
•6	10 — 12 miles easy
•5	1500 — 4.20/3 MR/1K — 2.50/1MR/500 — 80 over 2 hurdles
•4	1 hour with 2 x 4 min pick ups
•3	45 minutes easy with a few strides
•2	20 — 30 minutes easy with a few strides
•1	Stanford Invitational 3000 meters S/C 8:24.88 (first)

Summit High School

When I was hired by Summit High School, I decided I would utilize the same philosophy that I had used in the past coaching Olympians and club runners. The first thing I did was the following.

Set Up A Training Program
1. Determine how much time you have before the big event where you want the athlete to run their best.
2. Count back from this target time how many weeks you have for preparation.
3. Break this time period into segments.
4. Prior to the final phase, do the type of training that will prepare them for the final segment? Keep this segment under consideration which will dictate the type of training that will be used in the final part of the training.
5. In the final segment of training, do the type of training that is best suited for the situation and the particular event you are training the athlete for. Consider
   a. Individual strengths and weaknesses.
   b. The conditions under which the important race(s) will be run, i.e., if you know they will be racing in the heat and humidity, get ready for the heat and humidity or if cold, get ready for wet and windy.
6. Work on weaknesses.
7. Don't change intensity or amount of training any more often than every two or three weeks.

How much emphasis you place on any particular type of training is part of coaching philosophy and personality? What I have identified are types of training, along with proper intensities of training, which best benefit various systems physiologically. I have not tried to tell you whether intervals should be 400s, 800s, 1200s or a combination of distances.

It is important not to include too much quality work in a single training session. Easy days are important; if you think a complete rest is warranted, then that is the ultimate easy workout and the purpose is easily identified. There is always a purpose for every workout; try to have an answer for the question, "Why am I doing this workout?"

Cross Country

We start before the cross-country season, in July, with organized workouts on Mondays, Wednesdays, and Fridays.

Mondays are usually on the grass at Drake Park. I have a 400-meter circuit with running up one hill and then back to the start. I have several different types of workouts:

1. Three-person relay running 400 meters.
2. Repeat 400 meters depending on fitness level.
3. 4x 800 with 3 minutes rest between.

Wednesdays — usually an easy 30-45-minute run

Friday — Sawyer Park - grass — Fartlek running.

Rest of the week, they can run how they feel.

In August, we try to get the athletes to run most days. If not an organized workout, run up to one hour easy. Monday through Friday, we have the runners follow a schedule, which includes the following:

Daily Team Warm Up and Drills

800 meters easy warm-up run
Forward Skip - 50 yards
Backward Skip - 50 yards
Side Shuffle with arm swings - 50 yards
Backwards run - 50 yards
Knee Pulls — 6
Quad Pulls — 6
Toe Touch — 6
Side Lunges - 5 yards
Regular Lunges - 10 yards
A-Skips - 4 X 20 yards
B-Skips - 2 X 20 yards

We hold a 4K team time trial in late August and based on the runners' times, they are placed into three running groups called black, silver, or green, as laid out in Chapter 53. Runners of similar ability train together to get the most out of their training. Runners are often motivated to improve, and we allow them to run themselves up into different groups during the XC season.

When school starts, we get serious and introduce hill workout and hard sessions on the grass.

Hill Workouts (Monday)

For hill workouts, we ask our co-ed runners to run at 90-95% effort. We train on two hills that are about a half-mile from our school; the team can jog to these hills to start the workout. One hill where we train is 500 meters to the top, and I have it marked off in 100-meter segments. I instill in our runners that we run past the top, not just run to the top. The second hill is Overturf Butte, a loop that varies depending whether we are running clockwise or counterclockwise, 365 meters uphill and 425 meters downhill clockwise, or 425 meters uphill and 365 meters downhill counterclockwise. In a workout, I will mix up the direction; for example, six clockwise and then six counterclockwise.

Easy Runs (Tuesday, Thursday, Friday, Sunday)

Easy runs are 1.5 - 2 minutes slower than race pace. For example, if race pace is 6-minute miles, then an easy run is at 7.5 - 8 minute-mile pace. I don't have our runners do tempo runs because I believe easy days are very important to recover from hard days, and I believe that it is very difficult to get high school runners to do tempo runs in groups that are specific to their individual speed.

I do get questions asking if our team does tempo runs. Our grass workouts are the closest I get to doing them, and probably some runners are doing tempo on "easy days" because they are running with a group of faster runners and they don't know how to run easy or think it is helpful to have easy runs. This will compromise their training and ability to fully recover from hard training days, and it will show up in their practice and race performance. I do not recommend running fast on recovery days. This can be a recipe for injury or burnout and one that I try to avoid. Easy should be easy, recovery days are ways to consolidate all the hard training that was done, and easy days are when the body repairs itself and grows stronger. I tell kids to run easy, and if someone wants to show off by leading the run too fast, just let them go.

Grass Workouts (Wednesday)

At the beginning of every grass day workout, I put runners in co-ed groups based on similar pace. Depending on the workout, I tell them to run at either 80% or 90% of their race pace. The total distance of the grass loop is 800 meters. Specifically, the length of the grass they run on is long, there is a 10-meter hill that leads to a 200-meter slightly downhill asphalt section, and the remaining grass section of 400 to 600 meters is a mix of wet to swampy grass due to the sprinkler system putting too much water on the grass and a drainage issues which leaves up to two inches of water to run through. You need flippers, not training shoes.

Race Day

On race days, I will walk the course and tell our team where all the holes, wet spots, and dangerous corners are located. If I have any concerns about holes or dangerous parts on the course, I shares this information with the race organizer to try and make the course safe for all runners. I then meet with the varsity runners and tell them the race strategy for the day.

An hour before the race, the varsity girls will go for a group warm-up run. 15 minutes before the race, the team will go to the starting box and start their drills and strides. Coaches will be at the start with baskets to take clothing back to the tent. If it's a cold day, Coach Carol McLatchie will have olive oil on hand to give to the girls so they can rub it on their exposed skin to keep themselves warm at the start of the race. As the race progresses, the skin heats up and the layer of olive oil "sweats" off.

Coaches are strategically placed around different parts of the course to yell out split times, encouragement, and sometimes that all important, "Go now" (if you can) directive.

Getting ready for NXN

Our varsity girls' team raced ten races in the 2018 season. The team had seven races on their calendar, including districts, then our eighth race was State, the 9th race was Nike Cross Regionals (NXR), and the tenth race was Nike Cross Nationals (NXN). All season long, the whole team cheered each other. I trained the runners for early-season and mid-season races by training at "today's" race pace—the current pace our runners were racing at. Then I cranked up the training in late season for State, NXR, and NXN to goal pace, which I call "winning pace," the pace that I think each individual athlete will be capable of racing at on the big day.

I had the team train through State and NXR, meaning that they didn't taper during this time. From NXR to NXN, I had them taper for one week before NXN, where I eliminated hills and weights, and tapered overall running.

An important point to highlight is that to compete in the NXN and race our best, I needed our team to commit to staying in Bend and training with the whole team during Thanksgiving break. That conversation started well before State and the girls stated that they were staying in Bend during the holidays and were ready to train hard for the championship.

Runners and parents recognized this great opportunity to be

competitive at State, NXR, and NXN. Our whole team trained together for the first time ever over Thanksgiving and it ultimately showed in our NXN race results.

The NXN race strategy was to go out quick, but not too quick. I had to get the team to believe in themselves that they could win this. They put in the hard work and on the start line it was, again, time, "to take the lid off the kettle." And, at the 4K mark, it was time to go for it all in the final 1K. Below is the training that the girls did prior to Nationals:

November 2018

Sun	Mon	Tue	Wed	Thu	Fri	Sat
28 1-1 ¼ miles easy	29 Hills 8X400 Jog back 90%	30 45 — 60 minutes run, drills and core, 4x150 pick ups	31 3x800 grass last 400 on track 4MR	11/1 45-60 minutes Core 4x150 pick ups	2 Leave for State champs 30 minutes 4x150 at end	3 OSSA STATE
4 45 MIN EASY RUN	5 HILLS 5X100 jog back 5x300 jog back 90-95 %	6 45 — 60 minutes run, drills and core, 4x150 pick ups	7 GRASS 4x800 2MR	8 45-60 minutes Core 4x150 pick ups	9 Depart for Boise 30 minutes easy Strides core	10 NXN
11 Travel back to Bend	12 45-60 minutes Core 4x150 pick ups	13 Hills 8x 400 jog back 90%	14 45-60 minutes Core 4x150 pick ups	15 Grass: 4x mile with 4 minutes rest	16 30-45 minutes easy Core 4x150	17 45 — 60 minutes easy run Core 4x 150
18 Easy run 1 hour Or cross train	19 Hills 6(100/ walk 50/200/	20 45-60 minutes Core 4x150 pick ups	21 Grass 3x800 2MR Jog 5 minutes 3x800 2MR	22 45 — 60 minutes easy run Core 4x 150	23 Grass	24 1 hour easy

25	26	27	28	29	30	12/1
Easy run 1 hour Or cross train	GRASS 8x200 with 200 jog 95%	45 minutes Core 4x150 pick ups	Mile on track Race pace minus 20 seconds	30 minutes easy run Core 4x 150	30 minutes warm with strides	NIKE National Champs Team First

The above worked for the team. At one time, with my health issues, I was not so sure if I would be around to see the results of what I had planned. Now that we had won the big race, the challenge would be to see if we could repeat. Every year athletes change both physically and mentally.

Coaching teenagers brings with it a myriad of personal problems: puberty, in and out of love, break ups, school's not going well, worrying about college, etc. Coaching track is easy. Cross country is a different kettle of fish. There are seven personalities, and each has to be dealt with individually. This is what makes it exciting, as all girls have to be firing on top cylinders on the day of the race.

The Team won — excited

Training Schedules I Have Developed

At Summit, training for the track season usually starts at the beginning of January, with easy runs and an introduction to weights on Tuesdays and Thursdays. The schedule is dependent when the State Championships are being held. I will back off from that date and devise a training schedule to get the athletes ready to produce the goods at that meet.

Summit now belongs in 6A, which is much tougher than 5A. We won numerous titles against weaker competition, but this will be a tougher challenge. Our kids are up to it.

Since I was in the computer field for nearly 40 years, I have written several programs to determine workout times based on today's race time over a certain distance, which makes it easier for me than trying to guess what times the athletes should be training at. I tweak them occasionally as my calculations might be off a wee bit.

Here is a list of tables that I have produced and use for most workouts depending what I am trying to accomplish. The first table I use for cross country.

5K Time	400	600	800	1000	1200	1600	3000	3200
14.00	01:00	01:36	02:10	02:42	03:20	04:31	07:51	09:29
14.30	01:02	01:39	02:14	02:48	03:27	04:41	08:08	09:49
15.00	01:04	01:43	02:19	02:54	03:35	04:50	08:25	10:10
15.30	01:06	01:46	02:24	03:00	03:42	05:00	08:41	10:30
16.00	01:08	01:50	02:29	03:06	03:49	05:10	08:58	10:50
16.3	01:10	01:53	02:34	03:12	03:56	05:19	09:15	11:11
17.00	01:12	01:57	02:38	03:18	04:03	05:29	09:32	11:31
17.30	01:15	02:00	02:43	03:24	04:10	05:39	09:49	11:51
18.00	01:17	02:04	02:48	03:30	04:17	05:48	10:05	12:12
18.30	01:19	02:07	02:53	03:36	04:25	05:58	10:22	12:32
19.00	01:21	02:11	02:58	03:42	04:32	06:08	10:39	12:52
19.30	01:23	02:15	03:02	03:48	04:39	06:17	10:56	13:13
20.00	01:25	02:18	03:07	03:54	04:46	06:27	11:13	13:33
20.30	01:27	02:22	03:12	04:00	04:53	06:37	11:30	13:53
21.00	01:29	02:25	03:17	04:06	05:00	06:46	11:46	14:14
21.30	01:32	02:29	03:22	04:12	05:08	06:56	12:03	14:34
22.00	01:36	02:36	03:31	04:24	05:22	07:15	12:37	15:15
22.30	01:38	02:39	03:36	04:30	05:29	07:25	12:54	15:35

23.00	01:40	02:43	03:41	04:36	05:36	07:35	13:11	15:55
23.30	01:42	02:46	03:46	04:42	05:43	07:45	13:27	16:15
24.00	01:44	02:50	03:50	04:48	05:50	07:54	13:44	16:36
24.30	01:46	02:53	03:55	04:54	05:58	08:04	14:01	16:56
25.00	01:49	02:57	04:00	05:00	06:05	08:14	14:18	17:16
25.30	01:51	03:01	04:05	05:06	06:12	08:23	14:35	17:37
26.00	01:53	03:04	04:10	05:12	06:19	08:33	14:51	17:57
26.30	01:55	03:08	04:14	05:18	06:26	08:43	15:08	18:17

Here is a workout using the above table for:

3x1000 with 30 sec rest between
3-minute rest
2x1000 with 30 sec rest between
3-minute rest
1000

If an athlete has run 20.00 minutes for 5K find 20.00 minutes on table and read across using the table for example:

20 minutes 3K time is3.07 for 1000 meters. I add 5 seconds to the second set and 5 seconds to the first set.

Times are 3x1000 at 3.17/ 2x1000 at 3.12/ 1000 at 3.07.

TABLE USING 3000 METER TIME

TIME	C	A	L	C		
3000	1600	1200	1000	800	600	400
8.30	04:41	03:21	02:43	02:11	01:36	60
8.40	04:46	03:25	02:47	02:13	01:38	61
8.50	04:52	03:29	02:50	02:16	01:40	62
9.00	04:57	03:33	02:53	02:19	01:42	63
9.10	05:03	03:37	02:57	02:21	01:44	65
9.20	05:08	03:41	03:00	02:24	01:46	66
9.30	05:14	03:45	03:03	02:27	01:48	67
9.40	05:19	03:49	03:07	02:29	01:50	68
9.50	05:25	03:53	03:10	02:32	01:52	69
10.00	05:30	03:57	03:13	02:35	01:54	70
10.10	05:36	04:01	03:17	02:37	01:56	72
10.20	05:41	04:05	03:20	02:40	01:58	73
10.30	05:47	04:09	03:23	02:43	02:00	74
10.40	05:52	04:13	03:27	02:45	02:02	75
10.50	05:58	04:17	03:30	02:48	02:04	76
11.00	06:03	04:21	03:33	02:51	02:06	77
11.10	06:08	04:25	03:37	02:53	02:08	79
11.20	06:14	04:29	03:40	02:56	02:10	80
11.30	06:19	04:33	03:43	02:59	02:12	81
11.40	06:25	04:37	03:47	03:01	02:14	82
11.50	06:30	04:40	03:50	03:04	02:16	83
12.00	06:36	04:44	03:53	03:07	02:18	84
12.10	06:42	04:48	03:57	03:09	02:20	86
12.20	06:47	04:52	04:00	03:12	02:22	87
12.30	06:53	04:56	04:03	03:15	02:24	88
12.40	06:58	05:00	04:07	03:17	02:26	89
12.50	07:04	05:04	04:10	03:20	02:27	90
13.00	07:09	05:08	04:13	03:23	02:29	92
13.10	07:09	05:08	04:13	03:23	02:29	92
13.20	07:09	05:08	04:13	03:23	02:30	92
13.30	07:09	05:08	04:13	03:23	02:30	92

USE BEST   TIME FOR 3000 TO DETERMINE WORKOUT TIMES

EG: 9 MIN FOR 3000   READ ACROSS   IF RUNNING 1600/1200/800/400 WITH 3MIN

Track workout using 3000 table:

3000 Meter Workouts

CODE	DESCRIPTION
1	1600/1200/800/400 3 min rest
7	1600 4MR/ 800/ 4MR/1600
23	800/1600/800 4MR
26	1600 3MR/200 200JOG 200/ 1600
40	8x 400 rest = 1.45/90/75/60/45/30/15
45	4X800 3MR/J5/4X400 2MR/J5/4X200 1MR
50	4X 800 2MR/ JOG 5/ 4X 800 1MR
51	8X 400 WITH 90 SEC REST
53	5x 600 with 200 jog
54	800 - 400 - 800 4 MIN REST BETWEEN
M2	1000 3MR/ 400/ JOG 5 MIN/ REPEAT

Workout using the 1500 table:

1500 Meter Workouts

▶ 11 = 8X200 30SR/ JOG 5 MIN/ 800
▶ 14 = 4X400 5MR/10 MIN JOG/ 2X300 100 WALK BETWEEN
▶ 15 = 400/1200/400 / 5 MIN REST BETWEEN
▶ 16 = 5X600 WITH 3 MIN REST
▶ 19 = 3(400/ 100 walk/300) 4 MIN SETS
▶ 20 = 3X 300 WITH 100 walk/ 4MR/ REPEAT/ J 10M/ 400
▶ 22 = 800/ 600/ 400/ 300 3 min rest between
▶ 23 = 800/1600/800 4MR
▶ 36 = 1000 3MR/ 300/ 2MR/200
▶ 37 = 2X(400/350/300/250/200/150/100 3MR) 5 MIN SETS
▶ 40 = 8x 400 rest = 1.45/90/75/60/45/30/15

274

QUICK 800 WORKOUT

Best time	400	300	200	100
1.50	00:53	00:39	00:26	00:13
1.52	00:54	00:40	00:26	00:13
1.54	00:55	00:41	00:26	00:13
1.56	00:56	00:42	00:27	00:14
1.58	00:57	00:42	00:28	00:14
2.00	00:58	00:43	00:28	00:14
2.02	00:59	00:44	00:29	00:14
2.04	01:00	00:45	00:29	00:14
2.06	01:01	00:45	00:30	00:15
2.08	01:02	00:46	00:30	00:15
2.10	01:03	00:47	00:30	00:15
2.12	01:04	00:47	00:31	00:16
2.14	01:05	00:48	00:32	00:16
2.16	01:06	00:49	00:32	00:16
2.18	01:07	00:50	00:33	00:16
2.20	01:08	00:51	00:33	00:17
2.24	01:10	00:52	00:34	00:17
2.26	01:11	00:53	00:34	00:17
2.28	01:12	00:53	00:35	00:17
2.30	01:13	00:54	00:35	00:18
2.32	01:14	00:55	00:36	00:18
2.34	01:15	00:56	00:37	00:18
2.36	01:16	00:56	00:37	00:19
2.38	01:17	00:57	00:38	00:19
2.40	01:18	00:58	00:38	00:19
2.42	01:19	00:59	00:39	00:19
2.44	01:20	00:59	00:39	00:20
2.46	01:21	01:00	00:40	00:20
2.48	01:22	01:01	00:40	00:20
2.50	01:23	01:02	00:41	00:20

2.52	01:24	01:02	00:41	00:21
2.54	01:25	01:03	00:42	00:21
2.56	01:26	01:04	00:42	00:21
2.58	01:27	01:05	00:42	00:21
3.00	01:28	01:06	00:43	00:22

Workout — 800 IN 2:20 =400-5MR/300-4MR/200-3MR-100
Goals: 400- 68 /300- 51 /200-33 /100-17

TRACK WORKOUT USING CODED TABLE

36	1000 3MR/ 300/ 2MR/200
H8	3X150 PU WB/ 10MR/ 4X200 WITH 6MR/ 10MR/ 4X150 PU WB
H9	3X150 PU WB/ 10MR/ 300 5MR 300/ 10MR/ 3X150 WB
MO	4X400 REST-3/2/1 MIN/ JOG 5M/ 4X200 - REST 3/2/1 MIN
28	10 x 200 WITH 200 JOG BETWEEN
86	500 4MR 200 2MR 100
M6	8x200 rest = 1.45/90/75/60/45/30/15

List of Isabel Max 800 workouts leading to Summit HS record

Date	Code	Times
5/11/2019	36	3.09 47 29
5/13/2019	H8	27 28 27 28
5/14/2019	H9	47 47
5/16/2019	800	02:21.3
5/18/2019	800	02:13.4
5/20/2019	MO	64 65 68 75/32 31 31 31
5/22/2019	99	4X150 WB/5MR/300/5MR/4X150 WB - 45
5/25/2019	STATE 800 H	02:14.8
5/26/2019	STATE 800 F	02:12.4
5/30/2019	28	30 32 32 32 32 32 32 31
6/1/2019	86	81 29 14
6/3/2019	M6	31 32 32 32 31 32 32 33
6/5/2019	99	4X150 WB/5MR/400 100 WALK 300/10MR/2X150 WB - 63 47
6/9/2019	800 OPEN	02:10.6

All the workouts that I have designed are coded to make it easier to retrieve them when I am looking at an athlete's past history or deciding what workouts will be attempted today.

Here are a few coded workouts:

CODE	DESCRIPTION
1	1600/1200/800/400 3 minutes rest
2	400 8MR/300 6MR/200/4MR/100 (02)
54	800 - 400 - 800 4 MIN REST BETWEEN
57	2x600/2x400/300/200 2 minutes rest
MI	4X200 2MR/JOG 5 MIN/2X300 2MR/J 5/400

I have 32 student athletes. Below are a few times for some.

5/11/2019	1	JOE	4.59 3.39 2.24 64
5/11/2019	1	JACK	5.05 DNS 64
5/11/2019	1	TEAGHAN	5.20 DNS 2.31 XX
5/11/2019	1	FIONA	5.20 3.57 2.30 66
4/26/2019	2	SAM T	57 42 27 12
4/26/2019	2	IZZY	64 47 31 15
4/26/2019	2	KELSEY G	75 56 35 16
4/10/2019	57	AZZA	1.56 1.56 75 75 53 33
4/10/2019	57	STELLA	2.00 1.58 76 77 54 35

I can also extract individual workouts by code, showing if an individual has done this workout previously. See below for Olivia Brooks, who won six Oregon Division 5 State Championships. Code 15 shows that she had done this work out three times with improvement every year.

INDIVIDUAL BY CODE
Olivia Brooks

Date	Code	Times
3/14/2013	15	73 4.25 73
3/17/2014	15	72 4.11 73
3/16/2015	15	70 3.53 70
3/26/2014	20	54 54 55/ 54 55 56/ 70
4/3/2015	20	53 54 53/ 52 53 53/ 68
3/12/2014	21	72 75/ 72 55/ 74 55/ 78 56
3/30/2015	21	72 54/ 72 55/ 73 55/ 75 55
3/19/2014	28	35-36 ave
4/8/2015	28	35 38 35 34 34 35 35 35 34 34
3/12/2013	36	2.46 2.49/ 2.52 2.55
4/16/2014	36	2.47 2.48/ 2.46 2.48

Below are the workouts achieved by Matthew Maton prior to leaving Summit and running a sub-4-minute mile the following year.

Codes for Maton

51	8X 400 WITH 90 SEC REST
3	2x800 3mr/j 5 minutes/2x400 2mr/j5/2x200 1mr
2	1200 2MR 300/JOG 5 MIN /1200 2MR 300
M4	4X400 WITH 100 JOG BETWEEN
49	800 3MR/400/2MR/200 1MR/200
5	200 2MR 200/5MR/400 4MR 400/5MR/200 2MR 200/
MD	200/2MR/200/3MR/200/2MR/200
MF	400/4MR/4X200 2MR/4MR/400

Normal schedule for the week would look like this.

Sunday	Easy run up to 1 hour depending on time of the year
	If raced on Saturday or travelling home late from an away meet
	A day off would be ok or a walk
Monday	Warm up. which would include drills and strides before workout
	Time of season would determine what type of workout
	Cool down

Tuesday	Easy 45- 1 hour run with strides and then weights
Wednesday	Same as Monday
Thursday	Same as Tuesday
Friday	Early season 45 minutes easy
	Racing season 30 minutes warm up, drills and strides
Saturday	Early season 45 — 60 minutes easy run
	Race season —Race

Made in the USA
Middletown, DE
11 March 2020